Studies in Newspaper and Periodical History

1995 ANNUAL

Studies in Newspaper and Periodical History

1995 ANNUAL

EDITED BY

Michael Harris
and Tom O'Malley

GREENWOOD PRESS
Westport, Connecticut • London

British Library Cataloguing in Publication Data is available.

Copyright © 1997 by Greenwood Publishing Group, Inc.

ISBN: 0–313–29052–0
ISSN: 1075–0673

First published in 1997

Greenwood Press, 88 Post Road West, Westport, CT 06881
An imprint of Greenwood Publishing Group, Inc.

Printed in the United States of America

The paper used in this book complies with the
Permanent Paper Standard issued by the National
Information Standards Organization (Z39.48–1984).

10 9 8 7 6 5 4 3 2 1

Contents

Preface

The 1995 volume of *Studies in Newspaper and Periodical History* reflects a wide range of work on serial publication, chronologically, geographically and theoretically.

It traverses the period from 1700 to the 1970s and has a distinct international dimension with material covering the United States, England, Wales, Germany and Australia. In fact, two of our articles—Jamie L. Bronstein's on the Land Reform movement and Peter Dowling's on the illustrated press in the nineteenth century—illuminate the way in which traffic in serial publication crossed between countries, integrating elements within the different communities in the context of shared concerns over social issues or, simply, over maintaining some sort of personal contact with lands left behind. In this context serial publication both followed the expansion of international trade and acted as one of the sinews binding together different cultural elements of the ever-expanding global economic networks.

A number of theoretical issues are addressed in this volume. Michael Harris' piece raises questions about the way in which the serial is conceived of as an object of study and how it might be inserted into wider debates about the role of the serial in print culture and into the wider cultural processes of the eighteenth century. This is a theme taken up in a slightly different way in other contributions. Mark W. Turner argues that understanding the place of the literary periodical in the nineteenth century requires a sustained effort to theorize its relation to the contexts of production and the cultural mores of gender and class. For this he draws on poststructuralist insights into the nature of the text.

Tom O'Malley, Stuart Allan and Andrew Thompson explore the relationship between the newspaper press in Wales and issues of national identity. They point to the need to recognize the way in which the press reflected conflicts within Welsh society over the definition of Welsh identity at the end of the nineteenth century. Later in the volume Glenn R. Wilkinson stresses that a methodologically aware approach to newspapers as visual and textual artifacts, connected in a range of different ways with the society in which they functioned, is necessary if we are to develop a fuller understanding of the role of newspapers in society.

The other contributions in this volume focus on serial publication in relation to a wider set of cultural processes, including gender, religion, provincial politics, the relationship between the press and broadcasting, the politics of the Nuremberg trials and the effects of commercialization on countercultural publications in the United States. It is these links between serial publication and the wider public sphere that we consider still need to be more fully explored historically and theoretically. Bringing studies in serial history into a wider theoretical context, integrating the work of historians and bibliographers with some of the theoretical work of social and cultural theorists is one way of progressing toward a clearer understanding of the relationship of serial print to print culture in general and to wider processes of cohesion and change. This work has already begun but much remains to be done.

We also include our annual review of publications in the field and a review section. The review editor of *Studies* is Mark W. Turner and our associate editor in the United States is Amy Beth Aronson.

Michael Harris
University of London

Tom O'Malley
University of Glamorgan

I

The Eighteenth Century

Locating the Serial: Some Ideas about the Position of the Serial in Relation to the Eighteenth-Century Print Culture

Michael Harris

The worldwide appearance of projects concerned with the history of the book is running in tandem with the rapid development of electronic forms of communication. The new technology, which offers both a challenge to and a means of exploring print, seems to have provided a spur to action. There is now a real opportunity to build on existing lines of research and rethink some of the concepts around which histories of print can be constructed. A debate is beginning to take shape, though as yet in a highly fragmented way, and these remarks are intended as a contribution to the process.

As the projects proliferate, the general issue of how to approach the totality of the output of print and how to integrate its constituent elements in a convincing way has begun to sharpen. Part of a universal framework of organization is provided by the nation-state. The adoption of this form of cultural nationalism is usually said to be imposed by the availability of funding rather than by conceptual agreement. Histories of the book are constructed within the frontiers of countries whose pragmatic financial interests give a curious patchwork effect to the research process. In relation to Britain, with its far-flung empire, the possibility of geographical dislocation is considerable. In this case, the national approach is locked into a network of overlapping projects concerned not only with the book in Scotland, Wales and Ireland but also with the form as developed in the scattered components of the imperial past. In this respect Britain may, by default, become England, an isolated unit separated from its immediate neighbors as well as from its formative European connections.

The national approach, confused or enriched by a buildup in parallel histories of the book, can still provide an effective focus for an enterprise of this sort. It may be more straightforward to deal with the history of the book in, say, Iceland or Canada, than in Britain (whatever that portmanteau term may be taken to imply), but the problems of organization and methodology overlap at a variety of points. On the other hand, in Britain, as in France and America, the long-term perspective gives a particular urgency to the question of how to cope with a vast body of material that has been under close examination over a long period but whose character and outline remains disconcertingly hazy. These preliminary remarks are centered on the *History of the Book in Britain*, a heavily funded, multivolume, multiauthor enterprise organized chronologically and intended to provide a general view of the production of texts since the Roman period. The editorial hierarchy is in place, and the volumes concerned with the earliest periods are, apparently, well in hand. My interest here is how the serial, and serialization as a publishing strategy, can be accommodated within the account of a period extending from the late seventeenth to the early nineteenth century (volume 4 in the sequence).

It is sometimes suggested that any notion of an agreed structure is surplus to requirements. That given the state of play, an attempt at an integrated approach, in which the forms of print as well as the mechanisms of production and consumption are in some kind of balance, would be a recipe for delay and confusion. Under the circumstances, it seems to be argued, the chronological sequence itself, prefaced in each volume by a recurrent element of statistical information (databases constructed around the hierarchies of the book) and linked by bridging chapters is sufficient to carry the enterprise forward. Subsequently, chosen contributors can be slotted into a sequence in which any creative conflict of ideas can be mediated by editorial intervention, but through which the momentum of the output of print can be displayed.

This is a pragmatic approach, which may get the job done. But the question remains, what does it all mean? If the medium is intended to be the message and the "history of the book" is a mechanism for drawing attention to a subject not well represented within academic discourse, then it will surely do. Equally, if it is intended to provide an indication of the range and variety of research falling within its parameters, the project will serve a valuable and complementary purpose. If, however, the intended benefit is to give some sense of how the subject can be integrated with a broader view of the eighteenth century, then other considerations come into play. If the intention is, in fact, to indicate how the history of the book can be brought into balance with work in history, literature and areas of social science, then it will be necessary to confront the problem of structure. The purpose of this chapter is to suggest that any representation of print and the book between 1690 and 1820 must focus on the serial (and serialization) not just as a peripheral topic nor as a prelude to the nineteenth century, but also as a central component of the general analysis.

It can be said at the start that pursuing an argument of this sort is uphill work. Within the field of bibliography, which provides the base for the history of the book, the eighteenth-century serial has not been given a high profile. The reasons for this surprising absence can partly be identified in the academic alignment of the subject. Over a long period, the frontiers between bibliography and history remained closed. Hardly a whiff of the debates raging around the social and economic structure of England reached the bibliographers, while few if any of the notions of the construction and use of print have gone the other way. Within the field of history the serial was always on the agenda but its presence has been rigorously contained. The limited nature of the interchange was given a practical form in the work of Paul Langford. In two long and highly acclaimed books concerned with the middling sectors of English society in the eighteenth century, he was able to completely exclude the serial along with all the other components of the print culture.[1] One reason for this surprising absence seems to lie in a general consensus that serial print was mainly significant in relation to party politics. Given the long-term interest of a proportion of historians with party skirmishing this might have suggested an important line of analysis. However, because of the perceived nature of the political process in eighteenth-century England, dominated by closet intrigue with limited interventions through the blunt instrument of public opinion, print and the serial remained part of a largely unexplored periphery. The rather bizarre result of this can be seen in the work of Jeremy Black, whose book on the eighteenth-century newspaper targets the major component of this material.[2]

Partly because of the notions of the indestructible link between newspapers and party propaganda, a view given in its purist form by Stanley Morison in the 1950s,[3] Jeremy Black is completely unable to find a way of looking at this form of output generally. In his account the newspaper is squeezed into a corner where it can be represented as limited in distribution, marginal in its political use and restricted in its market potential. The view is not consistent and some elements of reality keep breaking through, but it is recognizably a reflection of the established way of looking at serial print in a historical context.

In the sphere of research concerned with the literature of the eighteenth century, in which an interest in the operation of print might be expected to take on a clearer form, another set of limitations have been in play. These relate to issues of perceived quality, to a willingness to accept a hierarchy of texts, whose pinnacle is represented by the books of writers whose work is fenced off within what has been referred to as "the canon." This extravagantly blunt statement is only intended to suggest a relationship between content and form that has operated to the disadvantage of the serial. Books have been the heart of the matter, and though the serial has been filleted for additions to the *oeuvres* of great writers such as Fielding and Swift among others, the serial as a product has not taken on any particular shape within the discipline. The heavy preoccupation with the *Tatler* and *Spectator* suggests a relationship that is distinctly hands off. These serials, in which the periodical essay was refined to a point of literary acceptability, became part of the culture of the book as their primary content was continuously recycled in multivolume form. In the closely related areas of bibliography, the hold of literary definitions of quality has only gradually been relaxed. The interest in workshop practice was geared to an interpretation of the plays, novels and general output of the great writers. The sense of bibliography as a part of an elite literary culture in which a particular kind of book-centered approach is predominant is suggested by the volume of work still centered on the great institutions of established authority, the libraries and presses of the ancient universities and the Stationers' Company in London. In these areas, a reassuring link is maintained with the high status products of the press.

Things have been and are changing. The mavericks in the disciplines of history, literature and bibliography whose work has been accumulating around the printed serials published in England during the eighteenth century are coming in from the cold. The emergence of new centers of research and teaching in which history and literature are linked and in which the application of ideas expressed through theory are applied to empiricist material, is beginning to shift the perspectives on print. Research organized through departments of cultural studies, communications and even journalism are intersecting with the established centers of history and literature and refocusing on areas in which serials have a more dynamic role. A single indicator of the benefits of the process can stand for many. The cultural historian Anne Goldgar, in her study *Impolite Learning* (1995), has suddenly brought into view a pan-European system of cultural formation during the later seventeenth century organized through serial print.[4] The work in itself shifts the perspective on the uses of the serial and suggests the importance of an integrated view of form and content.

In bibliography, the long march toward a more open and flexible approach to the products of the press has gathered some momentum, reflecting in turn the developments in related areas of research. Some of the activity involves a reworking of established lines of interest within the discipline. London, in its metropolitan character as the grand arena of the trade in print, has begun to assume a clearer shape both in relation to local centers and as an engine of commercial activity in its own right. At the same time, the external relationships of print within society at large are coming into focus. Research into the structures of publishing and into the more difficult but crucial area of reading is accumulating in ways that both enlarge and disrupt the established view. In almost all new areas of research, whether in history, literature or bibliography, the serial and serialization are on the agenda and can be said, in some respects, to represent a point of convergence between the disciplines.

Why has this shift in perspective taken so long? Some sort of answer has already been suggested but it may be worth trying to clarify the issue of status, a concept that has such remarkable force in the generality of human affairs. The peculiar forms of self-aggrandizement that are such an unexpected feature of academic life are geared to the hierarchical notions applied to the products of the press. In classifying and grading the output of print, not least in the pragmatic subculture of the library system where long-established categories remain in place, a line has been drawn dividing the modest, short-term items from those that have a permanent importance. On one side, books, pamphlets and associated material, on the other, ephemera. It is possibly that the notion of ephemerality has been responsible for shunting the serial into the sidings over such a long period. The effects of this are easy to identify. In the recent volume, *The Book Encompassed*, celebrating the progress of research in bibliography, no space was given to serial publication.[5] This clearly is a consensus view. The almost miraculous absence of the serial from the field of bibliography and from discussions about the history of the book is apparent in a recent essay by Thomas R. Adams and Nicolas Barker. Barker is a remarkably good writer whose main interests lie in the earliest periods of print as well as in the most prestigious forms of output. His attempt with Adams to give a shape to the history of the book generally, involving a flowchart set in the context of "The Whole Socio-Economic Conjuncture," is reasonably based on ideas about process rather than product.[6] How in doing this it is possible to avoid the idea and the brute fact of the serial is a mystery of a profound sort. It seems to arise from the author's underlying classification of the output of print into two categories. On one hand, books and related material, on the other, ephemera. This is going to be a hard view to sustain. It might be noted here that the whole representation of ephemera is undergoing a radical shift. The printed ticket, for example, takes on a dynamic character in the cultural analysis centered on issues of public access and exclusion during the eighteenth century. In other words, the jobbing work of the print trade is beginning to be related to the context of use.

The serial, particularly its central components—the newspaper and the periodical—is of an entirely different order but is benefiting from a similar shift of analysis. It is becoming clearer, on one hand, that the line dividing the serial from the book is part of a worn-out form of cultural elitism. There is, after all, a well-established, transformative process leading through the serial to the book as producers and readers engaged, through republication and the binding of copies, in the complicit construction of the permanent form. Books on the library shelf are not always what they seem, however large and elaborately cased. The process by which serial parts were reassembled by individual readers or their agents seldom has a high visibility in the finished product. On the other hand, serials cannot simply be defined as deconstructed books or alternative versions of the closed text. Transformations may be made but the primary functions of serial production, distribution and consumption remain distinct and powerful. It is the deep misunderstanding of the relation of the text to the serial process itself that has created most of the difficulty and that can be demonstrated most fully in relation to the newspaper.

The wish to apply the established forms of critical analysis to a clearly identified text, for whatever purpose, has tended to reinforce a view based on the dissection of the individual issue. Whether squeezed for information or used as an indicator of trade practice, the newspaper has been viewed as a static accumulation of single copies. As a result, it has been represented as a repository of a jumble of short-term, commercially oriented material, an item of ephemeral interest destined, in its contemporary setting, for reductive use in the kitchen or the lavatory. The eighteenth-century newspaper has limped into view in relation to the political process, but in many of these cases a lack of concern for the production-side system has had dire results.

And yet as time has passed, other ways of looking at the eighteenth-century newspaper and periodical have begun to impinge on research. To some extent the change of view has been imported from work based in later periods. Studies of both the Victorian and twentieth-century output of serial print have generated ideas and approaches that are transferable.[7] Like a long-unused engine, the eighteenth-century printed serial is spluttering into life. The great heaps of material often reluctantly accumulated in the library system and identified as part of the problem of space rather than the solution to understanding the collections, are beginning to be reassessed. The single-issue approach has to be extended to accommodate the dynamic of the serial as part of a continuous social and cultural process leading out of a past into an unknown future. Each issue becomes, in this context, part of something else. Like a frame of film it carries an image that in isolation is hard to assess; if not devoid of general meaning it is still enigmatic. Put into a projector and thrown onto a cinema screen, the single frame is sub-sumed into a moving picture having its own public resonance. It is an effect of this kind that is offered by the serial in relation to the print culture. At all events, the static notion of ephemerality has to be laid quietly to rest.

These remarks may be said to be tilting at windmills. It is easy to imagine the weary response that everyone knows about serials and has a sense of how they work even if the preference is for others to carry forward the research. Like any other line of investigation, it might be said, it will fall into place in time and become part of the patchwork of knowledge concerned with eighteenth-century English culture. This is not the point being made here. The accumulation of information about the serial is continuing. As lists, bibliographies, histories and edited texts roll slowly forward, there might be said to be a cumulative shift in the response to the material generally. The value of these enterprises is immense. However, the issue here is one of understanding, of locating the serial in a setting vaguely constructed around ideas about the book and of integrating a sense of the serial and serialization into something that might be called a history of the book in Britain.

Addressing this issue and reaching a resolution would require some sort of divine intervention. The purpose of this chapter is partly to identify an unacknowledged problem that the positive thinking of the promoters of the history of the book is tending to slough off. Even so, it may be possible to go a bit further here by considering, in a general way, the question of the importance of the serial and serialization in the organization of print and the print culture during the eighteenth century. In the first place, it may be useful to consider how the serial in general and the newspaper in particular interacted with the English book trades during this period.

As an opening proposition it could be suggested that serialization became a crucial organizing principle within the trade in print. The serial form itself, as it developed during the seventeenth century, di-versified around different timetables and forms of content. The process of elaboration, involving an increasing variety of output geared to dif-ferent audiences, was centered on material catering to the heavy and continuous demand for updated news and information. The newspaper, and the penumbra of forms within which it was constructed and dis-tributed, became the most effective mechanism for establishing a line of serial production. Offering as it did, to both producer and reader, the powerful benefits of regularity and cheapness, this material became the formative element in the construction of production schedules as well as in the process of marketing. The printed serial, whether in an open sequence as in the case of most newspapers, or with a specified limitation as with most part works, became in many ways the banker in the competitive environment of commercial print. The force of the serial in the context of workshop practice was demonstrated with some clarity during the diaspora of printers from London after the end of state control in 1695. The movement of individuals into local centers of population can be charted by the appearance, in widening geographical circles, of newspaper titles. Setting up in business, serial publication based on the addictive commodity of news offered both regularity of income and a mechanism for setting up lines of local contact through which other elements of print could be directed. In both cases the force of advertising represented a crucial ingredient.

Until the newspaper developed a level of commercial force that thrust it into a separate industrial existence, it remained a structural element within the book trades. In local centers it tended to continue as it began, the basis for the mixed activities of local printers.[8] In London it played a more complex role, particularly after the post-1695 regrouping. It was through the serial that the struggle for access to, and control of, the metropolitan and national market was worked out. Printers and booksellers, grouping and regrouping around strings of serial titles, struggled together in a process leading toward a form of bourgeois hegemony.[9] Through the established cartels of shareholding newspaper proprietors, the market was shaped and run by a respectable trade whose interests coincided in a variety of ways with masters/employers controlling other sectors of the metropolitan economy. The force of the serial as it interacted with commercial interests within the book trade was evident at all points. Stationers, the primary dealers in paper, were established at the upper (respectable) end of the trade and sailed into prosperity on the rising tide of the demand geared to the output of serial publications. Equally, as the lines of communication marked out by the flow of print were laid down and extended through the metropolis, across the nation and throughout Europe the sector of the book trade concerned with publication took shape around the serial. As Michael Treadwell has shown, the wholesalers, identified in his work as trade publishers, moved from an early specialization in pamphlets into the larger and more profitable field of newspapers.[10] Over time the functions focused on serial distribution developed a more general importance as part of the infrastructure of the trade.

Much of the detail of the commercial engagement suggested here has yet to be clarified or even investigated. It may be that the lack of systematic analysis relates in some way to the mercurial nature of the serial as a product. Its mobility and the nature of its external relationships seem to disrupt the production-side view. The assessment of how the serial fits the pattern of the output of the press is closely associated with its reactive character and its role in linking producer and consumer. The reading public was drawn to the serial form for a variety of overlapping reasons and its underlying appeal offered a way into the market to a widening range of economic, cultural and political interests. The flexibility of the serial and the line of public access it offered was exploited by outsiders as well as by respectable insiders. On one side, low-key, entrepreneurial printers were able to construct a business around forms of serialization leading directly into the market that challenged the vested interest of the respectable trade. On another, most writers made some use of the serial form on their way up or down the slippery slopes of the literary system. The sense of the serial as an open channel may have changed as the respectable trade moved into a dominant position, but its potential as a mechanism for evading commercial or political controls remained.

The difficulty of locating the serial as a structural component of the print culture lies partly in the intersection of different interests in this form of output, in other words, in sorting out how serials worked. The emphasis in historical studies on party politics suggests that this line may be the one of least resistance. However, questions about the way in which the serial, particularly the newspaper, functioned in society has to be given a more general context. If the newspaper is identified as the primary medium of communication running around a circuit that linked producer and reader and was accessible to a variety of external interests, a pattern begins to emerge that has been identified in other parts of the forest. Robert Darnton gave the notion of a circuit of print a tangible form and his idea has been modified by Adams and Barker.[11] The representation on the page of a circular form, along the circumference of which are strung out the people or the processes involved in the construction, distribution and consumption of print, are extremely helpful in conceptualizing some complex relationships. Such diagrams are also crucial in suggesting the organization of various cultural transactions. What I find disorienting is the subordination or absence of the serial as the inescapable material from which the circuit was constructed and by which it was maintained and developed. The shape is clearly identified; the primary structural component is not.

The circuit is clearly a fruitful way of bringing ideas about serial print into balance. However, one circuit is hardly enough even with the Sistine Chapel effect introduced by Adams and Barker. Circuits linking producers or readers or interest groups might be superimposed on the single shape proposed by Darnton. The wheels within wheels that drive the machine of cultural formation and that involve the printed serial require a combination of approaches relating to different parts of the system. In this respect the connections between the serial and its readers is of primary interest and it is in this area that the work of Jurgen Habermas and his commentators and successors has a particular force. In *The Structural Transformation of the Publick Sphere: An Inquiry into a Category of Bourgeois Society*, Habermas tracks the emergence and decline of a new form of public, developing in opposition to forms of established authority.[12] His analysis is centered on the nations of Western Europe and is set in the context of a specific historical period extending from the seventeenth to the twentieth century. It is hardly possible here to do more than acknowledge the ideological basis of his argument. Even so, its construction is particularly fruitful for any discussion of the location of serial print.

Habermas identifies the networks of print as crucial components in both the construction and the breakdown of the bourgeois public sphere. As the dispersed individuals coalesced within a commercial environment and began to move during the eighteenth century toward a political engagement, the networks of serial print assumed a crucial importance. The relationship that he proposes for the serial to the formation of a bourgeois public sphere is both recognizable and useful. The commercial origins of the English serial within the London business community and its relationship to an international traffic in commodities and news are seldom noticed. Other parts of the Habermas argument also fall into place. The way in which the force of a central authority gave way to pressures it had attempted to contain, as well as the shift from the private system of manuscript to the public sphere of print, were related directly to the emergence in England of serialization as a publishing strategy.

Predominantly, what Habermas provides is a framework that can accommodate the dynamic presence of the serial. The formation of the bourgeois public sphere took on a physical shape within the public spaces of European society. At the same time, the assembling of the new public through the voluntary association of private individuals was, Habermas suggests, geared to an integrative process of reading and conversation. What he is describing is the milieu of serial print, particularly as it was developed in eighteenth-century England. The material circulating in this form had a particular force in the individual lives of bourgeois readers whether as business people, theatregoers, cricket players or even as voters.

Without wishing to overemphasize the importance of the Habermas thesis, it may be worth noting two elements in his argument that are out of line with a detailed view of the English serial. These are issues forming part of a much more generalized debate and are bluntly stated here to suggest that serials and serialization could and should form part of the argument. First, identification by Habermas of a single public in the shape of the bourgeoisie. Print itself can be said to mark off other "publics" that, as already suggested, confronted a new hegemony. How far print in serial form, as a product of a particular commercial system, could assume a variety of roles in relation to different social sectors has yet to be considered in relation to eighteenth-century England.

In the second place, the Habermas formulation, first published in the 1960s and based on secondary material, is acknowledged to be empirically weak. It has been stated quite reasonably that if the general model holds up, the detail is expendable. However, this becomes a problem when a specific chronology is constructed from limited published research. A general identification of a process of change within the seventeenth and eighteenth centuries may be agreed upon. However, if it is focused on the period of the French Revolution some difficulties emerge. In England, the chronology suggested by Habermas looks increasingly shaky. In a recent restatement and critique of Habermas' ideas, Geoff Eley used the work of John Brewer and John Money to reaffirm the timing of a shift in the character of English society.[13] In this view the 1760s were identified as a critical turning point. As forms of commercialization were linked to an upswing in political engagement centered on the bourgeoisie and geared to serial print, so, it was suggested, a new phase in the cultural formation of English society began to open up. This timing has the advantage of compatibility with change in other European nations, particularly France and Germany. Unfortunately it is not a view that can be sustained against a background of developing research centered on the serial form. The poverty of active investigation has meant that any creative and detailed reading of the serial by individual historians has seemed, because of the unexpected force and interest of the material, to represent something new and original. Without a solid framework of information and some sense of a general process, every sample can be identified as a starting point. As the work of Anne Goldgar has suggested, serial print is a long-term phenomenon and as such has to be integrated with a more effective chronology than is provided by Habermas.

The operation of the serial within eighteenth-century English society is a complex matter that has hardly begun to be given close attention. One element consistently missing from existing studies is what might be called a holistic approach. The material is so vast in quantity and dense in content that personal survival seems to suggest the need for rigorous selection. However, as has already been suggested, the isolation of issues and titles as well as particular forms of content can have a distorting effect on any general view. There is a sense in which all forms, titles and constituent elements have to be viewed inclusively and brought into some sort of balance. Everything within the text, which was constructed and read as a composite form, will have to be reassembled within the research process. If the Habermas model is to be explored and tested in relation to eighteenth-century England, some way will have to be found of comprehending the totality of the material. In this respect the resources of the disciplines of history, literature, bibliography and social science will all be involved.

If there is an answer to the question about the importance of the printed serial it will have to accommodate the issues noted here. As well as representing a structural element in the book trades, serialization, as the printed sequences shaped and ran around the circuits linking producer and consumer, also became a defining element in society at large. This suggests that something more is needed than the occasional accumulation of research into the history of individual publications, valuable as this process can be, or of pinning down the bibliographical details of more and more serials in increasingly accessible catalogues. At the heart of the matter is an issue of will and imagination—a sense that the totality of print may perhaps, as Adams and Barker suggested, be better understood in terms of process than of product or personnel. While the serial is simply a looming shadow on the stair, there is no way a real sense of how print works can be achieved.

Finally, what about the serial in the context of the history of the book in Britain? The title of the project itself is an enigma. Talking to a scholar from Israel about the project, it became clear that he understood the use of "the book" as a reference to holy writ, and he expressed his amazement at the existence of such a large-scale enterprise devoted to a religious text. It is sometimes said that the ambiguity of the term *book* has some value. Whether the reference is to a genuinely book-centered enterprise or whether it is being used as a general signifier in relation to the construction of texts does not need to be clarified. Such ambiguities can, it is suggested, offer a useful way of the task to be open and inclusive. It might also be said that it can lead to the construction of a heap of disorderly and meaningless information that will clog the understanding of the force of print in society for years to come. At all events, a structure into which a chapter about serials and serialization in the eighteenth century is loosely inserted will not do more than reestablish the kind of disruptive inversion already noted. Perhaps existing notions about the history of the book need to be turned inside out. How else can the great engine of serial publication be given due weight in relation to the cultural and commercial formation of the long eighteenth century?

Questions are easier to come by than answers. There is plenty of room for consideration of a range of strategies, some of which have already been put into practice. At one end of the spectrum is the dual approach adopted in France. Here, the history of the book was constructed after the appearance of a multivolume history of the press resulting in a complete separation of forms.[14] At the other end of the notional spectrum, the history of the book could be organized within a structure defined by the interlocking circuits of production and consumption. Following this line would give the serial a central position, not as a distinct form but as a core element in the total output of print. As indicated here, my own preference would be for an agreed version of the latter. However, there are a range of intermediate alternatives, all of which still needing to be identified and discussed. Locating the serial is going to be a long but stimulating process.

NOTES

1. Paul Langford, *A Polite and Commercial People: England, 1727–1783* (Oxford: Oxford University Press, 1989); *Public Life and the Propertied Englishman, 1689–1798* (Oxford: Clarendon Press, 1991). The general omission of print from socioeconomic history is equally evident in the work of Peter Earle.

2. Jeremy Black, *The English Press in the Eighteenth Century* (London: Croom Helm, 1987).

3. Stanley Morison, "The Bibliography of Newspapers and the Writing of History," *The Library*, Ser. 5, ix (1954), pp. 153–75.

4. Anne Goldgar, *Impolite Learning: Conduct and Community in the Republic of Letters, 1680–1750* (New Haven: Yale University Press, 1995).

5. Peter Davison, ed., *The Book Encompassed: Studies in Twentieth-Century Bibliography* (Cambridge: Cambridge University Press, 1992).

6. Thomas R. Adams and Nicolas Barker, "A New Model for the Study of the Book," in *A Potencie of Life: Books in Society*, ed. Nicolas Barker (London: British Library, 1993).

7. For essays concerned with different approaches to the study of the periodical literature of the nineteenth century see, Laurel Brake, Aled Jones and Lionel Madden, eds., *Investigating Victorian Journalism* (London: Macmillan, 1990).

8. The complexity of local structures involving the newspaper are only just beginning to emerge. See C. Y. Ferdinand, "Local Distribution Networks in Eighteenth-Century England," in *Spreading the Word; the Distribution Networks of Print, 1550–1850*, ed. Robin Myers and Michael Harris (Winchester/Detroit: St. Paul's Bibliographies/Omnigraphics, 1990). A full-length book by the same author based on a close analysis of the organization of the *Salisbury Journal* during the eighteenth century, will be published by the Oxford University Press.

9. For a preliminary discussion of the commercial divisions see Michael Harris, "Paper Pirates: the Alternative Book Trade in Mid-18th Century London," in *Fakes and Frauds; Varieties of Deception in Print and Manuscript*, ed. Robin Myers and Michael Harris (Winchester/Detroit: St. Paul's Bibliographies/Omnigraphics, 1989).

10. Michael Treadwell, "London Trade Publishers, 1675–1750," *The Library*, Ser. 6, iv (1982).

11. Robert Darnton, *The Kiss of Lamourette: Reflections on Cultural History* (New York: Norton, 1990).

12. Jurgen Habermas, *The Structural Transformation of the Publick Sphere: An Inquiry into a Category of Bourgeois Society*, trans. Thomas Burger (Cambridge: Polity Press, 1989).

13. Geoff Eley, "Nations, Publics and Political Culture: Placing Habermas in the Nineteenth Century," in *Habermas and the Public Sphere*, ed. Craig Calhoun (Cambridge, Mass.: MIT Press, 1993), pp. 289–306.

14. Claude Bellanger, Jacques Godechot, Pierre Guiral and Fernand Terrou, eds., *Histoire Generale de la Presse Francaise*, 5 vols. (Paris: Presses Universitaires de France, 1969–1976); Henri-Jean Martin and Roger Chartier, eds., with Jeanne-Pierre Vevet, *Histoire de l'Edition Francaise*, 4 vols. (Paris: Promodis, 1982–1986). Whether or not this separation had any strategic purpose is unclear. Its use may relate to the idea that newspapers and periodicals were predominantly products of the nineteenth and twentieth centuries when they can be identified as part of a distinct commercial system.

2

Sons of Liberty and Their Silenced Sisters: "Ladies' Magazines" and Women's Self-Representation in the Early Republic

Amy Beth Aronson

The first American magazine for women, the *Ladies Magazine and Repository of Entertaining and Instructive Knowledge* (1792–1793), was a novel venture in a volatile age. The "American experiment in democracy," now a new and polyglot nation that was growing and changing at an unprecedented rate, had thrown many cultural rules and roles into question. Amidst this ideological flux, one prevailing orthodoxy was the idea that women were not expected to engage in the public sphere as speakers. Yet restrictions on women's self-representation faced the incursions of a democratic culture: Liberalizing standards for public speech were rousing and inflecting public debate, and the literary marketplace was also diversifying, expanding public access to a widening range of discourse.[1] The over one hundred "ladies' magazines" that were launched in America between 1790–1830 partook of these democratizing conditions to answer the presumption of women's silence in the public realm.

The American magazine itself was a form tailor-made for the self-representation deemed largely improper for a lady. Although conceived in imitation of Britain's popular eighteenth-century periodicals—the *Tatler, Spectator* and *Gentleman's Magazine*—the American "periodical miscellany" was distinctly keyed to the democratic conditions in which it was produced and consumed. From its inception in 1741, the American version was more inclusive, more multiple, more open than its

British forbearers. Where the *Tatler* magazine had its "Isaac Bicker-staff" character and the *Spectator* its "Mr. Spectator" persona, each of which worked to center commentary and organize contents, the eighteenth-century American magazine had no strong, controlling voice. The trendsetting *Gentleman's Magazine*, the forefather of America's gender-marketed magazines, was comprised of sequential entries linked through carefully composed editorial transitions, an organizational tactic absent from its early American kin.[2]

By contrast, the early American magazine was written and read more democratically. The American version was marked by openness to a range of contributions, by polyvocality and discursive competition between adjacent items on the page. Populated by contributions and perpetuated by reader response, early American magazines configured a dynamic forum. Thus, although American magazines as a group would not become profitable until about 1850, from the first they did succeed at promoting ideological and discursive commerce in public. They sustained a range and promoted the exchange of divergent viewpoints, qualities that compelled readers' active participation in the construction and perpetuation of meanings.

A brainchild of a democratizing print culture, the American magazine for women promised virtually revolutionary possibilities. Its democratic openness and participatory dynamics promised to subvert and to redress women's silence in the public sphere. This chapter will examine some of the ways in which contributors made use of the early women's magazine, helping to recode the "woman question" and to put forward strategic possibilities for women's self-representation in the new American nation.

These contributions are drawn from three of the most successful early American women's periodicals: the *Ladies Magazine and Repository of Entertaining and Instructive Knowledge* (1792–1793), printed by William Gibbons of Philadelphia, the first of the genre; Samuel B. White's unusually long-lived *Weekly Visitor or Ladies' Miscellany* (1802–1812), a New York City–based purveyor of fiction and the emergent sentimental mode; and the *American Ladies' Magazine* (1828–1836), out of Boston, the periodical in which Sarah Josepha Hale, the trendsetting editor of the best-selling nineteenth-century women's magazine, *Godey's Lady's Book* (1830–1898), got her start in the business.[3]

ROBBING THE CRADLE OF LIBERTY: THE PROBLEM OF THE SILENCED SISTER

Ironically, although early American women's magazines wanted women's words, their very democratic openness limited women's presence in their pages.[4] The earliest women's magazines were often monopolized by male voices, and they spoke for women in two major modes: negation and omission.[5]

The negating voice of a male speaker can be heard in a letter sequence published in the *Ladies Magazine and Repository* in 1792, "LETTERS From A Brother to a Sister at a Boarding School." The four-letter sequence is presented as authentic: The letters are printed in three consecutive issues of the magazine, and in letter format, including the original salutations and dates of writing. Yet the sequence, as published, tellingly distorts the definitive dynamic of the letter-writing process: the equal participation of writer and reader through which a collaborative building of meaning takes place.[6] Only the brother's letters appear in the magazine. The basic equality of the correspondence relationship is thereby warped in the *Ladies Magazine*, concentrating the brother's voice while utterly effacing the sister's response. Indeed, her voice is doubly suppressed—by the male author of the letters and the male-controlled *Ladies Magazine*.

The specific mechanisms of the sister's silencing are revealed over the course of the sequence. The brother begins with "an extract from Dr. Richard Hey's dissertation," which instructs that "the pleasures which have a tendency to dissipate and enervate, should be used with prudent reserve, lest they should introduce an habitual lassitude and depression, which may degenerate into melancholy." "Above all," the brother then quotes, "indulge your propensities of the benevolent kind." It is not difficult to imagine why a brother might choose this excerpt as a relevant lesson to his American sister. It conjoins two fundamental conceits of feminine gender obligations moving into the nineteenth century: "regulate . . . pleasures" and "indulge benevolence." The excerpt nicely conflates an obviated form of self-interest, the avoidance of "lassitude and melancholy," with the control of pleasure, suggesting that a woman's pursuit of happiness is linked with her virtuous self-restraint.

But the idiom of negativity can best be heard when we consider the brother's source. While he describes Dr. Hey's dissertation as "an excellent direction for the conduct of life," the work is actually a treatise about suicide. The brother's positive example is actually a negative antiexample and woeful warning.

The brother's second letter further expresses this emergent negativity. It begins with a backhanded compliment further attenuated by its faint praise: "Though your last letter is not free from errors," he points out, "accuracy is what I do not, at present, expect." He then writes of the sister's "freedom and fertility of thought" with the imputation of disease and catastrophe: "This letter," he writes, "abounds more with ideas than any former composition of yours that has come under my notice. This I consider a promising symptom," he explains, taking on an anxious edge. "Your mind will [now] begin to exert its powers of invention, and to think for itself," he continues. "This, then, is an important crisis."

The brother's negative reaction to his sister's expressiveness as a letter writer is particularly telling. Although a woman's epistolary competence is a signal of her attainment and breeding, the "freedom and fertility" of the sister's letter is not an unqualified sign of success, but is, ambivalently, a symptom, albeit initially pleasing, of something he cannot name. It is a signal of trouble or illness glimpsed, but not yet grasped.

The brother's mounting anxiety next condenses into anger, which is only accentuated for readers by Gibbons' placement of the next letter in the very next column of the *Ladies Magazine*. It opens with naked chastisement. "The principle reason [for writing] is that I think it necessary to mention your faults," the brother dashes, and "whatever pain it may cost you," he continues, "I think myself obliged to say that, after such expectations as I had formed of you, I am greatly disappointed." He finally resorts to denunciation, to outright negation, blaming the sister for an impudent or ignorant indifference to his instructions. "I kept in mind the directions I had given you," he thinks, "and was constantly cherishing the hope, that I could see them copied into your conduct; . . . if you had at all imbibed the Spirit of them," he persists, "you would have been a very different person from what you are."

Therein lies the rub. The male writer had intended to script his female reader's "character" and, in fact, apparently believed he was directing her effectively. But what is missing, at least for readers of the *Ladies Magazine*, is the authority and the informed discourse necessary to bring his designs to fruition. If only the sister had somehow comprehended the "Spirit" of his intentions, she would be different from "what"—not who—she is.

For female readers of the *Ladies Magazine*, the sway of the brother's ineffectual instructions, his language of male management, is both underlined and undermined. Even while the consolidated presentation of the sequence wants to foreclose possibilities for female response, the marked absence of the sister's voice, especially in light of the dynamics of the correspondence relationship, exposes the need for it. Her silence is pronounced, her absence highlighted, by her negation by the pens of men.

The second kind of male speaker, who writes in an idiom of omission with regard to women, is just as incapable of rightly representing them. A narrator, he propounds the many truncated parables of miserable and fallen females that appear in early magazines as cautionary tales. Foregrounding female suffering, these contributions encapsulate female experience as the inexorable onset of dire distress. While these pieces may represent the seeds of the emergent sentimental narrative, most lack coherent references to the process by which miserable women "fall." Indeed, some are mere one-paragraph deathbed scenes, in which female figures utter their tortured goodbyes.[7] Few of these stories offer so much as a spiritual rationale for the heroine's trials.[8] Unlike articles in contemporaneous British women's magazines, which mingled "compliment and chastisement in the service of didactic intent," these American versions would "entertain" by imponderable pathos and "instruct" by omission.[9]

Take, for example, "The Beggar Girl," a three-paragraph piece published in Samuel White's *Weekly Visitor or Ladies' Miscellany* in November 1803. "Have pity on a wretched orphan," it opens, with the nameless girl's "tears trickling down her care-worn cheeks, and her bosom heaving with sighs, that seemed to rend the heart from whence they came." The abject figure approaches a "beautiful young creature" on the street, as the writer "draw[s] nearer for the purpose of hearing their discourse." The abject girl then reveals to the woman passerby that her father died, and that her mother, too, "afflict[ed] by the dreadful news . . . withered and died," with her helpless daughter clasped in her arms. Immediately, "our little all was seized by merciless creditors," she continues, "and friendless and unprotected, I'm doomed to wander, and prey to misery and fatigue." The woman then murmurs, "God bless you, in such a tender, melancholy, impressive tone" that "borne on every breeze," it seemed telegraphed through town. Abruptly, the male narrator then admits that he cannot find the words to finish the story: " 'tis impossible to describe how affected I was," he submits. So, he ends it there, assuring readers that the beggar girl "is now in a place, secure from every evil."

"Sarah—A Fragment," published in the *Visitor* the year before (December 31, 1802) is similarly the plaint of an orphan which, in its three-quarters of a column, can hardly explain why its pathetic subject appears "with tears streaming down her cheeks," crying out, "Can I hope that Heaven will hear my complaint, when a father turns his ear from it? Can I hope that charity will relieve a child whom its mother has also forsaken?"

These estranged women, speaking in public only in desperation and heard only because they are overheard by male narrators, evoke the limitations on women's speech in the public domain. Controlled by sentimentality, encased in their own vulnerability, women speak publicly only when they must, when pleading for help. The male narrators who give them limited representation (at best), can neither elaborate their stories nor substantively assist them within the plot. Yet, these tales also suggest the role the early women's magazine would play in response. Everywhere these manifest expressions of woman's negated and needy condition elicited forms of constructive response from other women.

The early American women's magazines, as we'll see, worked especially on these two dimensions: They operated as a female forum, providing a site of collaboration and group support for women writers and readers. And, they made available a space for experimental self-representation, constructing new possibilities for argumentation, authorial subjectivity, language, narrative and reader response.

THE WOMAN'S ANGLE IN THE FIRST AMERICAN WOMEN'S MAGAZINES

Many apparently female-authored contributions discuss expected themes and practices, but in unexpected ways. These "feminine" interests include matrimony and its ominously autonomous opposite, "spinsterhood"; seduction and its consequences; and virtue, rightly defined. In the treatment of each, women contributors reveal some buried implications.

The matrimonial essay, for example, raises embedded questions about women's unequal status, about obedience, subservience and their limits. In the July 1792, issue of the *Ladies Magazine*, the female author of "On Matrimonial Obedience" talks in public, legalistic terms about the ostensibly "private" matter of marriage, pursuing this logic in an effort to recreate the partners as equals. The writer begins on confirmed ground, with an accredited claim of "feminine" propriety: "The word *obey*, in the promise or vow to be made by the *woman* [is] very improper," she writes, "and ought not to be." Continuing, she explains why: "Obliging a woman to make a *vow to obey* their husbands [is] . . . obliging them to perjure themselves." The promise cannot be made by anyone, she asserts, without "reservations." Balancing a "feminine" language of self-restraint with the judicial concept of "perjury," a public conception of wrongdoing based on discrepancy between inner belief and outward presentation, the contributor repositions "masculine" and "feminine" values, bringing both under a framing rubric of justice.

The point has been to create a suitable space from which to press the feminine case. The contributor offers an imaginary courtroom and undertakes a thorough cross-examination of the practice under review. "Why, therefore, is the word *obey* still preserved in our service, when it would be easy to leave it out; and when, in fact, we know that it is virtually left out by nine out of ten who enter into that holy state?" she asks, pointing out that the one-sided obligation to obey is quite undemocratic in a larger sense, too: the vast majority of marriages, she testifies, already begin on this rhetorically equal plane.

The scales of justice need adjustment. So, like an attorney, the writer demands that evidence be brought forward to support the continuation of the wrongful practice being tried: "You may say, perhaps, that the word *obey* as it appears in our service, means only that the wife is to obey in all things lawful.—Yes—But can you prove that *obey* will admit of this restrictive interpretation?—Can you also prove," she insists, "that husbands in general, will admit of the very favourable construction you are pleased to put upon it?" Her conclusion to this cross-examination is brief, but decisive: "I am afraid not."

The writer is now in a rhetorical position to offer a brief but broad-thinking summation. Proposing a reconfiguration, she suggests that the roles of leader and led, in general, ought to be gender-neutral, premised on merit, talent and intellectual ability, rather than on received convention or unreasonable law. "Suppose we leave out of our consideration the many women of superior judgment, of our acquaintance," she grants, "it will still be allowed that there is . . . no woman whose understanding is so very barren, but that she may at sometimes take the lead in command with a better effect than her husband." Appropriating public standards for private relations, the writer advances an egalitarian ideal of marriage in which the wife is not subordinate. At least by rhetorical formulation, wife and husband are hereby created equal. The writer is aptly tagged, "A Matrimonial Republican."

The issues of marriage and "spinsterhood" typify larger meditations in the magazines about the unwritten rules controlling women's stories. The "old maid" is a preoccupation because she raises the prospect of a contradiction in early nineteenth-century terms: the lady as autonomous individual.

Contributions like an 1807 letter "To the Editor" of White's *Weekly Visitor* pave the way for the potential accreditation of the autonomous lady. "There is something capriciously cruel in what most men expect from their wives," the writer observes. Reproving a gendered wrong, the writer relates that "a man dislikes that his wife should express any symptoms of discontent when he declares his intention to leave her and dine at a tavern with his friends," she notes, "yet he would not be pleased to hear her say, especially if he thought she spoke her thoughts, 'Pray, my dear, go: I shall be just as happy without you.'"

The contribution does not suggest that a husband's freedom to live and act as he chooses ought to be equally shared by wives; nor does it propose that a marriage ought to curtail a man's freedoms in leisure time, centralizing his wife, home and family. But the logical pivot for each of these lines of nineteenth-century American gender discourse can be read here. More important for now, by exposing that a husband probably would not appreciate the treatment he routinely proffers to his wife, this ordinary woman subtly proposes a more egalitarian understanding of the rights and responsibilities of married women and men. Turning the tables on the masculine prerogatives to autonomy, the writer implies that the same cultural standards might be applied to men's and women's conduct. Like the "Matrimonial Republican," the letter reveals a woman's perspective and is consequently suggestive of thinking about gender equality.

LETTER AND ADDRESS: GENDERED GENRES AND THEIR USES

This contributor's subtle suggestion (and warning) that "turnabout is fair play" is conveyed in the form of a letter. The understanding of the magazine as a nexus for the exchange of information largely controlled by participating readers explains why letters would methodize, emblematize and epitomize the American magazine.

For some readers, however, the letter constituted and conveyed different messages. Historically, the letter is a gendered genre, carrying particular meanings for women and men writers respectively. Although cultural prescriptions about letter-writing decorum shifted through the eighteenth century, generally with the result of degrading women's epistolarity as private, nonliterary and emotional, prohibitions against women's writing and reading never included letters.[10] The letter was perhaps the one genre that had always been available for women's use.

The "natural" affiliation of women and letter writing is affirmed in early American ladies magazines. Gibbons' *Ladies Magazine and Repository*, for example, headlines the publication of reader letters as "Specimens of Female Literature." Several magazines published letters as "models of female comportment." Over time, the letter's topography became a shorthand in some women's magazines for articles about culturally constituted "women's issues"; subjects such as virtue, marriage, motherhood and "female character" are collected across monthly editions under the generic editorial earmark "Letters On. . . ."

While early republican women and men shared equal access to letter writing, only women gained special access and status under the auspices of epistolarity, and women's magazines broadcast that fact. Under the letter's aegis, women contributors to early magazines make notable narrative shifts. "From A Young Lady To Her Seducer," published in White's *Weekly Visitor* in April 1807, uses the letter form to accomplish a crucial authorial turn for women and it enables the writer to pronounce her gender-determined yet "unladylike" outrage—both for all the journal's readers to see.

The writer uses the intimacy of the letter strategically, to pave the way for a heart-to-heart confrontation where, arguably, she would have the upper hand. "I write not to justify myself to yo[u]; you deserve not—" she begins, "but while I lay open my heart, I desire you would examine *your own—*," she writes. Having drawn the reader close, she then utilizes the letter's (and the magazine's) presumption of audience engagement to her advantage, questioning pointedly: "What must your sensations be when you recollect that you have violated all laws, divine and human; broken through every principle of virtue, and every tie of humanity; that you have offered an insult to the kind genius of hospitality, the benevolent spirit of good-neighborhood, and the sacred powers of friendship."

The rhythm and rhetorical structure of this opening paragraph, which initially emphasizes evocative dualities—"divine" and "human," "principles" and "ties"—soon foregrounds a woman's cultural perspective of the codes her seducer had breached. The "principles" at issue are not those of democracy, but of "virtue." He has scorned a gendered complex of values that women are meant to hold dear: "hospitality," "benevolence" and "the sacred powers of friendship."

The writer's anger and accusations intensify as she assaults the "masculine" characteristics and cultural privileges he has exploited: "Was it not sufficient that you added my name to the list of your infamous triumphs? . . . that you had ranked me among the daughters of wretchedness and ignomy?" she asks. But that's not all: "Deprived me of my father, my all of comfort, and my all of hope?" "Were not these things sufficient," she presses, "without adding to them the baseness of publicly speaking of me in the streets, in language that a gentleman would not have used to the vilest wanton that ever breathed." The writer's list of grievances bespeaks the absolute loss of her identity—personal, familial and cultural—at the hands of an ignoble man whose "triumph" is to "deprive" her of even those accredited markers of public identity allowed and allotted to women. What's worse, he has violated her in public. Exposed as an estranged woman, she is utterly undone. Yet, she turns her loss to consolation, her isolation to a kind of triumphant embrace: "Weak, unhappy man! I am not ashamed of defeat," she declares.

This letter writer's righteous anger about male mistreatment sets up an important reversal that represents at least a rhetorical victory for the woman's point of view. The seducer may have "ruined" his abandoned mistress by male-authored public standards, but, in the context of the woman's letter, his ignoble deceit, base language and inhuman rending of culturally ratified rules of interpersonal conduct *ruin him*. The ultimate effects of seduction and abandonment are rewritten here. The seducer, rather than the person seduced, is seen to be weak, miserable, debased and defeated. He, not she, is destroyed. Denouncing him as perverse and monstrous, the writer literally unmans him.

Such treatments of the issue of seduction set up critical authorial reversals that would have enormous ramifications for women's narratives in magazines and outside them in the decades to come. What's more, in the present, the abandoned lady is not alone. The magazine has created a space for her to expose her seducer publicly—to do unto him, through the magazine, what he can do unto her in the streets. Unmaking him in this public way, she also visibly constitutes herself. This self-making is marked by the attachment of her Christian name, "Eliza," to the letter.

And Eliza's act of self-creation invites readers' emulation. Eliza writes to the implied audience, readers of the *Visitor*, as much as to the intended audience of her letter, its addressee. These magazine readers are doubly engaged; they are compelled both by the reader-responsive climate of the magazine and by the dynamic expectations of the episto-lary form to enter Eliza's story. Such overlapping invitations to reader involvement promote audience ratification and reiteration of the act of self-representation that Eliza accomplishes.

AUDIENCE INVOLVEMENT: COLLABORATION AND THE REAUTHORIZATION OF GENDER DISCOURSE

The epistolary relations at play in Eliza's contribution are suggestive of the multiple forms of audience engagement encouraged by the mag-azine's format. Numerous early republican contributors utilized these various audience dynamics quite consciously to pursue their discursive goals. An 1809 contribution to the *Weekly Visitor*, "The Criterion of Virtue," raises with readers the politics of language as well as the lan-guage of politics. The writer, "V.," envisions reader collaboration in her effort to redefine the popular understanding of "feminine virtue," a piv-otal gendered term.[11]

"It is, I believe, extremely common, in the appropriation of words to ideas, to give them erroneous significations, or attribute greater latitude to general terms than they were originally intended to express . . . ," V. begins. Since her sights are set on reforming gender discourse by popu-lar consensus, the magazine is her best place to turn: "I have often, though vainly, wished to see the criterion of virtue, as it respects our sex, properly established," she writes, so "it shall be the employment of a serious hour to assign, with as much precision as my slender knowl-edge will admit, the distinct and proper claims of the highest grace a woman can possess."

Although officially attenuated by the writer's admission of "slender knowledge" (a frequent female disclaimer through the nineteenth cen-tury), the ensuing article pursues a larger understanding of a power-fully packed concept. Like so many others, V. begins by imagining a suitable space within which to work. Since she is seeking group consen-sus, she chooses not the contentious courtroom of the "Matrimonial Republican," but the more common conversation space of the "feminine" drawing room. She imagines herself surrounded by female company when she asks "a moment's indulgence," then proceeds to acknowledge her audience, cleverly promoting their continued "indulgence" by promising that their own virtue would be thereby confirmed: "She whose consciousness of integrity can give a decided affirmative to the following interrogatories," V. assures, "is, indisputably, possessed of that exalted characteristical excellence."

With her audience in tow, V. moves to the task before them all. "Virtue, if I understand its implications rightly," she proposes, "is a combination not a solitary grace, when meant to include female excellence." Continuing, she complicates the oversimplifying metonymy of chastity for virtue: "Chastity, (although the fairest ornament our sex can boast, and without which no woman can be estimable) is yet but a *single* virtue," she thinks, and so it hardly captures the whole of "female excellence." "Virtue is an aggregate, and contains the sum of human goodness."

A "new and improved" virtue would therefore require an expanded understanding of women's "estimable" qualities, beginning with chastity but also including intelligence, benevolence and moral strength. As V. propounds a new "feminine virtue," she simultaneously breaks it down and builds it up. The process implicates the current understanding of the term as faulty, while also raising it to an elevated standard more difficult to achieve. Does raising standards promote higher attainment and status, or prevent it?

Surely a telling answer depends on the conditions of reception. What V.'s letter captures is the expectation of reception, the hope of audience participation made possible by the early American women's magazine. The project of the contribution, to revise and then ratify gender discourse, also calls upon the *Visitor*'s potential to mobilize a female audience. It demonstrates the inclusion and consent of women in efforts to innovate, revise or recover the gender discourse that will govern them.

SEEING EYE TO EYE: ASSURED AUDIENCES AND WOMEN'S REVISIONS

As women's magazines began to proliferate after the turn of the nineteenth century, contributors showed an increasing consciousness of women audiences, of the conditions and possibilities of reception. More and more contributions, especially stories, are written for readers with whom writers can strategically see eye-to-eye—and who will meet them halfway, actively participating in the construction of critical meanings.

A striking reflection of these developments is an anonymous April 1828 story published in Sarah Hale's *American Ladies' Magazine*. The story rereads as it rewrites the tale of an autonomous woman, or "old maid," named Margery Bethel.

The story begins with a biographical sketch notable for the scantness of the evidence it supplies. "Margery Bethel was an inhabitant of Danvers, Mass. It is not certain that she was a native of that town, nor is the year of her birth accurately known; but in 1719, she bore such evident marks of age, that she became distinguished by the appellation peculiar to unmarried females . . .—she was called an old maid." Margery's story would have been a romance narrative, were it not for the dereliction of the male partner. She "had been a famous beauty;—had several admirers, and, it was conjectured, was once engaged to be married. But her lover, as lovers have often done since the example of Phaon, proved a recreant."

With this ruination of the "feminine" romance plot, Margery is on her own. Abandoned by a "recreant" man, "the disconsolate fair-one . . . neither rhymed nor raved, nor made any attempt to drown herself," the writer notes, merely alluding to the responses of abandoned heroines in many male-authored tales at this time. Instead, "she acted a much more common, and, indeed, more feminine part." She became "sad . . . and taciturn; and finally, as her beauty waned, she seemed to resign herself uncomplainingly, to neglect and celibacy. . . . She grew old, and she faded, as every fair girl will do . . . and was called ugly." The writer's elliptical structure and detached tone here suggest her confidence in her reading audience. She condenses whole volumes of Margery's history into a single sentence because she knows women readers will have heard this story before and will fill in the gaps for themselves.

As if this seemingly inexorable fate were not punishing enough, the writer then interjects a pointed parallel to the social conditions afflicting actual women living in the nonfiction world: "There is another evil to which women are subjected," she asserts. It is to have cultivated minds, and yet be confined to a society that does not understand and cannot appreciate their talents and intelligence. This frequently occurs. And so Margery Bethel's story becomes an allegory of the woman's silence, of the absence of her stories from the public mind.

The mystery of Margery's temperament slowly deepens into a larger communal distrust of its meaning. Since Margery lived alone, and "never received company, no one knew much about her management. But the less they knew, the more they guessed; till finally, as she grew older and more reserved, they first called her odd—then cross—then strange—and then a witch!"

"The case of Margery made a great bustle," drawing scrutiny from the highest authorities in the town. Their first response is to hurl negations, in an effort to suppress the powers they imagine her to possess: "Her supposed compact with the spirit of the devil was regretted, or condemned, sighed over, or inveighed against" until these measures proved insufficient. "Finally," it was "the opinion of all that something had to be done."

Not surprisingly, "the minister, the two deacons, and two of the most influential and pious men belonging to the church, were chosen to visit her, at her dwelling, and propound certain questions; and, from her answers, it was concluded, the full proof of her guilt, which no one doubted, would be obtained." The writer's elevated sarcasm conveys her contempt for this bogus interplay, in which male authorities blot out the possibility of a woman's self-expression by writing answers to their own questions before they are even asked—and at the woman's expense. Poor Margery "was totally ignorant of the honor intended her," the writer wryly remarks, "as it had been judged expedient to take her by surprise as the most likely method of eliciting truth from one whose study was to deceive."

Fearful and uncomprehending of Margery's story, the male leadership of Danvers becomes enmeshed in a tense mystery plot. "The gentlemen . . . silently drew near the door," led by the minister who "heard a sound within. He paused, then motioned the party to advance, and they all cautiously crept forward, and all distinctly heard the same noise." The men could not decipher it, but all agreed on what it was not: "It was not like mortal conversation; it was a low, but continued, and monotonous sound, such as none of them ever recollected before to have heard. They all trembled." Eavesdropping on Margery, they recognize only that she seems to be speaking a language alien and unfamiliar to them. "At length, as it did not cease, and as there was no window on the side they stood, through which to reconnoitre, the party was obliged to enter, in order to discover the cause of their alarm. The minister laid his hand on the latch—and the boldest deacon stood near to support him. They opened the door with the swiftness of lightening [sic], and stood before the astonished eyes of Margery."

Their sudden, uninvited appearance surprised her. But Margery Bethel showed "no dismay. Why should she? She was at the moment reading that consoling promise of the Saviour,—'Blessed are they that mourn, for they shall be comforted.'"

Both the cultural "logic" by which the merely unmarried Margery Bethel comes to be construed as a devil-worshiping witch, and the narrative logic by which the male authorities of Danvers are shown to have egregiously misread her, speak to the importance of women's self-representation in public. In the absence of a comprehensible story to explain and legitimize Margery's autonomous life, the community around her confabulates a phantasm with almost unending destructive potential. Silenced as to her own character and circumstances, Margery Bethel is construed as not merely wicked, but also monstrous. In contrast to the male "seducer" of Eliza's letter to the *Visitor*, who is transmogrified by his overt and unconscionable acts, Margery, omitted and storyless, is dangerous and inhuman due to the very absence of her narrative from the popular imagination.

The male authorities charged with containing this lurking peril on the margin of their town clearly lack the knowledge necessary to interpret and represent her. These pious men, pillars of their community, are so illiterate when it comes to women's stories that they misread the very text that authorizes them: They mistake the utterance of prayer for evil incantations. It is the woman writer of the contribution who can reveal Margery's true character and narrate her circumstances. As she exposes the inadequacies of the cultural authorities who license themselves to contain by interpreting Margery, the contributor also subtly instructs her readers in the significant art of reading and writing—of public self-representation—as a woman. As a tale told by a woman to be read by women, Margery's life story becomes not only visible, but comprehensible and, by ascendent cultural standards, exemplary. Deserted by a recreant lover and cruelly outcast by a community that ought to have embraced and protected her, Margery Bethel chose not to "rave" nor plead desperately for help; neither was she ruined and defeated, becoming "cross" and "taciturn," as many a male author would have her do. Instead, Margery Bethel can be seen as the heroine of an emergent woman's plotline: hers is the story of an autonomous lady who leads a benevolent, pious life of her own.[12]

WANTING WOMEN'S WORDS: THE APPEARANCE OF A NEW GENRE FOR A NEW AND DEMOCRATIC NATION

Using the democratic openness and audience participation of the early American women's magazine, contributors explored strategies of self-representation amidst and against the silencing idioms of male authority and authorship. By revealing previously invisible angles, writing new subject positions and collaborating in the creation and critique of gender discourse, communities of women's magazine readers and writers began to envision new cultural positions and elaborate new stories for themselves. As women's magazine contributors began to write "Woman" from a position of dutiful silence into a discourse of virtuous presence moving into the nineteenth century, women began to constitute themselves as a distinct public in American life and letters.

NOTES

1. Kenneth Cmeil writes that despite new "democratized" standards of speech, women's voices, if heard, "were viewed not so much as uppity women claiming equality, but as the wives and daughters of offending men." See

Democratic Eloquence: The Fight Over Popular Speech in Nineteenth Century America (New York: William Morrow and Company, 1990), p. 136. Regarding the diversifying marketplace, see Richard D. Brown, "From Cohesion to Competition" and Rhys Isaac, "Books and the Authority of Learning: The Case of Mid-Eighteenth-Century Virginia," both in William L. Joyce et al., *Printing and Society in Early America* (Worcester, Mass.: American Antiquarian Society, 1983). Women's responses to their own public silence is the subject of Glenna Matthews, *The Rise of Public Woman: Woman's Power and Woman's Place in the United States, 1630–1970* (New York: Oxford University Press, 1992). See also, Mary P. Ryan, *Women in Public: Between Banners and Ballots 1825–1880* (Baltimore: Johns Hopkins University Press, 1990).

2. Dorothy Foster, "The Earliest Precursor of Our Present-Day Monthly Miscellanies," *PMLA* 23, no. 1 (1917): 22–58.

3. The scholarship on early American women's magazines is sketchy in terms of the numbers. The difficulty of publishing any periodical in the early Republic—including cost of materials, poor transportation, cantankerous print technologies, unstable political conditions and a chronic scarcity of copy—certainly dampened magazine development. Frank Luther Mott remains the best descriptive source on the state of early American magazines. See *A History of American Magazines. Vol. I: 1741–1850* (New York: Thomas Nelson and Sons, 1931). A lighter overview is John Tebbel and Mary Ellen Zuckerman, *The Magazine in America 1741–1990* (New York: Oxford University Press, 1991). Bertha-Monica Stearns has written descriptively of early American women's magazines. See "Before Godey's," *American Literature* 2 (1930): 248–55. See also, "Early New England Magazines for Ladies," *New England Quarterly* 2 (1929): 420–57; "Early Western Magazines for Ladies," *Mississippi Valley Historical Review* 18 (1931): 319–30; "Southern Magazines for Ladies, 1819–1860," *South Atlantic Quarterly* 31 (1932): 70–87; "Early Factory Magazines in New England: *The Lowell Offering* and Its Contemporaries," *Journal of Economic and Business History* 2 (1930): 685–705. Finally, Patricia Okker has recently argued that the early nineteenth-century women's magazine "created the idea of a public space for women." Okker provides a register of more than six hundred women editors between 1800 and 1899 that is a godsend to scholars of women and/in the American magazine. See *Our Sister Editors: Sarah J. Hale and the Tradition of Nineteenth-Century American Women Editors* (Athens: University of Georgia Press, 1995).

4. As the vast majority of magazine contributions were published anonymously or were identified only by a pseudonym, it is impossible to know to a certainty the gender of the writer. It was not uncommon for men to write as women in colonial and early American periodicals—witness Benjamin Franklin's "Silence DoGood" series in the *New-England Courant* (1721–1723), which ran between April and October 1722. However, as I know of no cases, including Franklin's, in which a male writer posed as a female without alerting his audience to the charade, I have used pronouns and other self-references to infer the gender of the authors discussed herein.

5. Patricia Okker, *Our Sister Editors: Sarah J. Hale and the Tradition of Nineteenth-Century American Women Editors* (Athens: University of Georgia Press, 1995), p. 8.

6. The sexual and textual politics of the letter have been discussed in Janet Gurkin Altman, *Epistolarity: Approaches to a Form* (Columbus: Ohio State University Press, 1982); Elizabeth C. Goldsmith, ed., *Writing the Female Voice: Essays on Epistolary Literature* (Boston: Northeastern University Press, 1989); Michael Warner, *Letters of the Republic* (Cambridge, Mass.: Harvard University Press, 1990).

7. The deathbed scene has been seen as an organizing principle of the sentimental by Ann Douglas, *The Feminization of American Culture* (New York: Anchor Press, 1988).

8. The incompleteness of such narratives is underscored by Jane Tompkins' argument that sentimental novels are "spiritual training narratives in which God is both savior and persecutor and the emphasis falls not on last-minute redemption, but on the toils and sorrows of 'the way.' " See *Sensational Designs: The Culture Work of American Fiction 1790–1860* (New York: Oxford University Press, 1985), p. 183.

9. Kathryn Shevelow, "Fathers and Daughters: Women as Readers of the *Tatler*," in *Gender and Reading: Essays on Readers, Texts and Contexts*, ed. Elizabeth A. Flynn and Patrochino Schweikart (Baltimore: Johns Hopkins University Press, 1986), p. 107. See also, Kathryn Shevelow, *Women and Print Culture: The Construction of Femininity in the Early Periodical* (New York: Routledge, 1989).

10. Shifts in the cultural meaning of women's epistolarity are discussed by the following: Katharine A. Jensen; Elizabeth C. Goldsmith; Patricia Meyer Spacks; Susan K. Jackson, all in Goldsmith, *Writing the Female Voice*.

11. The redefinition of "feminine virtue" remains a central task of women's magazine writers through at least the antebellum period, spanning both "popular" and political women's magazines. A helpful article is Ruth Bloch, "The Gendered Meanings of Virtue in Revolutionary America," *Signs* 13, no. 1 (Autumn 1987): 37–58. See also, selected articles collected by Ann Russo and Cheris Kramarae, eds., *The Radical Women's Press of the 1850s* (New York: Routledge, 1991).

12. The sentimental-domestic formula is delineated by Nina Baym, *Woman's Fiction: A Guide to Novels By and About Women in America, 1820–1870* (Ithaca, N.Y.: Cornell University Press, 1978).

3

The *World* of Edward Moore and the World of the English Parson

Christopher T. Hamilton

The first number of Edward Moore's periodical the *World* appeared in London on January 24, 1753. For the following three years, on each Thursday, the *World*'s essays circulated throughout London coffee-houses and were devoured by readers (many of whom, as Macaulay reminds us, were "men of high rank and fashion"), who maintained that only the uncultivated were unfamiliar with the new periodical. Finally, on December 30, 1756, after 209 numbers, the journal expired, but only after enjoying almost unprecedented success, at least judging by the typical life span of the mid–eighteenth-century periodical.[1] By 1755 the *World* had reached sales of up to two thousand copies per week and was so popular that many of its numbers were strung up in coffeehouses for public perusal.[2] Under the pseudonym Adam Fitz-Adam, Moore gloried in his success and tentatively compared his work to the *Spectator* papers that had taken London, and indeed almost all of England, by storm some forty-two years earlier: "I have the pleasure, and something more than the pleasure, of finding that two thousand of my papers are circulated weekly. This number exceeds the largest that was ever printed even of the *Spectators*, which in no other respects do I pretend to equal" (*World* 111).

The comparison Moore draws between the two papers, and the very nature of the periodical press, which, as is frequently noted, offers a unique firsthand look at the represented society, invite further estimations of these two exemplary journals.[3] Since the press customarily records, or confirms by what it omits, contemporaneous social preoccupations, the *World*, when placed in juxtaposition with the *Spectator*, becomes a revealing social document. We have seen its contribution to the creation and formation of the English novel, providing the genre with themes, dictating its function, and even defining or creating a readership for the new suspect literature.[4] And we have recently seen how the periodical press reveals eighteenth-century attitudes toward literary critics.[5] But there has not been much detailed commentary on how the periodical press sheds light on eighteenth-century attitudes toward the clergy. My interest in this chapter is in how the *World*, and its companion and rival the *Connoisseur*, when compared with earlier prototypes, reveal the degree to which English clergymen of all denominations had lost, at least in the eyes of a large portion of London's literati, the respect and influence they held during Queen Anne's reign when Addison and Steele enjoyed their greatest popularity.

It is not my purpose here to discuss the actual, as opposed to the perceived, reputation of the English clergy in the mid-eighteenth century. During the past twenty years, scholars have studied many of the significant religious controversies challenging churchmen during the Enlightenment, and there still remains a healthy debate as to whether the clergy were or were not held in high esteem—whether the church felt the impact of such attacks to a very large degree, or whether these significant challenges are twentieth-century constructs of critics exaggerating the so-called "threat" to orthodox Christianity during the period under consideration. But critics are in general agreement that most attacks originated either in a distrust of the priestly function as practiced by politically interested churchmen or in the perception of dissenting divines that the Anglican Church placed too much emphasis on ethical behavior and not enough on faith. As J. A. I. Champion has noted, "the radicals were concerned to debunk the false [political] authority of the Church"[6] and not to raise doubts about the existence of God. Certainly, divines often found themselves at the center of debate, especially when they espoused iconoclastic ideas about the nature of sin and redemption. Samuel Johnson's arguments with the would-be dissenting divine Samuel Dyer, arguments appearing in several *Rambler* essays, originated in Dyer's belief in man's basic goodness, the belief in the doctrine of universal optimism that was in vogue during the period.[7] But generally, the clergy maintained and promoted orthodox views and were accepted, as in any age and with the usual exceptions, as highly respected and necessary figures in English daily life.[8] This in spite of the attacks from the periodical essayists, who might be likened to television producers today whose depictions of churchmen are almost always satirical.

I

The essays of the *World* (edited by Edward Moore) and *Connoisseur* (edited by George Colman and Bonnell Thornton) saturated readers with incriminating images of English clergymen. While the *Tatler* and *Spectator* papers (1709–1712) endeavored, among a host of other things, to reform clerical shortcomings, the *World* and *Connoisseur* essays (1753–1756) persistently maligned the one figure whom the earlier moral apologists vigorously upheld.[9] In *Spectator* 270, Steele admires a recent production of Beaumont and Fletcher's *The Scornful Lady*, but severely rebukes the authors for their portrayal of the parson:

I must confess I was moved with the utmost Indignation at the trivial, sense-less, and unnatural Representation of the Chaplain. It is possible there may be a Pedant in Holy Orders, and we have seen one or two of them in the World; but such a driveler as Sir Roger, so bereft of all manner of Pride, which is the Characteristick of a Pedant, is what one would not believe could come into the Head of the same Man who drew the rest of the Play. . . . It is so mean a thing to gratify a loose Age with a scandalous Representation of what is reputable among Men, not to say what is sacred, that no Beauty, no Excellence in an Author ought to attone for it.[10]

Steele would be the first to support satire aiming to expose corrupt church practices or to correct clerical foibles. But satire for the sake of satire is unacceptable to both Steele and Addison, who are inher-itors of the tradition of "advices." The clergyman is an enduring fig-ure in English letters, and if tradition has named religion "the serious business of the human race,"[11] it is no less traditional to view the clergyman, even given the individualistic bent of English Prot-estantism, as a vital link between God and the laity. Should the cler-gyman neglect his duties, or, worse still, violate Christian principles, serious repercussions, translating into a general loss of faith, are felt nationwide.

Attempting to avert such social dysphoria, or to root out any rudi-mentary growth of spiritual malaise, English writers have frequently penned "advices" to improve, reaffirm and encourage the pastor's vital performance. George Herbert, Richard Baxter and John Eachard, three of the more prominent religious men writing in the seventeenth cen-tury, were concerned to revitalize the parish clergyman, and in the eighteenth century the proliferation of "advices to the clergy" continued what had become a minor literary genre, albeit that many of the "ad-vices" were simply veiled political satires. Among the earnest advices, though, throughout the seventeenth and eighteenth centuries, four questions recur with revealing frequency:

- Does the clergyman, in his sermons, gravitate toward controversial matters?
- Does he flaunt his knowledge of Greek and Latin?
- Has he neglected the art of public speaking?[12]
- Has he avoided visiting his parishioners and performing his social duties?

Naturally, other questions arise, perhaps concerning the parson's personal habits; but on the whole these four predominate. An affirmative response to any one of them calls for unconditional and rapid remediation.

When, for instance, Steele puzzles over the intolerable dullness of all too many sermons, he is drawing upon, and reminding his clerics about, a generic tradition that urges the necessity for practiced and effective oratorical skill. The clergy, states Steele in *Tatler* 66, are

the most learned body of Men now in the World; and yet this Art of Speaking, with the proper Ornament of Voice and Gesture, is wholly neglected among 'em; and I'll engage, were a deaf Man to behold the greater Part of 'em preach, he would think they were reading the Contents only of some Discourse they intended to make, than actually in the Body of an Oration, even when they are upon Matters of such a Nature as one would believe it were impossible to think of without Emotion

However, in a characteristic turn that one generally finds in early eighteenth-century commentary on the cleric, Steele does not withdraw his pen after dealing a damaging and embarrassing blow; he quickly mollifies the critics by profiling, in the same paragraph, the great and esteemed Francis Atterbury, a preacher who "has a peculiar Force in his Way, and has Many of his Audience who could not be intelligent Hearers of his Discourse, were there not Explanation as well as Grace in his action. This Art of his is us'd with the most exact and honest skill: He never attempts your Passions, 'till he has convinc'd your reason." In this example, we see that the general negative is followed by a personal honorific; Steele, like most early eighteenth-century writers, is easily able to find a living testimonial in the church as an example of the ideal clergyman, and he does not hesitate to set this exemplar before the public eye. Steele's tendency to balance negative with positive comments links him with a benevolent theory of satire that aimed to reform by eschewing strictly negative types in favor of positive exemplars. His complaints of clerical abuses sweep over the English clergy as a general class, thereby avoiding Restoration finger-pointing, and his recommendations highlight a positive and well-known figure.[13]

Steele's concern with the image of the preacher also suggests the vibrant social position enjoyed by early eighteenth-century clergymen. Far from being the docile and harmless creature satirized by later essayists and novelists and portrayed, perhaps unwittingly, by Goldsmith, the parish priest played such a vital role, beyond the ecclesiastical and religious ones in his parish, in social and political arenas that government officials were both alarmed by inflammatory sermons and appreciative of politically correct ones. Their voices, for instance, are the most intrusive in the ideological debates following the Revolution of 1688, and, to take an example from Queen Anne's reign, it was the dashing clergyman Henry Sacheverell who in 1709–1710 was largely responsible for toppling the Whig government.[14]

The satirical portraits in the *Tatler* and the *Spectator* papers aim to correct misdirected zeal while, at the same time, reaffirming the parson's crucial spiritual role. But we must also qualify our statements concerning the representations in these papers. On the whole, there are admittedly few references to preachers. Only 7 percent (58 out of 827 essays) mention a parson at all, but the fact remains that the majority of those 58 references auspiciously illuminate clerical traits: 34 are either positive or, by mentioning the parson only in passing, neutral. The occasional satirical portrait aims to correct a preacher who fails to follow one or more of the "advices" outlined above, notably the preacher who, as *Tatler* 71 records, "stretches his Jaws so wide, that instead of instructing Youth, it [his sermon] rather frightens them" and who, luxuriating in pride, "will go but once to the Sick, except they return his Visit."

Though this cleric is treated comparatively harshly, the *Tatler*/ *Spectator* papers are usually gentle, and, without ridiculing or exasperating the clergy with untempered critical remarks, suggest ways in which clergymen might more effectively implement moral reform and remedy spiritual barrenness. In *Tatler* 205, Steele writes: "I have often wondered, considering the excellent and choice spirits that we have among our Divines, that they do not think of putting vicious Habits into a more contemptible and unlovely figure than they do at present." Some critics might point to certain political restraints operating beneath the surface of Addison and Steele's usually tempered satire; political activists after all, they avoid attacking the clergy during the intense political maneuverings that characterized Queen Anne's reign because any outspoken censure would alienate the clergy—would make them disaffected toward a Whig ministry they were traditionally and constitutionally hostile to. But considering the aggressive and fearless outspokenness of the age, I believe Addison and Steele's references to clergymen are conventional portraits that would neither astonish nor offend the majority of their readers; they conjure up fictitious clergymen when looking to remediate a general problem, and frequently cite a well-known contemporary when praising jobs well performed.[15] Indignant of any malicious portraits, Addison especially sees his job as complementing the clergyman's. But, as an important sidenote, Addison subordinates his role as satirist to the clergyman's role as spiritual leader; thus, a proper hierarchy, as Addison would see it, is preserved, the image of the clergyman unimpaired and even elevated. In the *Guardian* 116, for example, Addison acknowledges that the clergyman's duties are more crucial than the satirist's: "While [the clergy] are employed in extirpating Mortal Sins, and Crimes of a higher Nature, I should be glad to rally the World out of Indecencies and Venial Transgressions. While the Doctor is curing Distempers that have the Appearance of Danger or Death in them, the Merry-Andrew has his separate Packet for the Meagrims and the Toothach." The areas, then, in which the clergyman must improve do not undermine his social and religious importance, and are not highlighted simply to divert the reading public, as are those faults illuminated by Moore and Thornton some forty years later. By midcentury, when Edward Moore was publishing his journal, the satirist had assumed not only a more corrective role, but also a more judgmental and competitive one as well. It was now Moore's job to extirpate "crimes of a higher Nature."[16]

II

William Temple's fortitude in the face of his father's financial troubles struck a sympathetic chord in James Boswell. On April 3, 1763, Boswell writes of his intimate friend:

His father's affairs went wrong, and Temple is obliged to give up about a half of an independent estate of between 3 and 400 a year in order to relieve his parent from shame and distress. He talks of it like a philosopher, and says that out of the wrecks of his fortune he will be able to pick as much as will support him in studious retirement, which is the life that he likes. He is not yet fixed whether he shall go into the Church. I shall encourage him in that scheme. He will be just the clergyman in the *Spectator*.

Boswell knew both the *Connoisseur* and the *World*; yet in order to allude to a clergyman of distinction, he had to pass over these recent and popular journals, and marshal in an old favorite, the *Spectator*. Though the *World* and *Connoisseur* delineate a large number of English clergymen, their references are consistently derogatory; Boswell, even if he had tried, would have searched in futility for a parson suitable for an appropriate comparison.

The editors of and contributors to the *World* and *Connoisseur*, if one were to judge solely by the clerical portraits, firmly align themselves with a satirical mode that exposes and then destroys its targets,[17] and reject the Augustan ideal to "blame and praise in equal parts." Instead of beneficent and sincere suggestions for clerical improvements, pointedly satirical portraits abound. The same categories are present (the four questions listed above), yet Moore, Colman and Thornton appear unwilling to provide moral exemplars to offset portraits of bumbling, inept and pedantic clergymen. To illustrate how the image of the clergyman had deteriorated, at least in these selected popular magazines of the midcentury, a few examples will suffice.

The *World*, as does the *Spectator*, recounts the origin of a literary club, a feature that, since the *Spectator*, had become the pattern for many periodicals. As did its predecessor, the *World* boasts of a reverend divine, one Dr. Carbuncle, who plays a vital part in his fashionable society. However, juxtaposition of the two divines reveals a comprehensive role reversal. In the world of the *Spectator*, the divine is an essential character; essential, that is, for providing a moral norm, and he becomes the most respected man of the club: "The Whole Club pays a particular Deference to the Discourse of this Gentleman, and are drawn into what he says as much by the candid and ingenuous Manner with which he delivers himself, as by the Strength of Argument and Force of Reason which he makes use of" (*Spectator* 34). Elaborating and commenting on the traditional concerns enumerated above, Addison judges his clergymen according to their pastoral success. In *Spectator* 106, Addison describes the chaplain to Sir Roger as the perfect man of faith. He not only preaches well, but lives "a very regular life" and performs his social functions to perfection: "There has not been a Law suit in the Parish since he has lived among them." The *World*'s divine provides a stark contrast; Dr. Carbuncle is necessary, not to provide moral training and mature advice to other members of the club, but to afford comic relief for the more serious philosopher-rogues. Whereas the *Spectator*'s clergyman is a pattern to which one should aspire, Carbuncle is a Hogarthian caricature, a man to be laughed at, to be endured and perhaps cherished as a pet animal, but not emulated. Compare the earlier rendition of the *Spectator*'s divine with the following account of Dr. Carbuncle (*World* 90)—a portrait infused with irony and puns, damning in its humor, yet pointed and devout in its criticism:

[He] is an honest, jolly, merry parson, well affected to the government, and much of a gentleman. He is the life of our club, instead of being the least restraint upon it. He is an admirable scholar, and I really believe has all Horace by heart; I know he has him always in his pocket. His red face, inflamed nose, and swelled legs, make him generally thought a hard drinker by those who do not know him; but I must do him the justice to say, that I never saw him disguised with liquor in my life. It is true, he is a very large man, and can hold a great deal, which makes the colonel call him, pleasantly enough, a vessel of election.

A short time later Dr. Carbuncle attempts to raise a large bumper of wine to his lips, misses his mouth, hits his nose instead, and spills the wine onto his lap. Such a disjunctive series of actions contrasts sharply with the calm acumen of the *Spectator*'s clergyman, who creates an adhesive moral bond among fellow club members; Carbuncle unites his friends by being the focal point, the subject of laughter. He is expressly forbidden to reflect upon the actions of the other members, and "unrestrained" activity rules the club. In the *World* and *Connoisseur*, this is no isolated image. The bibulous Carbuncle is only one of many clerical personages devised by the *World*'s contributors; and though these contributors may not have intended to undermine clerical authority, the conspicuous lack of positive patterns relegates the English divine to a position of servility and lends credence to one foreigner's observations of the English divine: "It is pleasant to see how fat and fair these parsons are. They are charged with being somewhat lazy, and their usual plumpness makes it suspected that there's some truth in it. It is common to see them in coffee houses, and even in taverns, with pipes in their mouths."[18]

The *World* is most persistent in its ridicule of oratorical abuses. Twelve different numbers exhibit the folly of parsons trying to distinguish themselves by an unwarranted emphasis on their learning and vocabulary. In *World* 136, the contributor satirizes the preacher's skill in winning adherents: "In the pulpit, the preacher who declaims in the loudest manner, is sure to gain the greatest number of followers. He has also the satisfaction of knowing that the devotion of a great part of his audience depends more upon the soundness of his lungs, than the soundness of his doctrine." This particular complaint echoes frequently throughout the century (and remains today the greatest and most justifiable objection to media preachers). So common was the complaint that certain numbers, concerned with peripheral topics, made sudden references to the "grave airs" of the parson. Moore himself (*World* 99) while observing that his countrymen frequently and illogically lose present enjoyments by fearing some future disaster, halts abruptly and makes a revealing apology to his readers: "I avoid entering seriously upon the subject . . . that I may not give my paper the air of a sermon." It is an inherent feature of one-line asides (many of Jane Austen's minor characters specialize in such verbal ironies) that personal attitudes are revealed; here the subordinative remark indicates an unconscious attitude toward a class of men employed for the spiritual welfare of the country. The contributor to *World* 177 seems at first to credit a clergyman for possessing the ability to know and recognize a woman of beauty and worth, perhaps a strange concern for a parson to have regardless of the later dismissal encapsulated in the concluding rhetorical aside: "But what can a country parson know of accomplishments?"

These and other one-line commentaries add to the numbers that deliberately and explicitly denigrate the character of the English clergyman. Not only do the essays of the *World* and *Connoisseur* point strictly and intently to the weaknesses of spiritual leaders, but the relatively new practice of mocking Church of England clergymen also indicates a more serious upheaval of traditional values. Where does one go, to whom does one turn, for spiritual guidance? The answer seemed to be—by the time of Richardson's *Pamela* in the 1740s—to the novelists, essayists and dramatists, rather than to the established clergy,[19] an implication even more evident in the pages of the *Connoisseur*, which is unusually vitriolic in its portraits.

Thirty-three percent of the 140 essays constituting the *Connoisseur* make at least one reference to the parson, an unusually high ratio. Again, the contributors show that they are aware of the typical concerns of Caroline and Stuart reformers, but, in setting forth clerical images, Colman and Thornton make little effort to strengthen church pillars and instead make a concerted attempt to elicit laughter. Occasionally a number offers commonplace suggestions without ridicule: Clergymen who ignore their parishioners will "grow morose and severe" (*Connoisseur* 78); or clergymen who truly wish to affect change should "become examples of the doctrine they teach" (*Connoisseur* 133).

But almost without exception, the reference strips the parson of all honor or respect. He is either grasping for preferment, which, once obtained, forges him ahead of his former friends (*Connoisseur* 5) or he embarrasses himself because of his concern for fashion (*Connoisseur* 32) or he is a political spokesman who "thunders out his anathemas, and preaches up the pious doctrine of persecution" (*Connoisseur* 13). Another contributor notes that those few who attend church service are either "kept awake by a jig from the organ-loft" or they are "lulled to sleep by the harangue from the pulpit" (*Connoisseur* 26). The tone of these references is unmistakably severe, far more strident than that of the *Spectator* and even of the *World*.

To multiply examples here would be inappropriate, but it is clear that, in the mid-eighteenth century, a large number of the literati in London, especially those eager to leave their marks in the public press, in adhering to a satirical method professing to reform by negative example, pushed their satire to the limit. Disregarding the more moderate satirical form practiced by Addison and Steele and, paradoxically, going against the grain of satiric theory and practice of the "sensibility" poets of the midcentury, a significant segment of the social elite, at least in the printed pages of the journals, neither esteemed the clergy nor acknowledged their significance in promoting moral reforms. The following chart, indicating the number of essays alluding to a clergyman, provides fascinating evidence of the decline of clerical prestige over a forty-year period in eighteenth-century England.[20]

Table 2.1
**A Comparison of the Percentage of Positive to Negative Images
of the Clergy**

Journals	# of Essays	Refs. to Clergy	Percent	Pos. Images	Neg. Images	Neutral
Tatler	272	19	7	5	10	4
Spectator	555	39	7	13	14	12
Total	**827**	**58**	**7**	**18**	**24**	**16**
World	209	43	20	1	36	6
Connoisseur	140	47	33	0	32	15
Total	**349**	**90**	**26**	**1**	**68**	**21**

Juxtaposing these particular journals does create a desired effect, at least for the purposes of this chapter. Such positioning seems to exhibit a striking degree of journalistic scurrility toward a traditional and sacred figure in English culture. The statistics do, though, coincide with the generally perceived notion among eighteenth-century scholars that the English clergyman, by the mid-eighteenth century, suffered a certain degree of social alienation, despite the popularity of preachers like John Wesley.

III

At least three problems remain with such a study. Most obviously, the limited and somewhat arbitrary selection of journals for comparison—four out of tens of dozens—cannot possibly produce definitive evidence as to the consistency of clerical portraits throughout the century. But in this case the arbitrary selection is not necessarily an evil. That the selection was made with no intention, initially, of examining or recording the number of clerical images exonerates the study from any charge of exclusiveness, and raises the question as to whether or not the findings here are coincidental, whether the clergy did receive, in graduated frequency, the brunt of the satirist's pen. The images are obviously embedded in the texts, and my analysis of these images offers tentative evidence that the periodical press, at least those journals that enjoyed some degree of popularity, was largely antagonistic to the established church.

It was also not possible for me to examine the many journals circulating between the last issue of the *Spectator* and the first issue of the *World*. It is therefore not evident whether the declining image is gradual, whether the forty-year period separating the journals witnesses any slow, persistent attack on clerical imbecility. By examining these journals, one does notice an increasing inclusiveness in clerical satire: Church of England priests are mocked alongside the Methodists, Quakers and other sects traditionally satirized by literary figures. In the *Grub-Street Journal*, which ran from January 8, 1730, to the end of 1737, references to the clergy are notably more satiric than those references in the *Spectator*. But the main targets of its satire are religious groups "outside the pale of the establishment."[21]

A third problem is that it is difficult, perhaps impossible, to determine whether the images had any effect on the public at large. At its height, the *Spectator* reached a circulation of nine thousand, a number that does not take into consideration those who read them in coffee-houses.[22] But it would be too much to say that the positive images caused sympathetic responses to the clergy. And though the *World* and *Connoisseur* papers are persistently negative, it is certain that the majority of the populace, unable to read or unconcerned with events in London, maintained a respect for their parish priests in the same way that the majority of the populace does today, despite media assaults on church corruptions. The church was a symbol of God's presence in daily affairs and the clergyman, however he appeared to the public through a secularized press, and especially to a highly literate public sometimes vying for attention at the book stalls, was called upon to provide spiritual support and to conduct the ritualized exercises so dominant in the lives of those professing religious faith. But it is plausible that a persistently negative image repeatedly stamped on the public mind does make an impression, and if it is true that the reputation of the English parson was at a low point in the mid-eighteenth century, it is an open but important question as to what part, if any, the popular media played in contributing to that decline.

NOTES

1. Samuel Johnson's periodical, *The Rambler*, had completed its run of 208 numbers, some ten months before the appearance of Moore's. Still, it was unusual for periodicals to survive for 200 numbers.

2. George P. Winship Jr., "The Printing History of the *World*," in *Studies in the Early English Periodical*, ed. Richmond Bond (Chapel Hill: University of North Carolina Press, 1957), p. 193.

3. In fact, I will be discussing four periodicals, but since the *Tatler* and *Spectator* papers are customarily spoken of in the same breath, and likewise the *World* and *Connoisseur* papers, I will normally use the abbreviated references for convenience.

4. Early commentary on the *World* appears in George Marr, *The Periodical Essayists of the Eighteenth Century* (New York: D. Appleton and Co., 1924), and in Walter Graham, *English Literary Periodicals* (New York: T. Nelson, 1930).

An important study of the influence of the periodical press on the development of the novel is Robert Mayo's *The English Novel in the Magazines* (Evanston, Ill.: Northwestern University Press, 1962). For discussion of the *Connoisseur*, see chapter 2 of Lance Bertelsen's *The Nonsense Club: Literature and Popular Culture, 1749–1764* (Oxford: Clarendon Press, 1986).

5. See, for example, Zeynep Tenger and Paul Trolander, " 'Impartial Critick' or 'Muse's Handmaid': The Politics of Critical Practice in the Early Eighteenth Century," *Essays in Literature* 21 (1994): 26–42. The article provides details of Addison and Steele's images of critics in the *Tatler* and *Spectator* essays.

6. See J. A. I. Champion's *The Pillars of Priestcraft Shaken: The Church of England and its Enemies, 1660–1730* (Cambridge: Cambridge University Press, 1992). The introduction provides a thorough review of some of the controversies facing the church during the period under consideration, and works to revise some modern misconceptions of the nature of religious debate. The quoted passage is on page nine. Also, see Isabel Rivers, *Reason, Grace, and Sentiment: A Study of the Language of Religion and Ethics in England, 1660–1780. Vol. I. Whichcote to Wesley* (Cambridge: Cambridge University Press, 1991). In chapter 5, Rivers discusses some of the major controversies that sprang up from within the established church.

7. See Robert DeMaria Jr., *The Life of Samuel Johnson* (London: Blackwell, 1993), pp. 140–42 for a brief account of Johnson's relationship with Dyer. For a discussion of universal optimism, see Nicholas Hudson, *Samuel Johnson and Eighteenth-Century Thought* (Oxford: Clarendon Press, 1988), pp. 112–23.

8. Many critics stress an opposing view. James Leheny, in his edition of *The Freeholder* (Oxford: Clarendon Press, 1979), containing essays by Joseph Addison, remarks that "an increasing indifference towards the clergy and the Church by English subjects was a gloomy reality" (p. 12).

9. Bertelsen, *Nonsense Club*, notes that the editors of the *Connoisseur*, though appearing to accept orthodox religious values, nevertheless seem to be frighteningly skeptical. "They seem, beneath their flippancy, to be searching for a set of values they really can believe in—and not finding them" (p. 57).

10. All references to the *Spectator* are from Donald Bond's five-volume edition (Oxford: Clarendon Press, 1965). References to the *Tatler* are from his three-volume edition (Oxford: Clarendon Press, 1987).

11. Arnold Toynbee, *Civilization on Trial* quoted in Roland Stromberg, *Religious Liberalism in Eighteenth-Century England* (London: Methuen and Co., 1954), p. 170.

12. In the late seventeenth century, the art implied a clear, plain style. Gerard Reedy has written that "the age placed great emphasis on the plain style of writing and preaching. Even scriptural revelation was thought to be most divine when it spoke in clear prose." *Robert South: An Introduction to His Life and Sermons* (Cambridge: Cambridge University Press, 1992), p. 2.

13. Edward Nathan, "The Bench and the Pulpit: Conflicting Elements in the Augustan Apology for Satire," *English Literary History* 52 (1985): 375–96. On page 377, Nathan writes, "The *Spectator* defines (and practices) satire as a moral force which uplifts by creating models for emulation, as well as admonishing the foolish."

14. Dudley Ryder wrote in his diary for 19 December 1715 that "the clergy in the country have been the greatest instrument in raising this spirit of rebellion through the nation" (quoted in Leheny, *Freeholder*, p. 7).

15. Bertrand Goldgar, in "Satires on Man and 'The Dignity of Human Nature,' "*Proceedings of the Modern Language Association of America* (hereafter *PMLA*) 80 (1965): 538, recognizes Addison's approval of general satire "where 'general' means portrayal of types rather than particular individuals." Accordingly, Addison mentions individuals only when he exhorts others to like behavior. Robert South is commended in 307, William Fleetwood in 384, and Gilbert Burnet in 531. These are only a few of the divines lifted up as examples to an admiring community.

16. As early as 1704, in the preface to *The Storm*, Daniel Defoe had forecast that novels would supplant preachers as the most effective moral guides to the nation. But his reason for thinking so was not that preachers were corrupt, but that they were spatially and temporally limited. Samuel Richardson, on the other hand, noting the disesteem into which clergymen had fallen, recognized the great possibilities open to novelists to inculcate Christian doctrine and, thus, to preclude the preacher as the moral force in England. See John A. Dussinger, "Conscience and the Pattern of Christian Perfection in Clarissa," *PMLA* 81 (1966): 236. And although Richardson did revise passages in *Pamela* to ameliorate his clerical friends who objected to his portraits of the clergy, one senses that, for Richardson, the moral power of his novel was far greater than that of most sermons. Another advantage the novelist had over the clergy, as one critic has recently pointed out, was that "in contrast to the clergy the novelist could promise something new in both form and content, and present the whole in a diverting manner" (K. G. Hall, *The Exalted Heroine and the Triumph of Order: Class, Women and Religion in the English Novel, 1740–1800* [Basingstoke: Macmillan, 1993], p. 7).

17. Perhaps "scratches" would be a more appropriate description of the journal's satiric damage. Bertelsen calls the style "bantering" and notes that the "great value of this kind of essay series has always been its ability to capture the historical moment: the current jargon, the topical symbols, the passing fads" (*Nonsense Club*, p. 39).

18. M. Murault, *Letters Describing the Character and Customs of the English and French Nations* (1726), quoted in W. A. Speck, *Stability and Strife* (Cambridge, Mass.: Harvard University Press, 1977), p. 98. Speck's chapter, "The Established Church and its Rivals," gives valuable information as to the conflicts frequently breaking out among the clerical members of the Church of England.

19. Interestingly enough, even the clergy sometimes turned to literary figures for assistance. As is well known, a number of beneficed clergymen looked to Johnson for help in composing the sermons they would later preach. Cited in Donald Greene, *Samuel Johnson* (Oxford: Oxford University Press, 1989).

20. Following is a list of the numbers of the *Connoisseur* that include a reference to a parson: 1, 4, 5, 7, 9, 12, 13, 15, 19, 22, 26, 27, 30, 32, 37, 38, 41, 44, 47, 49, 52, 54, 59, 61, 65, 76, 77, 78, 79, 84, 86, 87, 89, 96, 100, 104, 105, 112, 113, 114, 116, 123, 126, 133, 134, 139. For references in the *World*: 3, 16, 21, 25, 31, 46, 85, 89, 90, 91, 93, 96, 99, 104, 112, 119, 125, 127, 131, 134, 135, 136, 138,

140, 148, 149, 155, 157, 160, 162, 163, 165, 169, 172, 176, 177, 178, 179, 182, 184, 185, 187, 192. I have not considered the remaining 80 numbers of the *Spectator*, which appeared in 1714, as 555 numbers is more than sufficient in establishing the pattern.

21. James Hillhouse, *The Grub-Street Journal* (Durham, N.C.: Duke University Press, 1928), p. 242.

22. See A. R. Humphreys, *Steele, Addison and their Periodical Essays* (London: Longmans, Green and Co., 1959), p. 39.

II

The Nineteenth
Century

4

Early Nineteenth-Century Reform Newspapers in the Provinces: The *Newcastle Chronicle* and *Bristol Mercury*

Peter Brett

Reform-minded provincial newspapers consciously regarded themselves as the voice of the liberal middle classes while at the same time seeking to reflect their predominant interests and concerns. The extent to which readers were influenced by information and comment contained in their newspapers was a question earnestly debated in all of the leading contemporary periodical magazines at one time or another,[1] and the question has continued to exercise historians down to the present day. Professor Aspinall went so far as to argue that, "It was the mass pressure of public opinion, formed by the Radical Press, acting on a reluctant Legislature which brought about the reform of Parliament in 1832."[2] If the press was neither as crude nor, indeed, as effective a mechanism as this, newspapers did undoubtedly form a crucial part of that amalgam of contradictory voices and interests known as public opinion. In any explanation of the elusive relationship between ideas and events at the center, and the actions and views of the rank and file in the constituencies, newspapers are both a major source of information often not available elsewhere and a significant subject of interest in their own right. There have been surprisingly few attempts, however, to build upon the work of historians such as Asa Briggs, Derek Fraser and Donald Read on early nineteenth-century newspapers in Birmingham, Nottingham, Leicester, Leeds, Manchester and Sheffield, mostly written over thirty years ago, and it would still be fair to say that "the relationship between the provincial press and provincial opinion has been largely ignored."[3] It was in their own localities that newspapers and their editors had most opportunity to influence not only opinion, but the course of events. Remarks seldom reached Parliament or the government, but local leaders, corporations and opinion makers were well within earshot. This chapter focuses upon the role and influence of the *Newcastle Chronicle* and *Bristol Mercury* in their respective key provincial centers.

Important changes took place in the content of several provincial newspapers in the early nineteenth century as editors ceased to derive all of their news and opinions entirely from London and sought to shape and make public opinion. Factors holding back the development of newspapers in the eighteenth century included mechanical difficulties hindering production, the backwardness of communication and transport systems, the level of illiteracy among the population, heavy taxation and legal restrictions on what was allowed to be printed, but many, if not all, of these problems were gradually overcome in the first four decades of the nineteenth century.[4] The newspaper stamp returns from 1837–1838 showed that provincial papers commanded half as much revenue again as the London papers despite the fact that they were published in the main on a weekly rather than a daily basis. Contemporary politicians may have underestimated the influence of the provincial newspaper, which was the only paper seen by considerable sections of the community and was thus arguably "far more extensive and absolute within its range" than a London journal.[5] Although the Whig Party held a potential command over a number of provincial newspapers it was not considered worthwhile to directly control or subsidize them. There were, however, attempts made to mobilize and encourage faithful London newspapers even if the Whigs "practical achievements with regard to the press were never proportionate to their avowed intentions."[6] Whig leaders might well have been advised to heed the advice of provincial editors such as Egerton Smith of the *Liverpool Mercury* who argued that were he in possession of an ample fortune he would:

Cheerfully devote no inconsiderable portion to the establishment of constitutional public journals, in those parts of the kingdom where there might appear to be the most occasion for them" and expressed surprise that "amongst the various means adopted by the *true friends* to the British constitution for the dissemination of political information, they have never yet adopted a plan so simple."[7]

There continued to be widely circulated provincial newspapers without original articles well into the nineteenth century. It is a chastening thought for historians scouring newspaper files for political intelligence that even in the 1830s papers that came closest to political neutrality such as the *Newcastle Courant* and *Bristol Mirror* were either the most popular local newspapers in their area, or at least sold extremely well. This is an important reminder that not all readers were looking for strident editorials and opinionated letter columns. The informative elements of a newspaper, features such as tide tables, shipping information, market prices, specialist advertising, accounts of fairs, bankruptcy cases, transport schedules and the everyday details of births, deaths and marriages, were in many cases what a reader was chiefly interested in. Certainly the influence that reform newspapers might exert through their editorial columns depended upon the quality and reliability of the rest of the paper. Having said this, it is possible to detect a distinct turning point that occurred simultaneously in the content of many provincial newspapers within a relatively short period of time around the end of the first decade of the nineteenth century. James Perry, editor of the *London Morning Chronicle* wrote in March 1812 that: "In every part of the Kingdom, independent journals are now established . . . spreading the light of constitutional knowledge over the mass of the people" and cited eight examples: the *Leeds Mercury*, *Stamford News*, *Nottingham Review*, *Liverpool Mercury*, *Leicester Chronicle*, *Manchester Exchange Herald*, *Aberdeen Chronicle* and the *Hull Rockingham*. The pioneering role of the *Leeds Mercury* under Edward Baines, which by 1811 was carrying two full columns of editorial comment with separate leading articles on two or more subjects, is well known, but it was only one example of a nationwide phenomenon.[8] William Cobbett had noted in April 1809 that, "Even the provincial papers, so long the vehicle for dull repetition, of borrowed and uninspired reflection . . . have now assumed animation of mind," and Francis Horner in 1810 referred to the importance of the press in educating and enlightening the people in respect of Catholic emancipation: "The immense influence of the press in making one democracy (as it were) of the whole population, has been gained within these few years."[9] After about 1810 political neutrality became increasingly difficult to maintain as local opinion polarized and newspapers emerged as representatives of different opinions. The views of reform newspapers were strengthened in the immediate postwar years when peace brought no economic relief and there was an intensification of reform agitation, with public meetings, petitions and the establishment of political clubs and societies.

The people writing and distributing newspapers such as the *Newcastle Chronicle* and *Bristol Mercury* tended to share the same basic circumstances and condition of life as their readers. They were often excluded from landed society, the local urban elite and the electorate, and thus, effectively, from the "political nation." The Hodgsons' personal experience at the Newcastle election in 1812, for example, can only have strengthened their desire to see household suffrage introduced. Sarah Hodgson wrote to her son James:

You are quite wide of the mark when you suppose Ellison will give his printing to Tom. . . . By way of letting you know how business is to be got—Frank Humble introduced himself to Mr Ridley by saying there are some 70 freemen in the family and he hoped to be favoured with his printing. The same means were resorted to by Ellison the old man—so what chance can non-freemen have at an election?[10]

Provincial editors were usually known personally to their readers and to be at all effective had to stand above suspicion and to be well informed. They were intermediaries between political, economic and social theorists and their local readership, and a high level of general knowledge was required to deal with a variety of topics. Gibbons Merle, author of an article in the *Westminster Review* in 1830, detected a vast improvement in the previous thirty years in the skill and talent with which provincial papers were conducted. The newspaper office was a gathering point for information from a variety of sources—news could be communicated to editors by word of mouth, letters or via inhabitants of the town, especially merchants and those who received regular letters. The office also tended to be a place where reform and other petitions lay for signature. Newspaper proprietors and editors were often active participants or interested parties in the events and meetings that they were describing—political insiders who sought to urge activity on sometimes reluctant readers. In general they were in a pivotal and highly visible position within the local community.[11]

Provincial newspapers were aimed at a readership of tradesmen, farmers, businessmen and the leisured classes, for whom Saturday was the best day of publication. As the editor of the *Bristol Mercury* put it in April 1832, "The tradesman at the breakfast table, finds time to glance over his paper, and lays in a stock of answers for the benefit of his customers." On market day the comfortable farmer had a habit "as old as the French Revolution, of taking a newspaper home in his pocket with him from town," while others relaxed on a Saturday evening at home by "conning the week's news."[12] Newspapers were, in a sense, free publicity for a town's ruling classes; the names of committee members of charitable organizations were minutely detailed for posterity, resolutions with proposers and seconders were printed in full and the names of subscribers with amounts given were listed for each new subscription, campaign or organization. One does not get a total picture of a town's life; stamped provincial newspapers provided a detailed reflection of the prevailing concerns of a community's wealthier inhabitants but they generally lacked an understanding of, or sympathy with, popular culture and preoccupations. The liberal *Bristol Mercury* gave short shift, for example, to the National Union of the Working Class and the Chartists when they established branches in the city. It stated frankly that "unless individuals of a certain status in society take part in the proceedings of a meeting, its decision does not produce any effect," although admitted that this was unjust.[13] Nevertheless, it was from provincial newspapers that many individuals chiefly derived their sense of the outside world. There was a widespread conviction among active local and national politicians that editorial support was an invaluable political asset. The most common reason for establishing a provincial paper was a perceived lack of journalistic support for a political or religious viewpoint. Reform newspapers in Newcastle and Bristol—fallible, prejudiced and impressionistic as they often were—provided an invaluable campaigning and publicity arm for the activities of the liberal middle classes.

Of the Newcastle newspapers in the early nineteenth century, hitherto the bulk of attention has been given to the radical *Tyne Mercury*. Its editor from 1815, W. A. Mitchell, became a well-known figure on Tyneside. He was a particularly effective critic of the unreformed corporation of Newcastle and wrote a series of vigorous letters under the pseudonym "Tim Tunbelly" detailing a variety of local abuses, which were published in the paper in 1822–1823. Mitchell spoke at many meetings in favor of parliamentary reform in 1831–1832 and was for a time an active member of the Northern Political Union before an acrimonious parting of the ways. Maurice Milne has interestingly delineated the evolving political line of the paper, particularly in relation to parliamentary reform, from 1802–1848, and there is no doubting the *Tyne Mercury*'s influence in certain quarters. Yet Milne both exaggerates the uniqueness of the *Mercury*'s political stance and overestimates its appeal. Unlike the other Newcastle papers it was published on a Tuesday, and Milne adds: "The *Mercury* differed from its rivals in more important respects than its time of publication. It set out to be a newspaper of comment, voicing its own opinions, or the opinions of contributors, rather than merely digesting the contents of London newspapers."[14] This is to diminish the admittedly more sober, but nevertheless much more weighty and influential judgments and opinions periodically expressed in the *Newcastle Chronicle*. There is evidence that several individuals and groups found it difficult to take the *Mercury* editor seriously. The *Northern John Bull*, for example, a popular satirical magazine aimed at the freemen, ridiculed Mitchell for his self-importance:

Nothing can be more amusing to a man of sense than to read one of the *Mercury*'s leading articles: the lectures he weekly gives to whoever happens to be our premier, the dignity with which he lashes and directs the different states of Europe, the solemn events which he foretells and has foretold, are all given with as much seeming consciousness of universal attention as if the whole world was actually cocking its ear.[15]

The Corporation Mirror of 1829 claimed to owe its existence to the fact that Tim Tunbelly had laid down his pen, and that the *Tyne Mercury* had blunted the cutting edge of its criticism of the corporation in order that the paper could receive the corporation's advertisements. Similarly, during the enormously expensive and bitter 1826 Northumberland election, it was strongly suspected that the paper had ceded all of its independence and hired itself out as a vehicle for the candidature of T. W. Beaumont.[16] Milne's own figures show that the circulation of the *Mercury* in the 1830s was considerably less than that of its rivals, and R. W. Hetherington, in a historical retrospect published in the *Newcastle Weekly Chronicle* in 1833, noted that the *Mercury* "never obtained the circulation or influence of its contemporaries." On occasions W. A. Mitchell tended to be too close to, and too actively involved in, many of the local political events he was describing for him to foster the necessary distance and perspective.

Thomas and James Hodgson, on the other hand, the conductors of the *Newcastle Chronicle* were quiet, unassuming men who did not mix with outsiders in the movements agitating public opinion, "but they were assiduous in the quiet recess of their office, directing and enlightening the public mind with their pens."[17] From an inauspicious financial base following the death of their mother in October 1822, the two brothers built up the business and remained as owners, editors and managers of the *Newcastle Chronicle* until the end of December 1849 when, on account of "declining health and failing energies" they sold the title. Together they made the *Newcastle Chronicle* arguably "the leading political organ between York and Edinburgh."[18] They held moderate, reformist views in politics and religion, were strong supporters, as their father had been, of parliamentary reform and were members of the influential Unitarian congregation in Hanover Square. James, unlike his brother, entered public life, being elected a councillor in 1835 and shortly afterward being made an alderman. He was elected mayor in 1841–1842 and 1851–1852 and was chairman of the corporation finance committee for over a decade from 1844.

In many respects the *Newcastle Chronicle* was the official Whig newspaper in the North-East, with particularly close ties to the Grey family. On at least two key occasions involving prominent local Whigs, every effort was made to ensure that the *Chronicle* published the "correct" version of events. Upon the resignation of Lord Grey as prime minister in July 1834, his son Lord Howick wrote to James Hodgson commenting that: "as it is very desirable that you should have an accurate account of what has recently happened I send you our only newspaper in which it is correctly stated." And following Lord Durham's resignation from the Whig cabinet in March 1833, James Losh reassured him, "As soon as I came to Newcastle this morning I sent for Hodgson . . . and he has undertaken to insert in his paper a full account from *The Times*."[19]

Lord Grey, in particular, tended to receive very favorable treatment from the *Chronicle*; in declaring support for Lord Howick at the 1826 Northumberland election, for example, the paper's editorial column declared that: "The house of Grey has claims, in our opinion, on every Englishman, which we should be ashamed if we did not feel and were not ready at all times to acknowledge."

In 1831 the Hodgsons admitted that they were generally associated in public opinion with Grey and professed to be honored by the connection and exultant that he had finally secured a position of power.[20] The leanings of the *Newcastle Chronicle* could also be seen in smaller ways as when, for its readers' information, the paper reproduced in January 1821 a keynote speech that Grey had made in the House of Lords in 1810 on the state of the nation.

The Hodgsons, however, took considerable pride in the avowed independence of the *Newcastle Chronicle*. The Chartist newspaper, the *Northern Liberator*, charged in February 1838 that "The Chronicle has always shown itself a ready and willing servant to its masters. It is bound to Downing St., by the tenderest sympathies." This was unfair, but it did prove more difficult for the paper to maintain a truly independent line once the Whigs were actually in power in the 1830s. James Hodgson attested that the paper never contained "a leader, or any political, electioneering, or controversial article, purporting to express the sentiments of the editor that was not written either by his late brother or himself." This, he argued, was a proof of independence—the sentiments expressed were their own and their columns were never under the influence or control of any individual or party.[21] They did not disown the label "Whig" but argued that the *Newcastle Chronicle* was never a party tool and that the paper was not blind to the Whigs' errors and defects—"Though attached to men, we are not devoted to them. The country is our party; its welfare our only object."[22] This rhetoric might have been supported by pointing to the editorial position that was taken in 1819. In the wake of events at St. Peter's Field, Manchester, the paper adopted the role of candid friend to the Whig leadership and spiritedly sought to articulate the sentiments of the North-East liberal middle classes while at the same time chiding them for their timidity. The

Hodgsons recognized that there was "a wide difference between the whiggism of middle life and the whiggism of upper life," and sent a brave and potentially unpalatable message to local aristocratic and gentlemen Whigs: "If the whig leaders do not now come manfully forward . . . openly and decidedly profess themselves the friends of reform, and make known to what extent they are ready to support it, they may rest assured that they will as certainly lose the support of the middle ranks as they have already lost that of the lower."

The *Chronicle* no more minced its words to the region's middle classes. If they refused to make any public declarations, but confined themselves to mere private expressions of their dissatisfaction, how was it possible that their political friends could know their sentiments? "They have been so long accustomed to act under the guidance of the upper ranks . . . are so fearful of imputations of vulgarity, or want of respectability, if they should venture to act without them . . . that they have almost lost the power of acting for themselves." The paper expressed loudly and clearly what many individuals were saying in private.[23] A major local public meeting received considerable coverage. The paper singled out the enormous meeting of thousands of working people on the Town Moor in October 1819 following the Peterloo Massacre as memorable and epoch-making: "assuming that this is merely a counterpart of the situation of other districts, numbers of the temperate inhabitants of this town feel convinced that if some concessions are not made by the government, the consequences may be most unfortunate."[24] Meeting reports were an important element in the formation and direction of opinion—there was a symbiotic relationship between the press and the platform. Speeches at meetings concerning themselves with parliamentary reform, the proceedings against Queen Caroline and Catholic emancipation were printed verbatim, as far as possible, and newspapers elsewhere used the reports as the basis for their own shorter accounts.[25]

The *Newcastle Chronicle* contributed to the success of the reform cause in the North-East in many ways, but there are perhaps four aspects of its content in the years up to 1832 that are worth drawing attention to in particular. The paper was a consistent force for unity and cooperation among reformers, retained a perpetual optimism by its selection of material, drew attention to welcome developments elsewhere in the country and gave detailed coverage to local initiatives and meetings. A keynote editorial advocated reform as early as June 1810: The people paid £70 million in taxes for which they deserved representation, and reform would render revolution unnecessary. The paper rarely advocated a specific line and tended to avoid the issue of the precise details of reform it would support—"The question of the superiority of the several plans of reform is a very fit subject for discussion among the several classes of reformers, but in all joint attempts to obtain the object of their wishes this question should be avoided."[26] In October 1821 it referred to "the unnatural estrangement which has taken place between the several classes of society" and regularly spoke out against a breakdown in social harmony and in favor of "the cordial union of all ranks."[27] The paper succeeded, even in quieter times such as the mid-1820s, in giving an impression of improvement and progress. One way to give an impression of momentum was to draw attention to noteworthy speeches, articles or meetings elsewhere in the country in order both to enlighten local opinion and encourage local activity. For example, the editors encouraged the people of Newcastle to follow the example of manufacturing towns such as Manchester, Leeds and Bradford in 1825 that had held meetings and organized petitions calling for a revision of the Corn Laws.[28] Widespread publicity was given not only to important set-piece occasions such as the Newcastle Fox dinners but also to political dinners that occurred elsewhere in the country, particularly in Scotland. In February 1824 the paper could comment that "unfortunately those who took an interest in politics tended to feel depressed if events did not take the desired turn at the precise moment wished for," but this view it argued was superficial—change was a gradual process but it was occurring.[29]

The paper provided a sterling service in the years 1830–1832, a period of almost perpetual agitation and activity. It viewed the recall of Grey in 1832 following the Days of May, as the successful outcome of public demonstration.[30] Thomas Headlam could write to Lord Durham in May 1833, "In this district the *Newcastle Chronicle* has done an important service by the vigorous and correct manner in which it has maintained sound opinions and so ably defended the measures of Lord Grey."[31] Yet the service that the *Chronicle* provided in aid of the Whig cause was less highly rated only a few years later. Part of the problem was that all the qualities that the Hodgson brothers could legitimately claim characterized their paper when they finally took leave of their readers—sincerity, courtesy, forbearance to opponents, toleration and a desire to preserve their columns from the contamination of private slander and public calumny—could in another light be viewed as weaknesses and symptoms of complacency. The arrival of the *Newcastle Journal* in May 1832, with its aggressive, sharp-tongued editorials, as an avowed party organ of the Tories, brought a new bitterness to North-East politics. As R. W. Hetherington subsequently wrote of the Whigs: "They were not in possession of the like ordnance, even if they had an equal amount of powder and shot. Their great gun, the *Newcastle Chronicle* was under the command and control of an officer who manfully refused the use of it for such a service."[32]

The *Journal* sniped effectively at Grey family "jobbery," sought to diminish the activities of the Northern Political Union and highlight divisions among radical leaders, and regularly crossed swords with Lord Durham. By April 1838 the *Journal* could comment of the Whig cause that "their 'public instructor' is regarded by their stoutest partisans as one of the feeblest and most inefficient party organs in the kingdom."[33] There was a strong element of truth in this latter charge, with the paper's unwillingness to declare itself wholeheartedly in favor of the Durham principles as propounded in October 1834, being held against it by several prominent local Whigs. When Headlam heard of the government's proposed reduction of the stamp duty in 1836, he wrote again to Lord Durham, in anticipation of the effects that this would produce in the provincial press, in order to consider how the changes could be rendered most beneficial in the North-East:

This town is increasing so much in trade and population and local importance that a paper might be circulated there twice a week provided it was steady in its politics and arranged and spirited in its execution. The Chronicle is an excellent groundwork for such a speculation but I fear much they cannot be roused to it. If they will not exert themselves to avail themselves of the opportunity of satisfying the increased demand for local and general news, it will be necessary to commence some new undertaking upon a respectable foundation to keep the business out of [improper] hands.[34]

Headlam's disappointment with the *Chronicle* prefigured a falling out in local politics a few months later.[35] Lord Durham's agent Henry Morton was more scathing in his description of the "unfortunate situation" in which the liberal cause in the North-East was placed by the "apathy" and "incapacity" of their press—"Such an influential district as the town of Newcastle and the banks of the Tyne and Wear, not possessing an able and talented liberal newspaper, reflects great discredit upon the activity of the liberal party." Three newspapers advocated good doctrines—the *Durham Chronicle, Sunderland Herald* and *Tyne Mercury*—but possessed "no influence whatever, from the circumstance of their circulations being so limited": "As for the *Newcastle Chronicle* it is an emasculated liberal, feeble and indolent to a celebrated degree—it has a large circulation and might in good hands be made immediately and highly influential in disseminating liberal doctrines."

Morton favored a plan to buy the *Chronicle* from the Hodgson brothers by raising money through a share issue and finding a good editor "to advocate the principles of Lord Durham." He was persuaded that if the scheme could be established on fair terms, "the liberal cause would soon again be triumphant."[36] Lord Durham himself preferred the idea of relaunching an established paper to setting up a new press in Gateshead, but the Hodgson brothers, after entering into negotiations, refused to sell, and the *Gateshead Observer* was established in November 1837, initially under the control of W. H. Brockett. The paper was favored with government advertisements and a great deal of advice from William Hutt, M.P. for Hull, and Lord Durham, although the latter was "averse to do any act by which he could be implicated as a party in the concern."[37] For all of its problems in the 1830s, however, the *Newcastle Chronicle* outlived a host of other reform and radical papers such as the *Tyne Mercury, Northern Liberator, Newcastle Press* (1833–1834), and *Newcastle Standard* (1836–1837), and survived competition from the *Newcastle Journal* and a resurgent *Newcastle Courant*. The paper had an effective distribution network that extended into Cumberland and Yorkshire, as well as Northumberland and Durham, and kept pace with new inventions and printing techniques leading to clearer type and enlarged pages.[38] The reduction of the stamp duty in 1836 had led to a weekly increase of six hundred copies—over 25 percent up on its former circulation. The Hodgson family was an influential force on Tyneside for well over half a century.

Bristol, too, was the center for a flourishing weekly press; by the early 1830s all the established weeklies had achieved healthy sales of over two thousand copies a week and were voraciously perused in taverns and clubrooms.[39] The city's newspapers have been the subjects of more than one scholarly study,[40] and were also the objects of contemporary analysis. The relative success of newspapers maintaining differing political stances was taken to be a barometer of the city's opinion by outside observers. Thus the *Westminster Review* in 1830 saw the success of the *Bristol Mercury* as "a proof that all the Bristolians certainly are not opposed to the diffusion of correct opinions," and *Tait's Edinburgh Magazine* commented favorably in December 1836 on the sales of each of Bristol's liberal newspapers. It argued, admittedly from a radical perspective, that "the state of the Bristol press shows what progress Liberalism is making in that city."[41]

It had been a talented Tory editor, J. M. Gutch, who in 1811 initiated original editorial comment in Bristol in *Felix Farley's Bristol Journal*. He was the author of a notable series of letters signed "Cosmo" between 5 October 1822 and 19 April 1823 that dealt critically with every aspect of the management of the port of Bristol. Later, he was a leading advocate of the Provincial Newspaper Society established in 1836 and became its first president.[42] In contrast, the liberal *Bristol Mercury* was an ailing newspaper in 1818, with a weekly circulation of only about three hundred. It was sold for £600 to a group of seven liberal proprietors who planned to meet monthly in order to manage the paper, and "the newspaper at once gave evidence that new blood had been put into it. It was enlarged by a widening of its columns, and at once began to publish leading articles, hitherto unknown to it." T. J. Manchee, a printer and bookseller soon became its controlling spirit, and was sole editor by the end of 1819 and the sole proprietor by October 1823.[43] The purchase and regeneration of the paper was considered important enough for a Whig agent in the West Country to pass on to Lord Grey: "I believe I neglected acquainting your Lordship that Moggridge has succeeded in establishing a whig paper in Bristol; after the election it was found that the Tories derived great strength from the whigs having no channel for their opinions to be communicated to the public."

He reported that the main financial backing had come from Charles Elton, a Bristol banker, "who overlooks the editors and publishers" and was confident in October 1818 that "the good effects are already beginning to be felt."[44] In January 1819 Moggridge forwarded the *Mercury's* leading articles to Lord Grey at Howick. His letter further confirms the importance that reformers placed upon having reliable and effective support in the press. He reported, "we were losing everything in Bristol, as I had long and painfully noticed," but concluded of the transformation of the *Mercury* that: "The leading articles, the papers under the head 'State of the Country' & c., and the letters of Aristides have excited vast attention, more than doubled the circulation of the paper, and are evidently effecting the public's opinion."[45] That the paper explicitly sought to appeal to Bristol's liberal middle classes was seen by the titles given to some of its early leading articles: "Superior Importance of Reform to the Middle Ranks of Society," "Emigration of the Middle Classes of Society its cause and remedy," "Effects on Taxation upon the Middle Classes of Society and upon Trade and Commerce." It was obviously in the paper's interests to use this umbrella concept loosely, and it caught many occupations in its net—"the mechanic, the tradesman, the farmer, the manufacturer, the yeoman, the merchant, and the country gentleman."[46]

By 1840 the *Bristol Mercury* was the leading newspaper in the west of England, but it did not achieve this position of preeminence under the editorship of Manchee, who was a better journalist than he was a businessman. Nevertheless, Manchee could claim credit for stimulating debate and raising reform awareness. He published a series of nine articles in 1819, for example, entitled "Historical Review of the Progress of Public Opinion on Parliamentary Reform," and he reported on the efforts of reformers elsewhere in the country such as the Liverpool Concentric Society and the Essex and Cheshire Whig Clubs.[47] If Manchee ultimately failed to arouse apathetic Whiggism in Bristol in the 1820s it was not for lack of effort. After describing the proceedings at a number of country meetings in various parts of the country in favor of parliamentary reform in January 1823, the *Bristol Mercury* struggled in vain to exhort local leaders and reformers to exert themselves: "Let us hope that Bristol will rouse herself from [its] apathy; that her citizens will not let it be said that while they were contemplating internal improvements which affected only the local interests of their city they were insensible to the more powerful chains which they shared in common with the country at large." The reform spirit was a long time coming to Bristol. Parliamentary reform lacked the immediacy as an issue that it possessed in cities such as Manchester, Birmingham and Leeds that had no independent spokesmen in Parliament and were represented by county M.P.s. Overall it tended to be the case that Bristol followed in the wake of other cities rather than taking a lead.[48]

In November 1829 Manchee argued that "the *Mercury* was the first paper that made the local civic officers feel that there was such a thing in Bristol as public opinion." By this time, however, he had frankly confessed in an article that he was unsuccessful in the competition for advertisements that were the means by which papers survived: "We may exercise our talents, we may direct our zeal, we may stimulate our industry; the only thing we may deserve, but cannot command, is—success!"[49] The *Mercury* was further undermined by the success of the unstamped *Bristolian*, skillfully edited by James Acland, which sold at 1½ d. and conducted small-scale investigative journalism on local issues. Acland reported that the *Mercury* had been surviving on an average of only twenty to twenty-five advertisements, but by August 1829 this was down to less than twelve. He brought a variety of charges against Manchee including local corruption and political inconsistency, claiming, for example, that Manchee's motive for "political tergiversation and editorial inconsistency" was a desire to ingratiate himself with the corporation and thus receive their advertisements.[50] By November 1829 the lack of commercial success forced Manchee to sell. One of the problems that he had faced was a lack of access to key corporation meetings, and in 1828/29 the *Mercury* was excluded from those newspapers made available at the Council House.[51]

Competition between newspapers for a limited market was fierce, and the *Bristol Gazette*, also proreform Whig in its political stance, ran regular editorials from 1817. John Mills, its editor from 1809, like Manchee, also figured prominently as a leader of public opinion in the city. At a key Whig selection meeting in February 1812, for example, he spoke in favor of Samuel Romilly as the Whig candidate to replace Evan Baillie in the election and was a member of the Whig Anchor Society, becoming president in 1834. He was a zealous advocate of parliamentary reform, frequently addressing meetings, and was elected as a Liberal councillor in November 1837, retaining his seat until his death in 1849.[52] The *Gazette*'s Whiggism was also compromised, however, by its close relationship with Bristol's Tory corporation. Mills was invited by the mayor to attend a ceremony at the Mansion House in January 1825 when the freedom of the city was conferred upon George Canning and Lord Liverpool, while Manchee was pointedly excluded.[53] The *Gazette* could later be accused of making "eternal shuffling excuses" for the "self-elected junta" at Bristol's Council House and of pandering to the Tories, the West India interests and the corporation,[54] and the *Gazette*'s policies probably contributed to its comparative decline in the 1830s. Yet while the *Mercury* criticized the cozy arrangement between the *Gazette* and the corporation, the *Mercury*'s own lack of establishment credibility may have damaged it in the eyes of its potential respectable readership. In a "Farewell Address to his Readers," Manchee argued that he had "not met with that support which he has endeavoured to deserve." A libel action in August 1823, after he published anonymous letters that called into question a military officer's courage and modesty and then refused to reveal the identity of the author, had brought further adverse publicity.[55]

W. H. Somerton assumed the management and editorship of the *Mercury* in 1829, which led to a shift in the paper's declared purpose. While Somerton still aimed "to DIRECT the public mind," and to "ever maintain the liberal tone of our politics," his editorial line was more politically independent than that which Manchee had managed to achieve: "We confess that the *Mercury* is, and will always be, a party paper—of the party of the people—but not a party tool."[56] While this was a standard claim, the paper largely managed to live up to it, and it proved to be an effective and astute strategy. Unlike Manchee, who was a habitual speaker at public meetings, Somerton did not enter public life as a political partisan or councillor, and he retained a perspective on Bristol and national politics in the 1830s that John Mills and J. B. Kington, editor of the short-lived *Bristol Advocate*, perhaps lost through their close involvement with the Bristol Liberal Association. In January 1837, for example, a balanced line was adopted by the *Mercury* when it considered a keynote political article by Sir William Molesworth, "Terms of Alliance between Radicals and Whigs." It considered that the article was too severe on the Whigs but nevertheless called for "a vigorous system of policy" that included the ballot and the abolition of church rates—"the conduct of ministers upon some questions may not have been fully satisfactory, but progress was still onward, although the enthusiasm that carried reform had died away."[57]

Somerton also aimed to provide a family newspaper that appealed to a wider readership, and adopted a more formal and reserved tone; by September 1833 he claimed to have more than trebled the paper's circulation to over one thousand copies per week. He switched the day of publication to Saturday so that it was "the only organ of the Liberal party published at the end of the week" in Bristol, and extended the paper's circulation through Somerset, South Wales, Gloucestershire and other Western counties.[58] Somerton also argued that the *Mercury* was more widely read than any of its contemporaries and stressed that its circulation was "confined to families of respectability and intelligence, to the substantial yeomanry of the adjoining counties, and to hotels, inns, and reading rooms of the first character,"[59] although these claims are obviously difficult to substantiate. He really made his name by providing the fullest and most comprehensive eyewitness account of the Bristol riots, in October 1831, which provided the empirical basis of many subsequent analyses.[60] Like the Hodgsons at Newcastle, Somerton sought to keep up with the latest technology and innovations; he bought a new Napier machine in May 1836, and in October 1839 the *Mercury* became one of the first provincial newspapers to double in size and change to eight pages with six columns on each page. By the end of the decade the parliamentary stamp returns indicated that the *Mercury* was the leading Bristol newspaper, with a flourishing circulation throughout the west of England.[61]

It was indicative of the power that contemporaries attributed to the press that the most popular Tory account of the Bristol riots, written by Reverend J. Eagles, could blame the events largely upon a sustained and deliberate campaign on the part of a liberal press that had "fearlessly encouraged and demanded violence" and which was "constantly issuing most inflammatory language." And in a pamphlet written in dialogue form after the riots, a farmer was made to conclude that: "These newspaper fellows do all this mischief for no better reason than these riots make people more fond of buying newspapers than they would else."[62]

These accusations were largely groundless, and papers like the *Bristol Mercury* kept as cool as possible in the circumstances and dissociated respectable opinion from the violence,[63] yet the fact that such charges could be brought at all was significant in itself. Like the *Newcastle Chronicle* and other influential liberal provincial newspapers, the *Bristol Mercury* acted as an advocate and catalyst for further reforms. On the question of the secret ballot in September 1837, for example, the paper asked: "Why should the city of Bristol be behind her neighbours? We call upon our fellow citizens to discharge this one most important act of duty to themselves and to their country . . ." In March 1840, on the Corn Laws, the paper concluded that: "Action, energy, and unanimity ought to be the motto of our citizens. They must not look coldly and apathetically at each other and enquire 'what is to be done?' "[64]

A study of the liberal press in Newcastle and Bristol indicates that liberal middle-class reformers increasingly recognized the value of possessing a newspaper that both expressed their views and propagated selected events and meetings throughout the country that tended to show reformers in a positive light. The view from London was that the provincial press represented an echo of what was happening in the capital, albeit on occasions an impressive and resounding echo. Lord John Russell wrote in 1821: "What statesman can bear with unshaken nerves that voice which, beginning in the whispers of the metropolis, rises into the loud tone of defiance within the walls of parliament, and is then prolonged by means of the hundred mouths of the press until its innumerable echoes rebound from the shores of Cornwall and the mountains of Inverness?"[65]

The evidence from Newcastle and Bristol suggests that rather than representing a mere echo, reform newspapers maintained an independent and self-sustaining agenda of their own and could possess considerable local influence.

NOTES

1. E.g., *Blackwood's Edinburgh Magazine* XXXVI (1834): 373–91; *Fraser's Magazine* IV (1831): 127–42, 310–21; *Edinburgh Review* LXV (1837): 196–213.

2. A. Aspinall, "The Circulation of Newspapers in the Early Nineteenth Century," *Review of English Studies* XXII (1946): 43.

3. Asa Briggs, "Press and Public in Early Nineteenth Century Birmingham," *Dugdale Society Occasional Papers* No. 8 (Oxford, 1949); Derek Fraser, "The Nottingham Press 1800–1850," *Transactions of the Thoroton Society* (Nottingham, 1963), pp. 46–66; "The Press in Leicester c. 1790–1850," *Transactions of the Leicestershire Archaeological and Historical Society* 42 (1966–67): 53–75; Donald Read, *Press and People* (London, 1961); "Reform Newspapers and Northern Opinion c. 1800–1848," *Proceedings of the Leeds Phil. and Lit. Soc.* VIII (1959): 301–14. The phrase quoted is taken from this latter article (p. 301). Exceptions to this general rule include Michael Murphy, *Cambridge Newspapers and Opinion 1780–1850* (Cambridge, 1977) and Maurice Milne, "Survival of the Fittest? Sunderland Newspapers in the Nineteenth Century," in *The Victorian Periodical Press; Samplings and Soundings*, ed. J. Shattock and M. Wolff (London, 1982), pp. 193–223.

4. Cf. A. E. Musson, "Newspaper Printing in the Industrial Revolution," *Economic History Review* X (1957–58): 411–26.

5. "The Journals of the Provinces," *New Monthly Magazine* XLVIII (1836): 142.

6. I. Asquith, "The Whig Party and the Press in the Early Nineteenth Century," *Bulletin of the Institute of Historical Research* XLIX (1976): 283.

7. *Liverpool Mercury*, 3 June 1814.

8. *Morning Chronicle*, 8 March 1812; Read, *Press and People*; Edward Baines, Jr., *The Life of Edward Baines* (1859), p. 36.

9. *Cobbett's Political Register*, April 1809; L. Horner, ed., *Correspondence of Francis Horner*, 2 vols. (London, 1853), pp. ii, 17, Letter to Lord Webb Seymour, 3 Jan. 1810.

10. *Hodgson MSS* (Tyne & Wear Record Office) File: 13/13/9, Sarah Hodgson to James Hodgson, 5 Oct. 1812.

11. *London and Westminster Review* XXIII (1830): 75–103; D. Fraser, "The Editor as Activist: Editors and Urban Politics in Early Victorian England," in *Innovators and Preachers: The Role of the Editor in Victorian England*, ed. J. H. Wiener (Westport, Conn., 1985), pp. 121–42.

12. *Bristol Mercury*, 3 April 1832.

13. Ibid., 8 June 1833. Also 10 Aug. 1833, 26 April 1834, 4 May 1839.

14. M. Milne, "The *Tyne Mercury* and Parliamentary Reform, 1802–1846," *Northern History* XIV (1978): 227–42; "Strikes and Strike-breaking in North-East England, 1815–44: The Attitude of the Local Press," *International Review of Social History* XXII (1977): 226–40; R. Welford, *Men of Mark 'Twixt Tyne and Tweed,'* 3 vols. (Felling, 1895), pp. iii, 199–205; *The Letters of Tim Tunbelly: Gent, Free Burgess, Newcastle-Upon-Tyne . . .* (Newcastle, 1823); M. Milne, "Periodical Publishing in the Provinces: The Mitchell Family of Newcastle-Upon-Tyne," *Victorian Periodicals Newsletter* (1977): 174–82.

15. *Northern John Bull* II (Dec. 1830): 129–36, (Feb. 1831): 183–87. For additional comment on the limitations of Milne's use of the *Tyne Mercury* see J. V. Corrigan, "Strikes and the Press in the North-East, 1815–44: A Note," *International Review of Social History* XXIII (1978): 376–81.

16. *The Corporation Mirror* I (1829): 3; *Newcastle Chronicle*, 20 May 1826.

17. *Newcastle Weekly Chronicle*, 14 July 1883, "Newcastle Fifty Years Ago XIII: Newspapers."

18. *Newcastle Chronicle*, 4 Jan. 1850; R. Welford, *Men of Mark*, pp. ii, 548. For details of Sarah Hodgson see *Correspondence and Diaries of James Losh*, ed. Edward Hughes (2 vols., Durham, 1962), pp. i, 170–71; *A Sermon Preached in Hanover Square Chapel, Newcastle-Upon-Tyne 15 Sept. 1822 upon the Death of Mrs. S. Hodgson* (Newcastle, 1822).

19. *Hodgson MSS*, British Library Additional Manuscripts 50240, Lord Howick to James Hodgson, 14 July 1834; *Lambton MSS* (Lambton Estate Office, Chester Le Street) James Losh to Lord Durham, 20 March 1833.

20. *Newcastle Chronicle*, 18 March 1826; 29 Jan. 1831.

21. *Northern Liberator*, 3 Feb. 1851; *Public Dinner to William Ord Esq., at the Assembly Rooms, Newcastle, 8 Sept. 1852 on his Retirement from the Representation of Newcastle* (Newcastle, 1852), pp. 3–4.

22. *Newcastle Chronicle*, 27 Nov. 1830, 29 Jan. 1831.

23. Ibid., 20 Nov. 1819, 27 Nov. 1819; see Hughes, *Losh,* pp. i, 104, 2 Dec. 1819.

24. *Newcastle Chronicle*, 6 May 1820, 16 Oct. 1819.

25. Ibid., 29 Jan. 1820, 13 Jan. 1821, 14 March 1829, 25 Dec. 1830.

26. Ibid., 23 June 1810.

27. Ibid., 27 Oct. 1821.

28. Ibid., 2 April 1825.

29. Lord Cockburn, *Life of Lord Jeffrey*, 2 vols. (Edinburgh, 1852), pp. i, 267; *Newcastle Chronicle*, 9 April 1825, 7 Feb. 1824.

30. Ibid., 26 May, 2 June 1832.

31. *Lambton MSS*, Headlam to Durham, 30 May 1833.

32. *Newcastle Chronicle*, 4 Jan. 1850; *Newcastle Weekly Chronicle*, 14 July 1883.

33. *Newcastle Journal*, 28 April 1838; cf. *Blackwood's Edinburgh Magazine* XXXV (1834): 307–10, "Whig Prosecutions of the Press."

34. *Lambton MSS*, Headlam to Durham, 1 March 1836.

35. See *The Corporation Annual: or Recollections (Not Random) of the First Reformed Town Council* . . . (Newcastle, 1836), p. 9.

36. *Brockett MSS* (Gateshead Public Library) Henry Morton to W. H. Brockett, 31 Aug. 1837, vol. VII f. 325.

37. Ibid., William Hutt to Brockett, 2 Aug. 1837, 22 Nov. 1837, vol: VII f. 319. M. Milne (*Northern History*, 1978) refers to these discussions from the point of view of their effect upon the *Tyne Mercury*.

38. *Newcastle Chronicle*, 8 Jan. 1825, 5 Jan. 1828, 5 April 1834.

39. "Under Five Monarchs—Bristol in the Old Days—Veteran Citizen Reminisces" (extract from *Bristol Mercury* 1907? Bristol Ref. Library B3630); C. A. Elton, *An Apology for Col. Hugh Baillie* . . . (Bristol, 1819) p. 4.

40. E.g., D. F: Gallop, "Chapters in the History of the Provincial Newspaper Press 1700–1855" (master's thesis, University of Reading, 1956); A. P. Hart, "The Bristol Riots and the Mass Media" (Ph.D. diss., Oxford, 1979). Older accounts include A. Allen and A. G. Powell, *Bristol and its Newspapers* (Bristol, 1934) and A. B. Beaven and E. R. Norris Matthews, "History of Bristol Journalism," *Bristol Times and Mirror*, 1 Dec. 1909.

41. *Westminster Review* XXIII (Jan. 1830): 75–76; *Tait's Edinburgh Magazine* III (Nov. 1836): 689; (Dec. 1836): 803. The short-lived Liberal paper the *Bristol Advocate* claimed the highest circulation of any paper in the west of England, the *Bristol Gazette* claimed a 25 percent increase in circulation since the reduction of the stamp duty, while the *Bristol Mercury* had reportedly increased its weekly circulation from about 1,150 to over 1,850 and was receiving a great many more advertisements.

42. *Felix Farley's Bristol Journal*, 5 Jan. 1811; H. Whorlow, *The Provincial Newspaper Society 1836–1886, A Jubilee Retrospect* (London, 1886), ch. 1; *Gentleman's Magazine* CCXI (Dec. 1861): 683.

43. H. Lewis, "A History of the *Bristol Mercury* . . . from 1715 to 1886" (Bristol, 1886?), *Bristoliana* (Bristol Ref. Library 21964), pp. 7–8. The proprietors included H. H. Moggridge, a Monmouthshire landowner, Edward Kentish, M.D., C. A. Elton, S. J. Browne, Daniel Day, Francis Short and T. J. Manchee.

44. *Grey MSS* (University of Durham) John Goodwin to Lord Grey, 17 Oct. 1818.

45. Ibid., J. H. Moggridge to Grey, 15 Jan. 1819.

46. *Bristol Mercury*, 8 March, 18 Oct. 1819, 7, 14 Feb. 1820. The quotation is from the issue of 7 Feb. 1820.

47. *Bristol Mercury* 12, 19 April, 3, 17 May, 7, 14 June, 19 July, 2 Aug., 20 Sept. 1819. For the reports on reformers activities in Liverpool, Essex and Cheshire, cf. 21 Dec. 1818, 21 Nov. 1821, 11 Oct. 1824.

48. Ibid., 20 Jan. 1823.

49. Ibid., 9 Nov. 1829, 15 Jan. 1827.

50. *Bristolian*, 20 Dec. 1828, 22 Aug. 1829. For Acland and the *Bristolian*, cf. A. P. Hart, *The Bristol Riots*, pp. 148–53. T. J. Manchee, *Licentiousness of the Press* (1829?) (Bristol Ref. Library 1490 d. 14 [2]) and *The Bristoliad: Or,*

Incidents in the Life of James Acland, Omitted in his Memoirs by the Auto-biographer (Bristol, n.d.) were attempts to counter Acland's charges.

51. E.g., *Bristol Gazette*, 24 May 1827—Manchee was refused permission to be present at a meeting of the Grammar School Trustees; *Council Cash Book 1826–32*, p. 102 (Bristol Record Office); *Bristol Mercury*, 29 Sept. 1829.

52. For examples of Mills' political stance, cf. *Bristol Gazette*, 10 Jan. 1811, 23 July 1812, 24 Sept. 1818. For details of his municipal election results, cf. A. B. Beaven, *Bristol Lists* (1880), p. 31 et. seq.

53. *Bristol Mercury*, 17 Jan. 1825. For criticism of the *Gazette*'s relationship with the corporation and Mills' defense of his position, cf. *Bristol Mercury*, 22 May 1826; *Bristol Gazette*, 25 May 1826.

54. *Bristol Mercury*, 12 Jan., 28 Dec. 1833.

55. Ibid., 9 Nov. 1826; *Report of the Trial for Libel, Rex V. Manchee at the Prosecution of Sir Alexander Wilson before Mr. Justice Burrough, and a Special Jury . . . at Bristol 13 Aug. 1823*. (Bristol Ref. Library 1493 w. 28).

56. *Bristol Mercury*, 3 April 1832.

57. Ibid., 7 Jan. 1837. For a keynote political editorial, cf. 8 July 1837.

58. Ibid., 17 Nov. 1829, 17 Nov. 1832, 7 Sept. 1833.

59. Ibid., 12 Jan. 1833, 7 Sept. 1833.

60. W. H. Somerton, *Narrative of the Bristol Riots on the 29th, 30th., and 31st., of October 1831* (Bristol, 1831).

61. *Bristol Mercury*, 21 May 1836, 19 Oct. 1839; *Jefferies Collection* IX, p. 156, "The Leading Bristol Paper," a poster giving the parliamentary stamp returns for the three months ending 31 March 1839.

62. Rev. J. Eagles, *The Bristol Riots, their Causes, Progress, and Consequences* (Bristol, 1832), pp. 85, 467, 481; Anon., *A. Whisper from Devonshire, or, A Dialogue on the Reform Bill* (London, 1832), p. 8.

63. Cf. Lant Carpenter, "On the Bristol Riots," *Monthly Repository* 4 (1831): 842; the *Bristol Mercury* of 25 Oct. 1831 exhorted "all persons to use their influence to repress, on that occasion, [Wetherell's visit] the least appearance of disorder."

64. *Bristol Mercury*, 9 Sept. 1837, 14 March 1840.

65. Lord John Russell, *An Essay on the History of the English Government and Constitution* (new ed., London, 1865), p. 321. (Two previous English editions were published in 1821 and 1823.) Lord Brougham held similar views—see A. Aspinall, *Politics and the Press. c. 1780–1850* (London, 1949), p. 5.

5

Land Reform, Community-Building and the Labor Press in Antebellum America and Britain

Jamie L. Bronstein

The 1840s saw a peculiar convergence of ideas in Britain and America, leading to working-class movements intended to achieve private or public redistribution of land, encourage small farming and alleviate urban overcrowding and poverty. In Britain approximately seventy thousand men and women bought shares in the Chartist Co-operative Land Company; combined with the contributions of thousands of others, their money would be used to purchase houses and smallholdings when estates came on the market in England. In the Staffordshire potteries and throughout the north of England, approximately three thousand people purchased shares in the Potters' Joint Stock Emigration Society, in hopes of winning a free Atlantic passage, a house and twenty acres of land in Wisconsin. In America, self-proclaimed National Reformers petitioned Congress, held industrial congresses that attracted reformers throughout the north and printed a newspaper that became a powerful agent of propaganda for their cause—legislation to provide free allotments of the public lands for actual settlers, freedom of the homestead from the threat of confiscation for debt and a limitation on the amount of land that one might legally own.[1]

Each land-reform movement employed lecturers who traveled the circuit of town halls and temperance halls, sharing a message of redemption from the evils—present or prospective—of factory labor. But the printed word, the labor newspaper and pamphlet, held the movements together. This was especially true in the United States, where urban working people were largely literate and had neither a history of national protest comparable to British Chartism, nor loyalties to a particular leader of the stature and fame of a Feargus O'Connor. In the United States, the popularity of land reform in the 1840s is an object lesson in the role and importance of the press—here the labor press—in encouraging social change. Labor newspapers in the northern United States, catering to the cooperative movement and to factory reform as well as land reform, created a national and international sense of community among the "producing classes."

Although their primary function was to disseminate a worker-centered ideology through editorials, land-reform newspapers also reported on workers' meetings and demonstrations, recreated meetings by reproducing speeches in full and printed petition forms to be cut out and sent to Congress. Because editors of provincial newspapers often filled their columns with excerpts from other newspapers, single copies of the land-reforming *Working Man's Advocate* and *Voice of Industry* could be sent to the hinterland with huge effect. Copied-out articles reached the woods of Maine and Wisconsin, sharing the tantalizing idea that small farms were the only possible levers to raise American society, to rescue it from the specter of European-style worker degradation toward which it so steadily tended. These ideas were directly responsible for a flood of land-reform petitions that cascaded into Congress between 1845 and 1855.

The popularity of land reform as a working people's issue can be attributed in large part to the efforts of a small cadre of New York workers. Chief among these was George Henry Evans, formerly editor of the *Working Man's Advocate*, organ of the 1829–1830 New York Working Men's movement. Oppressed by debt, Evans moved from Manhattan to New Jersey to become a melon farmer during the economic depression of 1837. There he published his first newspaper avowedly devoted to land reform, *The Radical in Continuation of the Working Man's Advocate*. Arguing that only the land was a proper outlet for surplus labor, Evans advanced a plan for distribution of the public lands into one hundred–acre lots for farmers and three-acre village lots for mechanics. He created an ideological synthesis, an Anglo-American philosophical heritage of land reform—Thomas Spence, Thomas Skidmore, Thomas Jefferson—and a career of hands-on experience as the tribune of working men. He also mooted new organizational ideas, including National Reform's "agrarian pledge," with its overtones of political temperance:

No working man, no democrat, ought hereafter to give his vote for any candidate for a legislative office who is not pledged to support these measures. . . . I am ready to join a Union, no matter how small may be the number to commence it, of which the qualification for membership shall be, an oath or other solemn obligation, to support or vote for no man for any public office who will not pledge himself to exercise all the proper influence of his station to restore to the people, in some equitable manner, the Equal Right to Land.[2]

In addition to land reform, *The Radical* promoted universal freedom, universal suffrage for "all free citizens," secret ballots, popular election of all officers, free trade, direct taxation, demilitarization, gradual repudiation of state debts, the repeal of all bank charters, the simplification of existing laws and the submission of all laws to the vote of the people.[3] Evans produced 1,250 to 2,500 copies of each issue, and those he did not sell he gave away on the grounds that

there may be working men in New York who . . . may not understand how the proposed . . . making the public lands free to actual settlers can benefit those who may not feel able or willing to make a settlement thereon. . . . The equal right to land would create the proper equilibrium between the agricultural and other occupations, leaving a surplus of neither, and no man dependent on another for the right to work for a living, or with the power to extort the labor of others without equivalent.[4]

Among the audience for Evans' ideas on land reform were likeminded printers with experience, variously, in Chartism, Owenism and trade unionism. In 1844, Evans, Thomas Devyr, John Windt, Lewis Masquerier, James Pyne and James Maxwell met in Manhattan to reform a workingman's paper to support the new land-reforming movement, which they called "National Reform."[5] Renting a printing office at the northeast corner of Ann and Nassau Streets in Manhattan, the coterie began to print the *People's Rights*, a triweekly paper devoted to land reform. They hoped to distill its news and editorials into a weekly newspaper. Although the *People's Rights* soon folded, it gave way to a reincarnated *Working Man's Advocate*.[6] This newspaper would be the primary organ of propaganda for National Reform, its larger size and longer preparation time enabling it to bring theory and land-reform activity to its readers each week.

Buoyed by the reputation of its 1830s' namesake, the attractive *Working Man's Advocate* (later retitled *Young America* in emulation of Benjamin Disraeli's Young England parliamentary grouping) had an impact out of proportion to its circulation.[7] Over six hundred of the two thousand editors of newspapers in the United States were said eventually to have endorsed the idea of free homesteads due to its instigation.[8] At least one working man prized the newspaper enough to bring an entire run of it to Council Grove, Kansas, in 1870.[9] The newspaper certainly attracted able agitators to the movement. National

Reformer Joshua King Ingalls reported discovering Evans' newspaper, "a working man's paper, which drew my attention to the question of Private Landownership with great force, and at once convinced me, of what I had inferred . . . that usury of land (rent) was the basic usury, on which that of money, and of other property chiefly rested."[10] The newspaper was produced at least until 1850 and possibly later, since George Henry Evans' printing press was still among his effects when he died in 1855.[11]

Sold at a price the working man could afford ($1.50 a year, or 4¢ a single copy) Evans' newspaper professed an educational mission. As Evans wrote regarding the paper's 1830s' incarnation,

We are sometimes told by our agents that our paper would be liked much better by our female readers if it contained more anecdotes, stories, and other light reading . . . we have no doubt that such is the case, but we think it highly important that a different taste should be created, if possible. To those who can afford to take only one paper, it is highly necessary . . . that the paper they take should furnish them with correct political as well as other intelligence, for without it how can they be qualified to participate in their choice of public agents?[12]

The universal aims of the newspaper were emphasized by the banner engraving (carried over from *The Radical*) of a nude man sitting atop the world, pointing at the earth with one hand and in the other wielding a banner reading, "For me, for Thee, for All." Besides illustrating the inseparability of man from the soil and its products, this image indicated both the "naturalness" and vulnerability of the reformer in society—expressed through nudity—and his privileged position.[13] From atop the world, one could see, and change, everything.

In addition to the *Working Man's Advocate / Young America*, the New York center of National Reform produced cheap tracts which provided a summary of land-reform arguments and often testimonials from respected figures. A pocket-sized *National Reform Almanac for 1848* bore the motto "Free Soil for a Free People!"[14] "A man has a right to himself and to the use of enough of the earth's surface to sustain himself and his family as an inviolable HOMESTEAD. To secure this right is the first and highest duty of every state. Homes for all is the end, land limitation, homestead exemption and the Freedom of the Public Lands are the measures, the ballot is the means." The almanac contained not only the expected tables of eclipses, sunrises and sunsets, but also full reportage on the 1848 Industrial Congress.[15] In an early attempt at merchandising, the almanac was sent to all *Young America* subscribers as a premium.[16]

Land-reform tracts like *The Jubilee, Young America* and especially the one-page sheet *Vote Yourself a Farm!* could be printed up cheaply by the thousands and sold or given away by peripatetic National Reform lecturers, one of whom requested "5000 YA and 300 Jubilees" to be sent to him via canal as he perambulated upstate New York.[17] These pieces alternately played upon working-class fears and exploited pride in the newly acquired right to vote by suggesting that people vote themselves farms. They gave citations supporting their cause from friendly newspapers to illustrate that National Reformers were neither outsiders nor simply a handful of strange idealists. By autumn of 1845, *Young America* was in print to the tune of four thousand copies, and the goal was to circulate one hundred thousand.[18]

The Massachusetts *Voice of Industry* soon followed the example of the *Working Man's Advocate* by devoting substantial space to land reform and incorporating in its banner the National Reformers' motto, "For Me, for Thee, for All," as well as iconography joining industry and agriculture.[19] Most of the editors of this labor newspaper were clearly National Reformers. Former farmer-cum-harness-maker William Field Young, who edited the *Voice of Industry* and appeared at many industrial congresses, believed nine out of ten workingmen-reformers were in favor of land reform. "The people are beginning to realize that the nation's independence and property are based upon the landed interest of the country. We must have a landed Democracy or a ragged Democracy."[20] Young regarded speculation in the soil as the greatest evil affecting the agricultural interest and stressed the importance of preserving the family homestead from mortgage or execution. An evangelical believer in moral regeneration, he opposed striking as a labor tactic not because he felt that it was immoral, but rather because he believed that land monopoly and an overcrowded labor market were the real problems besetting New England.[21] As did George Henry Evans, Young gave land reform an international aspect by following the progress of the British land reform movement during his tenure as editor, and even defended the reputation of "Fergus O'Conner" [*sic*] against the disparagement of other newspapers.[22]

A series of land reformers replaced Young as editors of the influential *Voice*. D. H. Jacques was a professed National Reformer and a defender of Feargus O'Connor.[23] John Allen, impelled by a belief that under present conditions no one could afford to turn down a job, toured New England promoting National Reform in 1846. Allen and John Orvis, besides filling the *Voice* with land-reform editorials and articles, spent August and September 1847 lecturing in Springfield, Massachusetts, Albany, Troy, Rochester, Syracuse, Batavia and Buffalo, New York, and

Pittsford, Vermont.[24] That that congress received land-reform petitions from these areas is no mystery.

Although George Henry Evans, William Field Young and other work-ingmen-printers did much of the spade work necessary to make National Reform a thriving movement, *New York Tribune* editor Horace Greeley has received much of the credit for popularizing the homestead idea.[25] At first suspicious of land reform, Greeley eventually evolved to a position of sympathy with labor and, like Evans, envisioned the West as a healthier sphere for the operative:

We consider the Cities overcrowded already, and most Labor therein compara-tively ill rewarded. We believe the current of population should set not to but from Cities, and that the colonization of many of our City Artisans and laborers abroad in the open country, where their children may have free scope, free air, healthy exercise, and the constant companionship of nature, would be greatly beneficial to them and to all.[26]

By 1848, at least in public, Greeley had become an avowed friend of land reform, writing and speaking on the issue in fora that transcended class boundaries. He even introduced a homestead bill into Congress, where it was promptly tabled.[27] "National Reform is the broad and sure basis whereon all other Reforms may be safely erected," he wrote in George Lippard's journal *Nineteenth Century*.[28] In the main, working-class land reformers gladly accepted his support, until it ebbed in the early 1850s in favor of other reforms. Although Greeley may have been a too-convinced Whig politician to even have voted for the land-reform candidate in 1848, his decision to support the National Reformers at least through the *Tribune* increased the probability of land-reform sen-timent being propagated by the provincial press.[29]

Few newspapers bothered to show outright hostility to the National Reformers; those that did take a negative interest were often reforming papers whose editors worried National Reform might distract from their own hobbyhorses. As Greeley's *Tribune* commented,

The present silence of the Commercial Press and of those above it in the social hierarchy only proves that the idea is yet novel; not that it must ever be un-popular. . . . Already within the last year, four States and one Territory have in-scribed on their statute-books the pioneer measure known as 'Homestead Exemption' . . . within twenty years of agitating the subject, three fourths of the States composing this Union will have secured the home of every family against legal confiscation for debts of its owner.[30]

The *Albany Freeholder* labeled the National Reform movement a for-eign import, advocated by frustrated Chartists; but faced with the popularity of the proposed reform in the anti-rent region, its editor eventually gave his qualified support to National Reform measures.[31] He was not alone.

Newspapers' endorsements of land reform brought results. Over the period 1845–1855, the U.S. Congress and the Senate received at least 64,800 signatures endorsing either land reform generally or homestead exemption in particular, on 533 separate petitions; Congress received more petitions for land reform in 1849 than for any other measure save

Table 5.1
Newspapers Supporting National Reform, by State

State	Newspapers
Illinois	Chester *Reveille*, Chicago *Tribune*, Randolph *County Record*
Massachusetts	Boston *Chronotype*, Boston *Laborer*, Boston *Live Radical*, Fall River *Mechanic*, Boston *Social Reformer*, Lowell *Voice of Industry*, Lowell *Vox Populi*
Maine	Augusta *Age*, Gardiner *David's Sling*
Michigan	Alphadelphia *Tocsin*
New Hampshire	Concord *Freeman*, Concord *Herald of Freedom*, *White Mountain Torrent*
New York	Adams *Jefferson Democrat*, Albany *Anti-Renter*, Albany *Freeholder*, Albany *Knickerbocker*, Albany *Patriot*, Canandaigua *Day-Dawn*, Syracuse *Democratic Freeman*, *Evening Mirror*, *Fowler's Phrenological Journal*, Oneida *Gospel Reflector*, *Irish Volunteer*, *Landmark*, Rochester *National Reformer*, *Onondaga Standard*, *People's Rights*, *Plebeian*, *Precursor*, New York *Tribune*, *True Sun*, *Volkstribun*, *Young America*, *Wall Street Reporter*
Ohio	Steubensville *American Union*, New Lisbon *Aurora*, Cincinnati *Herald of Truth*, Cincinnati *Herald of Progression*, Cleveland *Home*, Salem *Homestead Journal*, Ohio *Eagle*, Ohio *Farmer*, Ohio *Self-Examiner*, Ohio *State Tribune*, Cleveland *Universalist*
Pennsylvania	Philadelphia *Ledger*, Pittsburgh *Daily*, *Quaker City*
Wisconsin	Milwaukee *Commercial Advertiser*, *Free Democrat*

Source: The list is compiled from various issues of the *Working Man's Advocate* and *Young America*, from the pamphlets *Jubilee* and *Young America* (New York: Young America Extra, n.d.), Gerrit Smith collection nos. 216 and 217, John Goadby Gregory, "The Land Limitation Movement," *Parkman Club Publications*, no. 14, 13 April 1897, *National Reformer*, vol. 1, no. 33, 15 May 1847.

cheap postage.[32] New York, Ohio and Pennsylvania—the presses of the former two being bastions of National Reform—amassed the most signatures in favor of the homestead measure.[33] Similar petitions were sent to state legislatures.

The forms onto which National Reformers affixed their signatures fell into five basic types: printed forms that called for approval of the homestead exemption measure but that were not obviously a product of the National Reform Association; handwritten forms simply calling for approval of homestead; printed forms prepared by National Reformers on their own presses; long handwritten preambles; and petitions supporting homestead sent by a separate group influenced by National Reform ideas, the Western Farm and Village Association. Some petitions of the total number may have been sent by nonworkers; National Reformer and trade unionist John Commerford sent Senator Andrew

Table 5.2
Petitions Sent to Senate and House of Representatives, 1845–1855

State	Number of Petitions	Approximate Number of Signatures
Alabama	1	7
Arkansas	1	16
Connecticut	6	460
Delaware	1	500
District of Columbia	1	73
Iowa	3	373
Illinois	41	5,717
Indiana	15	2,197
Massachusetts	20	1,441
Maryland	3	166
Maine	4	609
Michigan	9	781
New Hampshire	4	274
New York	160	18,960
New Jersey	7	251
Ohio	152	16,193
Pennsylvania	41	9,726
Rhode Island	2	294
South Carolina	1	63
Vermont	4	432
Virginia	4	457
Wisconsin	25	2,211
Origin Unknown	28	3,612
Total	**533**	**64,813**

Johnson a petition signed by one hundred and fifty businessmen who supported land reform because they had "been injured in their finances by having their customers appropriate the money that was due them for speculation in lands."[34] Nonetheless, the vast majority seem to have been signed by working people, many clearly catalyzed by the work of radical newspapermen.

National Reformers in New York, Ohio and Philadelphia produced their own petition forms either as newspaper "extras" or separate printed sheets.[35] The first form produced by the editors of *Young America* contained fourteen reasons for the redistribution of the public lands, but these were soon pared down for faster signature.[36] Aaron Hinchman, editor of the National Reform *Homestead Journal* of Salem, Ohio, drafted a form used for twenty-one petitions between 1845 and 1855. On each form, "we, the undersigned, legal voters of _____, being fully impressed with the evils of LAND MONOPOLY, and firmly believing that man has a natural right to a sufficiency of the SOIL from which to draw a subsistence," prayed that the Senate would pass the Homestead Bill that had just passed the House of Representatives.[37]

One of the most prevalent petition forms featured the figure from the banner of *Young America*, the unclothed everyman perched atop the world.[38] One *Young America* petition form called the "system of Land Traffic" a European import:

fast debasing us to the condition of dependent tenants, of which condition a rapid increase of inequality, misery, pauperism, vice and crime are the necessary consequences . . . in the infancy of the Republic, we should take effectual measures to eradicate the evil, and establish a principle more in accordance with our republican theory, as laid down in the Declaration of Independence . . .[39]

A later version of this document added an additional sentence, "The expelled Aristocracy of European Despotisms are buying up our Lands for speculation, while American Republicans are *homeless*. The case admits of no delay."[40] Another popular National Reform petition proclaimed "Freedom of the Public Lands" in a stars-and-stripes type font.[41] A third, "Give Land to the Landless," suggested a Disraelian "Two Nations." "Wherever the curse of Land Monopoly has become fully developed, its legitimate fruit has been to create the extremes of society, the Landlord and the Landless—the Rich and the Poor—the Oppressor and the Oppressed."[42]

These petitions were probably not set up for signature on street corners as they would have been in urban England. The National Reform lecturer for Genessee County, New York, suggested interested parties visit each family in a school district to collect signatures and encouraged the ladies to circulate during the day and sign their own petitions.[43] The names on a petition from one Massachusetts town all appear on the same two pages of the census enumeration, indicating the signers were neighbors and that someone had probably gone door-to-door in that instance.[44] Petitions also may have been signed outside the workplace and left for signature at National Reform meetings.

Fourierite settlements were particular strongholds of National Reform sentiment. Ceresco, Wisconsin, site of the Wisconsin Phalanx, not only yielded two petitions, but also saw an attempt to convert a communal village in Waukan, Wisconsin, into a "National Reform Village" (by laying out two hundred acres of ground in one-acre lots for separate homes while still conducting the mills, bakers and wash house on a joint system).[45] Monmouth County, New Jersey, home to the North American Phalanx, originated five petitions, three on National Reform sheets and a fourth even containing an imaginative etching of a village laid out on the National Reform plan. Although Virginia was otherwise devoid of land-reform petitioners, the town of Wheeling was home to a Fourierite phalanx and the point of origin for four petitions. Pittsford, Vermont, is another such example; besides being the location of a Fourierite group it yielded two petitions with handwritten preambles.[46]

The growth of National Reform sentiment within these settlements again can be traced to press influence. Before it expired in 1849, the *Harbinger*—official newspaper of the Fourierite movement—came out in tacit if incomplete approval of the National Reform scheme. At the least, its editors averred, freedom of the public lands was a step in the right direction.[47] Many writers for the newspaper also worked for the National Reform movement, occasionally managing to insert a reference to Association in some National Reform document. National Reformers courted this support; the first *Young America* petition form advertised freedom of the public lands on the grounds that, "Great facilities would be afforded to test the various plans of Association, which now engage the attention of so large a portion of our citizens."[48] With the decline of organized Fourierism around the time homestead was beginning to emerge as a plausible plan, energies seem naturally to have drifted into National Reform.

If the labor press was largely responsible for the success of land reform across the industrial north, a similar exchange of ideas occurred across the Atlantic.[49] Even as they denied that the National Reform movement was the brainchild of expatriate Chartists, the editors of the *Working Man's Advocate* admitted that "one of the things which cheered us on, when preparing to embark in this movement, was to learn that Feargus O'Connor was engaged, by lectures and by his papers, in promulgating the doctrine that 'The land makes the man.' "[50] "Thank God a poor Irish demagogue had forced the land question on the press of the country, and done something towards leading Republican America on to an examination of the all-important question," Feargus O'Connor exclaimed from a Manchester podium in 1845.[51] The *Working Man's Advocate* later noted that a recent issue of the *Northern Star* "has nearly a whole page respecting the National Reform and Anti-rent movements, including some of our most radical proceedings. If our movement has had no other effect than that of laying so much essential truth before the working men of Great Britain, I should consider that we had done well."[52]

The American and British land-reform movements communicated early and often. The Chartist *Northern Star* was particularly well-connected to the *Working Man's Advocate* and later to *Young America* through the person of former Chartist Thomas Devyr; moreover, the doings of the National Reformers bore out O'Connor's preoccupation with the land; for even in the United States, where men had the vote, corruption's tree—land monopoly—was growing.[53] A *Northern Star* editorial, noting the deteriorating position of American workers, urged every Chartist to read about American working men. "It will . . . show our readers that their American brethren are, like themselves, fast learning the secret of their deliverance; *that it is to THE LAND they look as Nature's resource, to which they must betake themselves as a refuge from man's oppression*, and that the Land they are determined to have."[54]

The editors of the *Northern Star* considered themselves part of a transatlantic "Movement Party," and continued to reprint material from *Young America* until the demise of that newspaper in the early 1850s. Among the articles was a comprehensive account of the origins and progress of the National Reform movement that ensured loyal Chartists would know more about National Reform than would most middle-class Americans.[55] Excerpts presented National Reform as demonstrative of unity in a common cause. "Reformers, Socialists, Fourierites, and Anti-Renters all seem to have acknowledged this 'great fact': and similar parties in this country and in Ireland might take a lesson from our American friends in this particular matter . . . were the several sections of the movement party in this country combined under one standard, inscribed, 'Political Equality the Means, Social Equality the End,' no power could long oppose the progress and success of the British movement."[56] In response to professed interest in their movement, Evans and his compatriots used the front page of the *Working Man's Advocate* to declare, "The people of England will be astonished to learn, that, although it is ten weeks since we commenced our movement, we have only hundreds instead of thousands of names to our *Pledge*, and only thousands instead of hundreds of thousands taking a lively interest in our movement."[57]

The British Potters' Joint Stock Emigration Society, headquartered in Staffordshire, also inaugurated its own relationship with the American National Reform movement. In the summer of 1845, George

Henry Evans reprinted a letter from the *Potters' Examiner*, the newspaper of the Potters' Joint Stock Emigration Society. Perhaps through this early connection, William Evans, head of the Emigration Society, acquired a copy of one of the National Reform pamphlets, which he published in parts throughout 1846 and 1847. Potters could read about the National Reformers' doctrines, study a map of a hypothetical township in the West, read a memorial which the National Reformers had sent to Congress in the 1844–1845 session, and note support for land-reform principles reprinted from various American journals.[58]

National Reformers and British land reformers addressed open letters to each other, and encouraged individual members of their respective movements to do so;[59] such letters were reprinted in labor newspapers on each side of the Atlantic, capitalizing on the low cost of mailing newspapers and attracting the greatest possible audience.[60] American and British workers thus could see common problems and feel part of a common dialogue, and both sides benefited because representing land reform as an international movement increased the ostensible authority of its proponents.

The attention paid to the redistribution of land in American labor newspapers, combined with the flow of petitions to Congress from 1845 until the passage of the Homestead Act, strongly suggests that the distribution of land was as much a central concern for American workers as were the conditions for, or remuneration of, labor. Land impinged upon health and housing as well as upon the labor market, and its redistribution was viewed as a more all-encompassing and permanent solution than reform of either wages or hours alone. Nor is the correlation between the spread of land-reform sentiment in newspapers and land-reform petitioning a coincidence. Rather, radical printers, with experience in a number of reform movements on both sides of the Atlantic, actively and effectively promoted both the issue and a particular course of action.

Far from being marginalized by the advanced information technology of their time, working men and their tribunes could fairly easily access the mass print media. Land reformers in the United States, by virtue of their connection with the printing trade, used this access and the customs of swapping newspapers and copying out articles to craft a multistate social movement. They perpetuated a discourse of land reform that even crossed the Atlantic, enabling British and American reformers to gain "authority" from each other. Taken together, the labor newspapers these men used to communicate their ideology and garner support for an eventually successful petitioning campaign represent a far-reaching, at least temporarily successful, attempt to build a feeling of community based on a shared interest as workers rather than on shared space.

NOTES

1. For the Chartist Land Company, see W. H. G. Armytage, "The Chartist Land Colonies, 1846–1848," *Agricultural History* 32 (1958): 87–96; Alice Mary Hadfield, *The Chartist Land Company* (Newton Abbott: David and Charles, 1970); Joy MacAskill, "The Chartist Land Plan," in *Chartist Studies*, ed. Asa Briggs (London: Macmillan, 1960): 302–41. For the Potters' Joint Stock Emigration Society, see Grant Foreman, "Settlement of English Potters in Wisconsin," *Wisconsin Magazine of History* 21 (June 1938): 375–96. For National Reform, see Helene Zahler, *Eastern Workingmen and National Land Policy* (New York: Columbia University Press, 1941); Sean Wilentz, *Chants Democratic* (New York: Oxford University Press, 1984). All three movements are discussed in Jamie Bronstein, "Under their Own Vine and Fig Tree: Land Reform and Working-Class Experience in Britain and America, 1830–1860" (Ph.D. dissertation, Stanford University, 1996).

2. *Radical, in Continuation of the Working Man's Advocate* (Granville, N.J.: George Henry Evans), vol. 1, no. 9 (Sept. 1841): 130.

3. *Radical*, vol. 1, no. 1 (Jan. 1841): 12; vol. 1, no. 2 (Feb. 1841): 17.

4. *Radical*, vol. 1, no. 6 (June 1841): 85.

5. Thomas Devyr, *Odd Book of the Nineteenth Century* (New York: The Author, 1882), American Section, 39.

6. C. K. McFarland and Robert L. Thistlethwaite, "Twenty Years of a Successful Labor Paper: The Working Man's Advocate, 1829–49," *Journalism Quarterly* 59 (1983): 35–39. McFarland and Thistlethwaite noted the potential of the newspaper to build social cohesion, but underestimated its contribution to promoting direct action on land reform.

7. *Working Man's Advocate*, vol. 1, no. 37, 7 Dec. 1844.

8. John Stanford Bradshaw, "George Henry Evans," in *American Newspaper Journalists, Dictionary of Literary Biography*, vol. 43, ed. Perry J. Ashley (Detroit: Bruccoli Clark, 1985): 184–88.

9. Newman Jeffrey, "The Social Origins of George Henry Evans, Working Man's Advocate" (Master's thesis, Wayne State University, 1960), x.

10. J. K. Ingalls, *Reminiscences of an Octogenarian* (Elmira: Gazette Co., 1897), 25.

11. Bradshaw, "George Henry Evans," 187–88.

12 *Working Man's Advocate*, vol. 5, no. 35, 12 April 1834.

13. Between September 1848 and 1849 the formerly naked man acquired a suit of clothes. *Young America*, vol. 6, no. 8, 12 May 1849.

14. Radical printers were common—according to Horace Greeley, only one in twenty printers became a master. *New York Daily Tribune*, vol. 5, no. 132, 11 Sept. 1845.

15. *National Reform Almanac for 1848* (New York: N.p., 1848).

16. *Young America*, vol. 6, no. 8, 12 May 1849.

17. *Young America*, vol. 1, no. 50, 7 March 1846.

18. *Jubilee* (New York: Young America Extra, n.p., n.d.); Gerrit Smith collection no. 216, Syracuse University; *Young America* (New York: Young America Extra, n.p., n.d.); Smith collection no. 217, Syracuse University; *Vote Yourself*

a Farm!, Smith collection no. 218, Syracuse University; *Working Man's Advocate*, vol. 2, no. 23, 30 Aug. 1845.

19. *Voice of Industry*, vol. 1, no. 31, 12 Feb. 1847. See also Norman Ware, *The Industrial Worker: 1840–1860* (Boston: Houghton Mifflin, 1924), 213. *Voice of Industry* was published in Massachusetts by Fitchburg, Lowell and Boston from 1845 to 1848.

20. *Voice of Industry*, vol. 1, no. 20, 2 Oct. 1845.

21. Lowell *Tri-Weekly American*, vol. 2, no. 205, 27 Sept. 1850; Jama Lazerow, "Religion and Labor Reform in Antebellum America: The World of William Field Young," *American Quarterly* 38 (1986): 265–86.

22. *Voice of Industry*, vol. 1, no. 41, 27 March 1846.

23. *Voice of Industry*, vol. 3, no. 31, 11 Feb. 1848.

24. *Harbinger*, vol. 4, no. 1, 12 Dec. 1846; *Voice of Industry*, vol. 2, no. 15, 23 Sept. 1846; vol. 2, no. 16, 2 Oct. 1846; *Harbinger*, vol. 5, no. 3, 26 June 1847.

25. Roy Marvin Robbins, "Horace Greeley: Land Reform and Unemployment, 1837–1862," *Agricultural History* 7 (1933): 18–41. Norman Ware rightly characterized Greeley as an editor first, a Whig second and a friend of labor third. Ware, *The Industrial Worker*, 21.

26. *New York Daily Tribune*, vol. 5, no. 141, 22 Sept. 1845.

27. Robbins, "Horace Greeley," 31.

28. *Nineteenth Century* (Philadelphia: Burr and Coffroth, 1848), vol. 1, no. 1 (Jan. 1848): 13–17.

29. Letter, Horace Greeley to Colfax, Sept. 5, 1848, Box 6 Folder 5, Horace Greeley Papers, New York Public Library.

30. *New York Tribune*, quoted in *Albany Freeholder*, vol. 6, no. 3, 16 Jan. 1850. On homestead exemption legislation, see Paul Goodman, "The Emergence of Homestead Exemption in the United States: Accommodation and Resistance to the Market Revolution, 1840–1880," *Journal of American History*, vol. 80, no. 2 (Sept. 1993): 471–98.

31. *Albany Freeholder*, vol. 2, no. 7, 20 May 1846.

32. The petitions are available at the National Archives, Tabled Petitions and Committee on the Public Lands records for both houses of Congress, under the following classification numbers: HR 29A G17, HR 30A H1.3, HR 31A G18.4, HR 32A H1.9, HR 33A G20.2, HR 30A G19.2, HR 32A H1.6, LC HR (Library of Congress House of Representatives Collection in the National Archives) Box 227, LC HR Box 232, LC HR Box 237, LC HR Box 243, LC HR Box 246, LC Territorial Papers (1 Box), Sen 28A G17.2, Sen 29A G19, Sen 29A H7, Sen 30A H17.2, Sen 31A H19.5, Sen 31A J4, Sen 32A H20, Sen 32A H20.2, Sen 32A H20.4, Sen 32A J2. The number of petitions is exact, but the number of signatures was estimated rather than counted on the longer petitions. Having settled on sixty signatures per page as a rough average for a sheet with two columns of names and thirty per page for one column of names, I multiplied that figure by the number of pages per petition. On the *Chicago Daily Democrat*, see Joe L. Norris, "The Land Reform Movement," *Papers in Illinois History, Transactions for the Year 1937* (Springfield, 1939), 80.

33. Robert Fogel, *Without Consent or Contract*, pt. 2 (New York: W. W. Norton & Co., 1989), 310.

34. Letter, John Commerford to Andrew Johnson, New York, 9 Feb. 1858, Sen 35A J1, National Archives, Washington, D.C.

35. In the absence of a printed blank, petitioners might copy the wording from such a *Young America* form. Petition from Duaresburgh, Schenectady County, NY, 22 March 1852, Sen 32A H20, National Archives, Washington, D.C.

36. Petition from Kalamazoo, MI, 9 Feb. 1846, Sen 29A H7, National Archives, Washington, D.C.

37. Petition from Washington Co., OH, 12 July 1852, Sen 32A H20; Petition from Ohio, 24 Jan. 1855, HR 33A G20.2, National Archives, Washington, D.C.

38. Petition from James Townsend and others, OH, 13 Feb. 1847, HR 29A H1.5; petition from New York City, 17 Jan. 1851, Sen 31A J4, National Archives, Washington, D.C.

39. Petition from D. Lamb and others, 21 March 1848, Sen 30A H17.2, National Archives, Washington, D.C.

40. Petition from Dunleavy, Ohio, 19 Jan. 1852, Sen 32A H20.4, National Archives, Washington, D.C.

41. Petition from New York, 12 July 1852, Sen 32A H20, National Archives, Washington, D.C.

42. Petition from Pope Leo, Illinois, 6 July 1852, Sen 32A H20, National Archives, Washington, D.C.

43. *National Reformer* [Rochester] vol. 1, no. 49, 31 Aug. 1848.

44. Massachusetts House unpassed legislation (1850) Box 290, no. 2910, Massachusetts Archives at Columbia Point, Boston, MA.

45. *Harbinger*, vol. 5. no. 10, 15 Aug. 1847. National Reformer and associationist Lucius Alonzo Hine visited Ceresco in that year. *Harbinger*, vol. 5, no. 11; Zahler, *Eastern Workingmen*, 47; *Weekly Tribune* [London] vol. 2, no. 52 (Enlarged series no. 1) 16 Feb. 1850.

46. Petitions from Pittsford, Vermont: 25 May 1852, HR 32A H1.6; 18 March 1850, Sen 31A H19.5. Wheeling, Virginia: 27 May 1852, Sen 32A H20; 3 June 1852, Sen 32A H20; 21 June 1852, Sen 32A H20. Monmouth County, New Jersey: 3 June, 7 June, 8 June, 1852, Sen 32A H20, 28 Jan. 1850, 8 Aug. 1852, HR 31A G18.4; Ceresco, Wisconsin: 7 June, 14 June, 1852, Sen 32A H20, National Archives, Washington, D.C.

47. *Harbinger*, vol. 3, no. 18, 10 Oct. 1846; *Harbinger*, vol. 4, no. 17, 3 April 1847.

48. Petition from Kalamazoo, Michigan, 9 Feb. 1846, Sen 29A H7, National Archives, Washington, D.C.

49. The extent, length and significance of the transatlantic connection between the working-class, land-reform movements, and its impact on their shape, have been underestimated by those historians who have written on this issue. See Zahler, *Eastern Workingmen and National Land Policy*, 78; Dennis Hardy, *Alternative Communities in Nineteenth Century England* (London: Longman, 1979), 244. Hermann Schlueter may have been the first to note the correspondence between American and British land reform in *Lincoln, Labor and Slavery: A Chapter from the Social History of America* (New York: Socialist Literature Co., 1913).

50. *Working Man's Advocate*, vol. 1, no. 9, 25 May 1844; on their insistence that land reform originated in America, see vol. 1, no. 24, 7 Sept. 1844. For

contemporary association of radicalism with English emigration, see Robert
Ernst, *Immigrant Life in New York City* (New York: Kings Crown Press, 1949),
19; but compare Ware, *Industrial Worker*, 171, who notes that "alien ideas" do
not take root unless the soil is primed for them.

51. *Northern Star*, vol. 8, no. 398, 28 June 1845.

52. *Working Man's Advocate*, vol. 1, no. 52, 22 March 1845. See also Evans'
response to a letter from O'Connor, *Working Man's Advocate*, vol. 2, no. 15, 5
July 1845.

53. *Northern Star*, vol. 8, no. 392, 17 May 1845. Devyr told New York audiences that the arguments of the National Reformers had been read by 2 million
English readers, *Northern Star*, vol. 7, no. 348, 13 July 1844. The *Star* was also
receiving Devyr's *Williamsburgh Democrat*. *Northern Star*, vol. 7, no. 336, 20
April 1844.

54. *Northern Star*, vol. 7, no. 337, 27 April 1844.

55. *Northern Star*, vol. 7, no. 338, 4 May 1844; vol. 9, no. 473, 21 Nov. 1846.

56. *Northern Star*, reprinted in *Working Man's Advocate*, vol. 2, no. 17, 19
July 1845.

57. *Working Man's Advocate*, vol. 1, no. 10, 1 June 1844.

58. *Potter's Examiner and Workman's Advocate*, vol. 6, no. 25, 17 Dec. 1846.

59. *Northern Star*, vol. 7, no. 345, 22 June 1844.

60. *Working Man's Advocate*, vol. 1, no. 37, 7 Dec. 1844; *Spirit of the Age*, no.
24, 6 Jan. 1849; *Northern Star*, vol. 10, no. 432, 21 Feb. 1846.

6

Destined Not to Survive:
The Illustrated Newspapers
of Colonial Australia

Peter Dowling

Published in Britain, North America and Australia, the illustrated newspaper is one of the most distinctive periodical forms of the nineteenth century. Illustrated newspapers epitomize the "explosion of imagery" brought about by the commercial application of Thomas Bewick's wood engraving process to mass produced, mass circulation serially issued magazines in the 1830s.[1] Charles Knight's *Penny Magazine* (1832–1845) was the first.[2]

The rise of the illustrated newspapers occurred at the same time as the invention of the photograph, announced independently, by Louis Daguerre and William Henry Fox Talbot in 1839. It could easily be assumed by many people in the late twentieth century that the explosion of imagery refers to the nineteenth century's embrace of photography rather than to illustrated newspapers. There was, however, to be a half-century hiatus between the development of photography in the 1830s and the development in the 1880s of the photomechanical, or halftone process, for reproducing photographs in print.[3] It is too often and too easily overlooked that the early daguerreotype process could only produce a single, positive (although reversed) image. By contrast, the negative-positive collodion wet-plate process developed in the 1850s allowed for multiple copies, as exemplified by the popular *carte de visites*.[4] However, the only way a photograph could be reproduced in a newspaper prior to the development of the halftone process was for the image to be copied onto a woodblock and then manually engraved.

Notwithstanding the *Penny Magazine*, the age of the illustrated newspaper carrying wood engravings covers almost exactly the half-century between the invention of photography and the invention of the halftone process. In Britain, the *Illustrated London News* was established in 1842 and in the early 1890s it adopted the new halftone process. In the United States, *Frank Leslie's Illustrated Paper* (1855–1922) and *Harper's Weekly* (1857–1916), its leading and arguably better-known competitor, both began publishing halftones in the late 1880s. In colonial Australia, the *Illustrated Sydney News* was launched in October 1853, and three weeks later, the *Melbourne Illustrated News*. While the latter only lasted two issues, the former ran for nearly two years. This dramatic contrast in fortunes was to set the trend for the next forty-three years of illustrated newspaper publishing in Australia. Of more than twenty-five papers founded, a few prospered; the remainder folded as suddenly as they appeared. However, with the advent of the halftone process, even the successful illustrated newspapers had all closed by 1896.[5]

This chapter will discuss the success and failure of illustrated newspapers in nineteenth-century Australia. The critical factors include the availability of start-up capital, production issues, consumer dynamics in a colonial market, competition from other papers and the social make-up of targeted audiences. This chapter divides the forty-three–year time span of illustrated newspaper publishing in colonial Australia into three periods: 1853–1862; 1862–1880; 1880–1896. Each paper has been allocated to one or more periods according to when it was founded and the length of its publication run.

1853–1862

With the discovery of gold in Australia in 1851 a new era was born that supplanted the convict image of the colonies. Within a decade the population grew 140 percent—from 438,000 to well over 1 million.[6] In economic terms, the value of produced gold quickly exceeded the pastoral industry's production of wool. It was a period of trial and error for illustrated newspapers. Of the nine papers founded, seven were weeklies and six closed within only a few issues. Of these nine newspapers, eight were founded in Victoria, which had become the richest colony because of its extensive gold deposits. Indeed, for the rest of the century its capital, Melbourne, was to be the production base for the majority of illustrated newspapers. Sydney and Adelaide (the capital of South Australia) were the only other cities to produce them.

The importance of start-up capital is highlighted by the fact that three of the four successful papers launched in the following period,

1862–1880, were stablemate publications of already established daily papers. The *Illustrated Australian News* (1862–1896), one of the earliest of these papers and running for over thirty years, was published by the *Melbourne Age* (1854–   ). As illustrated papers were expensive to produce, this arrangement allowed for much stronger financial backing during the difficult period of establishing a readership to the point of becoming self-supporting. By contrast, many of the earlier, unsuccessful papers launched in the 1850s were independent publications financed by either an entrepreneurial proprietor or by partners who were often directly involved in producing the paper. Two of the three partners in the *Illustrated Melbourne News*, which ran for six weeks in 1858, were the artist Nicholas Chevalier, who was the principal illustrator for the paper, and the wood engraver Frederick Grosse, who did the engraving.[7] When the paper closed, a brief article in the *Illustrated Journal of Australasia* dissected the cause: "The *Illustrated Melbourne News* deserved better success than it has met with. It has fallen, through the general cause of such failures—the absence of capital to carry on during its first struggles. The illustrations were excellent, the literary matter good, and the general conduct able."[8]

The earlier illustrated newspapers in their usually briefer publishing runs presumably had even less capital: *Melbourne Illustrated News*, two weekly issues in 1853; *Cassell's Illustrated Family Paper and Melbourne Advertiser*, eleven weekly issues in 1854; *Melbourne Pictorial Times*, two weekly issues in 1855; *Illustrated Melbourne Family News*, four weekly issues, also in 1855; and *Australian Home Companion and Weekly Illustrated News*, weekly, for four months, 1856–1857.[9]

Problems with production were a second factor inhibiting the success of early illustrated newspapers, although more in terms of limiting efficiency than as an outright cause of closure. In 1854 Victoria had only been settled for twenty years, and despite a rapidly growing population, there were shortages in labor—engravers, compositors, pressmen—inadequate machinery (the first steam press had only arrived two years earlier) and difficulties in ensuring a regular supply of materials: ink, paper and woodblocks.[10] The prospectus for the *Illustrated Melbourne Family News* confirms some of these problems. Acknowledging the superiority of wood engraving as the graphic medium most suited to long press runs, it went on to state that in situations calling for more limited runs due to smaller circulation, several factors mitigated against its use. There was the difficulty of obtaining the boxwood blocks, the lack of skilled engravers, and finally, the dryness of the Australian climate, which increased the susceptibility of the blocks to splitting. The publisher proposed a new system that involved producing the illustrations by lithography and the text by letterpress. He claimed the technique had never been used before in the world, for although he knew of journals being produced by lithography in Germany, he had never seen a newspaper combining the two mediums. Printing innovations like this were not uncommon during the gold rush period, a case of necessity being the mother of invention.[11]

The proprietors and publishers of illustrated newspapers adjusted to the consumer dynamics of a colonial market through a process of trial and error. The issues involved centered on the nexus of demographics, distribution and regularity of issue. In the decade 1851–1861, Victoria's emigrant European population experienced a sevenfold increase from 77,000 to 540,000. Melbourne's population, however, was not to increase at the same rate. After trebling between 1851–1845 to 69,000, to nearly 30 percent of Victoria's population, its growth flattened out to 125,000 in 1861, or 23 percent of the population; the lowest proportion ever reached.[12] In terms of newspaper circulation, these figures meant Melbourne became a proportionately smaller base population, a fact that increased the pressure to circulate in the goldfields and elsewhere outside of Melbourne. Complicating distribution, however, was the lack of an adequate transport network. Not until the mid-1850s did the government initiate a coordinated road construction program linking Melbourne to major regional towns. While this would have aided circulation, the weight and bulk of newspapers also meant added distribution costs. Only with the construction of railways was distribution made viable. Melbourne and Geelong were connected in 1857, Geelong to Ballarat in 1862 and Melbourne to Bendigo later the same year.[13]

In adjusting to the problems presented by colonial demographics and transport, the key to success was regularity of issue. The model for most colonial Australian illustrated newspapers was the *Illustrated London News*, which had been published weekly since 1842. From a first issue sale of 26,000 copies, circulation increased to 130,000 in the late 1840s, and to 300,000 in 1863. This was relative to a population in England and Wales of approximately 20 million, including sixteen cities of over 100,000 people. England also had a rapidly expanding railway network.[14] Despite Victoria's considerably smaller population base and the fact that Melbourne's population was only in the vicinity of 100,000, six of the eight illustrated newspapers from this period imitated the London model and were published weekly. From a production perspective, the logistics of weekly issue relative to the time-consuming wood engraving process, compounded by the lack of start-up capital, made them unviable.

The two exceptions were the *Illustrated Australian Mail*, which ran for fourteen months, 1861–1862 and the *Newsletter of Australasia*, which ran for over six years, 1856–1862. Both papers were published monthly, which meant not exhausting start-up capital so quickly and allowing more time to prepare a greater number of illustrations per issue. The *Illustrated Australian Mail* contained ten or more illustrations per issue compared to an average of three in the earlier papers. In the end, though, it failed due to a lack of capital backing as it was not the stablemate of a daily paper. The more unusual case of the *Newsletter of Australasia* will be discussed below.

In the 1850s gold rush era the main source of competition for illustrated newspapers came from their model the *Illustrated London News*, which was freely available in the colonies. Nostalgia for home was an understandable trait of the many recently arrived emigrant gold seekers—predominantly single men from Britain. Many came to seek their fortune, not intending to stay and settle. As the governor of Victoria pointed out in 1854:

The population here is essentially migratory, the Man of commerce strives to accumulate wealth, the Capitalist invests his money in land, the Miner seeks for gold, but none of these persons contemplate making this land their homes or endeavour to do more than amass sufficient money to enable them to return to England.[15]

Under these circumstances, many gold seekers adopted a sojourner *mentalitie* and initially took little interest in colonial affairs, preferring to keep track of news from home. In a June 1854 issue of the *Illustrated London News*, an article, "News-store in the Ballarat Goldfields," asserted that almost half the copies sent to Melbourne were sold through this outlet.[16]

Labor and machinery costs for newspapers and periodicals published in Britain were cheaper than in Australia, and postage rates were far from prohibitive. An English publication could be mailed from Great Britain to any part of Australia for 1p. The same item posted in Melbourne to a Victorian country town cost 3p and 6p to other Australian colonies depending on weight. Australian publishers were consequently forced to produce their newspapers and journals at competitive prices regardless of production and distribution costs.[17]

Furthermore, colonial publishers and editors were reluctant to compete against the metropolitan paper, preferring to view their papers as its provincial counterparts. The *Melbourne Pictorial Times* in its "Introductory Address" stated its aim as being not to compete with the illustrated papers of the mother country but to depict the colonial scene.[18] The following week in its "Principals and Prospects" the paper expanded on this position: "The extent of pecuniary resources, as well as the amount of versatile talent, enjoyed by the London journal, have already placed it beyond the arena of competition."[19] Although the editor expressed confidence in the paper's future, it was never seen again.

Nevertheless, it is arguable that the most important factor contributing to the lack of success of illustrated newspapers published in gold rush era Victoria was the targeting of too narrow an audience. In Victoria during the 1850s there were two almost mutually exclusive potential audiences for illustrated newspapers reflecting, in what was essentially a commodity-producing colony, the basic division between the production of wool and the production of gold. On the one hand were the merchants and the pastoralists who were investing in land, and on the other, miners seeking gold. For the former, wool was the true basis of prosperity, law, order and a hierarchical social structure; a kind of imitation of pre–Industrial Revolution England. Their vision of Australia was of the colonies being an Arcadia.[20] It was an ideal integral both to their own economic self-interests and to those of the woollen mill owners of Lancashire; of pastoral properties producing Merino wool to supply the factories of England.[21] Central to the Arcadian ideal of the colonial elites was the virtue of rural work for their shepherds, shearers and other employees. And when these employees had made enough money to buy their own land, they could become self-sufficient yeoman farmers working in the fields while their wives tended to home and hearth. This, then, was an ideology fusing agrarianism with domesticity.[22] The discovery of gold proved highly disruptive for this Arcadian ideal because it diverted the supply of labor to the goldfields. Instead of wealth from wool accumulating in the hands of a few, wealth from under the ground was available to all.

In the eyes of the ideologues of agrarianism and domesticity, gold seeking was a quintessentially masculine pursuit invoking a self-centered, antisocial, independence-seeking mode of behavior.[23] Not only had the gold seekers confused wealth with gold, they were the antithesis of domesticity. Leading an itinerant life rushing from one discovery to another and developing a single-minded work ethic devoted exclusively to finding the precious metal, the diggers were seen to live beyond the pale of civilization. Their lives were perceived as consisting of nothing but hard and dirty work, exposure to the elements and the absence of all domestic comforts. Success at gold digging also had overtones of a lottery, with the luck of the gambler rather than virtue governing the outcome. This dependence on luck implied that the digger was avoiding the opportunity for moral improvement afforded by steady labor, especially rural, agrarian labor. Furthermore, in leisure time the gold seeker was led further astray by the cycle of dissipation and regret associated with exclusively male behavior; a life of alcohol, gambling and whoring.[24] It was a world in which there was little room for women to provide, in the privacy of the home, a moral haven where the husband could recuperate from the corrupting influences of the outside world.

It was in the context of these two conflicting approaches to life—of agrarian prosperity and domesticity versus the lottery of gold and masculine culture—that four of the seven illustrated newspapers published in Melbourne during this period targeted too narrow an audience by promoting themselves as respectable family papers. In three cases the titles alone are indicative of the contents: *Cassell's Illustrated Family Paper*, the *Illustrated Melbourne Family News* and the *Australian Home Companion*. The *Melbourne Illustrated News*, meanwhile, specifically stated in the preface of its first issue its intention of being a family newspaper. Furthermore, all four papers were founded between 1853 and 1857 when the goldfields' population was at its greatest compared to that of Melbourne. None of these papers lasted longer than a few weeks. Although they had obvious appeal to the families of those whose wealth was based on trade and wool, given the way the papers moralized against gold and all the values associated with it, they had very little to offer the diggers.

By contrast, the most successful illustrated newspaper of 1850s Victoria was the *Newsletter of Australasia*, which, in running for over six years (1856–1862) actively catered to the requirements of the diggers on the goldfields, as well as to people living in Melbourne. The irony of this unusual publication was that it was primarily produced for a British, or "home" audience.

The *Newsletter of Australasia, or Narrative of Events to Send to Friends* was arguably one of the most innovative publishing ventures of colonial Australia. It was intended as a concise monthly summary of colonial news in a newsletter style, with additional blank space left for private correspondence. In appearance, the *Newsletter* comprised two sheets of rice paper folded crosswise, with one folded into the other, to form a quarto-sized, eight-page booklet. On the frontispiece page was the masthead, an illustration, and sometimes, an accompanying article. Overleaf, pages three to six were taken up with summaries of colonial Victorian news under various titles: "Journal of Politics"; "Journal of Social Progress"; "Journal of Science and Industry"; "Journal of Literature and Art." Pages two, seven and eight were left blank for writing on.

This format had two advantages compared to the illustrated newspapers of the period. First, its light weight meant the *Newsletter* could be registered with postal authorities as a letter and so assured of relatively safe delivery. (The overseas delivery of newspapers was still fairly unreliable.) Second, the "journal" style summaries of local news saved correspondents the dilemma of attempting to convey the breadth and variety of colonial life, allowing them to concentrate instead on their private news.[25] In addition, the single frontispiece illustrations of each issue covered a wide variety of subject matter aimed at informing friends and relatives back home about the different way of life in the colonies. In devising this format for the *Newsletter* the publishers were bearing in mind the hardworking diggers who could not afford the time to write lengthy and comprehensive letters about life in the colonies. The *Newsletter* also needed to be distributed on the goldfields, and in a listing of country agents, all the major gold towns were covered.[26]

In stark contrast to the number and variety of illustrated newspapers launched in Melbourne during the gold rush era, in Sydney only one paper was founded. It was also an anomaly for the period. The independent weekly *Illustrated Sydney News*, founded in October 1853, ran for nearly two years, closing mid-1855.

Although an independent paper lacking the capital backing of a parent daily paper, the *Illustrated Sydney News* was much better served in its production. One of the original partners in the paper and principal engraver, Walter Mason, had previously worked (before emigrating to Australia) on the *Illustrated London News*, *Punch*, and other illustrated publications in England.[27] Not surprisingly, then, of all colonial illustrated papers published during the trial and error period, the *Illustrated Sydney News* was the paper most closely modeled on the *Illustrated London News*. So, while the latter paper was undoubtedly a source of competition, its colonial imitator under Mason's guidance was much more astute in its choice of image, subject matter and quality of production. As for the issues of consumer dynamics and targeted audience, New South Wales, despite being where gold was first discovered, did not experience the social upheaval generated by Victoria's considerably richer deposits. The colony's population only doubled in size, to 351,000, in the period 1851–1861. Sydney's population as a proportion of the New South Wales population was also much smaller at 16 percent. Its population increased to only 56,000 in the course of the decade, a figure less than half Melbourne's population in 1861. New South Wales was also a much more established colony than Victoria. Its civic life was pervaded by a citizen *mentalitie* compared to the sojourner *mentalitie* of Victoria. So, while the *Illustrated Sydney News* understandably targeted the respectable among the colony's population, it aimed to have a multifaceted appeal for all colonists.

1862–1880

This was a period of stability and steady expansion for all the eastern colonies. With the one million population mark already passed by the beginning of the period, in 1873 the number of native born Australians exceeded those born overseas. Furthermore, the value of wool to the economy once more exceeded that of gold. In Victoria and New South Wales it was the era of land selection policies aimed at encouraging the development of agriculture; Victoria also saw the beginnings of local manufacturing. During this period two of the most distinctive elements of Australian popular culture began to emerge. First, the love of sport, with the first Melbourne Cup horse race and the arrival of the first touring English cricket team, both in late 1861. Second, the celebration of the "bush ethos" with its focus on the colonial Australian as exemplified by the stockman.

For illustrated newspapers it was a period of success during which the four longest-lived papers were all launched. Three of the four papers had the capital backing of a parent daily newspaper. All of them had sound production values in terms of labor, machinery and materials. Most important, they were all issued monthly in response to the consumer dynamics of the colonial market. The four papers were the *Illustrated Melbourne Post* (1862–1868) published by the *Herald* (1840–1890); the *Illustrated Australian News* (1862–1896) published by the *Age* (1854–   ); and the *Australasian Sketcher* (1873–1889) published by the *Argus* (1846–1957). These were all Melbourne-based papers. The only independent paper was a second series of the *Illustrated Sydney News* (1864–1894). All of these papers, especially the Melbourne ones, were pitted against one another. As for targeted audience, all the papers in their price and format—contents, layout, image, subject matter, range—aimed at a predominantly urban, respectable, middle-class audience. The editorial theme of the papers was the celebration of progress in the colonies.

These four most successful papers were not, however, the only illustrated newspapers launched during the 1862–1880 period. There were also three short-lived papers, two longer-lived Adelaide-based papers and the weekly stablemates of the east coast, capital city dailies.

Mostly established in the 1860s for rural distribution, this last category of papers was comprised of the *Leader* (1856–1957) published by the *Age*; the *Australasian* (1864–1946) published by the *Argus*; the *Weekly Times* (1869–   ) published by the *Daily Telegraph* (1869–1892) but taken over by the *Herald* in late 1869; the *Sydney Mail* (1860–1938) published by the *Sydney Morning Herald* (1831–   ), the *Australian Town and Country Journal* (1870–1919) published by the Sydney *Evening News* (1867–1931); and the *Queenslander* (1866–1939) published independently. Except for the *Australian Town and Country Journal*, none of these papers were illustrated when founded. Illustration came to these papers in the 1870s and 1880s, and then fairly sparsely. However, the weekly papers successfully survived the technological transition of the 1890s brought about by the introduction of the halftone process. Most lived on until either just before or after World War II when better distribution systems for their parent dailies and changing audience tastes took their toll.

In contrast to the weekly stablemates of the capital city dailies, there were the three short-lived papers, the *Illustrated Weekly Herald* (1872–1873), the *Graphic News of Australasia* (1873) and the *Australian Pictorial Weekly* (1880). All three were independent papers published in Melbourne. Their production values were not very high, and in the case of the *Australian Pictorial Weekly*, the illustrations possessed an almost crude, woodcut quality. They also attempted to launch themselves as weeklies. The *Illustrated Weekly Herald* ran for three months and the other two lasted only five weeks. Possibly the most crushing factor, however, was that all three papers were unavoidably in direct competition with both the rural weeklies and illustrated monthlies. The *Illustrated Weekly Herald* changed to monthly issue after nine weekly issues but lasted only one more issue.

The two longer-lived South Australian papers fail to fit the pattern established by the successful monthlies. Owned, printed and published by the same firm, but independent of a parent daily, one was the monthly *Illustrated Adelaide News* (1875–1895), the other *Frearson's Weekly Illustrated* (1878–1884). While the twenty-year lifespan of the *Illustrated Adelaide News* is comparable to the other papers, its longevity, given the size of its market, is unexpected. South Australia's population grew from 185,000 in 1871 to 358,000 in 1901, which very approximately was only one-third of the populations of both Victoria and New South Wales. In addition, Adelaide comprised only 12 percent of the colony's population, rising from 27,000 to 39,000 over the same period. In addition to the comparatively smaller population base supporting the *Illustrated Adelaide News*, the paper was rarely seen beyond the borders of South Australia. In many respects, it was a local paper when compared to the Australasia-wide Melbourne and Sydney papers, produced to show that the colony had a quality illustrated paper of its own.[28] Despite poorer production values compared to the other papers it survived by virtue of strong partisan support.

1880–1896

Initially this was a boom period due to the growth of local manufacturing and the emergence of an urban bourgeois, as epitomized by the experience of "Marvellous Melbourne."[29] The 1880s also witnessed the fiftieth jubilee celebrations of settlement in Victoria in 1884, and the centenary celebrations of European settlement in Australia in 1888. In the following decade there was a depression coupled with rural drought, bank crashes, widespread unemployment and a series of great strikes (maritime, 1890; shearers, 1891; coal miners and Broken Hill miners, 1892). For many people, the old faith in progress had collapsed, and the middle-class federation movement seemed a poor substitute.[30]

For illustrated newspapers, this period was both their heyday and their swansong. The three leading papers, the *Illustrated Australian News*, the *Australasian Sketcher* and the *Illustrated Sydney News* continued to prosper in the 1880s. During these years the population of Australia grew from 2.25 million to 3.5 million, with nearly three-quarters living in Victoria and New South Wales alone. The prosperity of the papers was underpinned by an efficient Australasia-wide distribution system based on coastal shipping and railways. Production values had also been given a fillip with the arrival of the New School style of wood engraving from North America.[31] The showcase for this new style of wood engraving in Australia was the serial publication of the *Picturesque Atlas of Australasia* (1886–1888) in anticipation of the centenary.[32]

Competition from new papers was slight. In Sydney, the monthly *Australian Graphic* was launched in late 1883, but only lasted five issues. In Melbourne, in 1888, the *Illustrated London News* launched an Australian edition. Essentially, this consisted of the weekly London paper carrying a monthly supplement devoted exclusively to Australian subject matter. On the one hand, the *Illustrated London News* was recognizing colonial pride in Australia, and on the other, catering to the continued nostalgia for home, especially among Melbourne's cultural establishment.[33]

There were, however, warning signs. In mid-1889, a second, unrelated *Australian Graphic* was launched. An independent, fortnightly paper, its distinguishing feature was its illustrations: photographs reproduced by photolithography. It lasted only eight issues, presumably for the usual reason of lack of capital. Later in the same year, a second paper, the fortnightly *Graphic Australian*, which used the same image reproduction technique, was launched. It lasted only three issues.

In terms of image reproduction technology, both papers were false starts. In August 1888, the *Illustrated Sydney News* became the first Australian paper to reproduce a photograph using the new photomechanical, halftone process. Two weeks later the *Sydney Mail* became the first weekly paper to use the same process.[34] The heyday of illustrated newspapers carrying labor-intensive and expensive-to-produce wood engravings was over. Their swansong had begun.

The repercussions were quickly felt. First to close was the *Australasian Sketcher* in December 1889. The *Illustrated Sydney News*, which in early 1888 had had a change of proprietor, went from a newspaper-style format to that of a magazine. The following year it changed to fortnightly issue, all the while steadily increasing the number of halftones per issue. It ran until 1894. Last of all was the *Illustrated Australian News*. It published its first halftone of a photographic image in September 1889.[35] Retaining a newspaper format, it continued running until mid-1896, by which time nearly all of its illustrations were halftones.

An era in Australian newspaper publishing was over. In the process, the pattern of factors influencing the success or failure of illustrated newspapers over the forty-three years of their publication had changed. By far the most important factor contributing to their demise was the introduction of the much faster and cheaper halftone process that rendered the monthly illustrated newspaper obsolete. In terms of competition, they had been usurped from within, for it was their weekly issue stablemates that had forced them out of production. Significantly, however, even the weeklies needed the capital backing of a parent daily. The targeted audience of the illustrated papers, notwithstanding the gold rush era, remained the same—a predominantly urban-based, respectable middle class keen to have its belief in progress confirmed by its visual representation. Finally, in terms of consumer dynamics, in 1896 colonial Australia's 3.5 million population was served by a transport network, which relative to distribution, was both constantly expanding and getting faster, thus facilitating the growth of the weekly illustrated newspaper.

NOTES

*I would like to thank John Arnold and Dr. John Rickard for their support, encouragement and comments in writing this chapter.

1. G. Needham, *19th Century Realist Art* (New York: Harper and Row, 1988), p. 36.

2. P. Anderson, *The Printed Image and the Transformation of Popular Culture, 1790–1860* (Oxford: Clarendon Press, 1991), ch. 2.

3. E. Jussim, *Visual Communication and the Graphic Arts: Photographic Technologies in the Nineteenth Century* (New York: R. R. Bowker Co., 1983) (orig. pub. 1974), pp. 66–68, 161, describes the twelve-year period (1881–1893) covering the development of the halftone process.

4. A-M. Willis, *Picturing Australia: A History of Photography* (Sydney: Angus and Robertson, 1988), pp. 10–11.

5. A distinction has been drawn between news-oriented illustrated newspapers like the *Illustrated London News* and humorous illustrated papers like *Punch*. Colonial illustrated humorous papers are not being discussed in this chapter.

6. *Australians: Historical Statistics* (Sydney: Fairfax, Syme and Weldon Associates, 1987), pp. 26, 41, for all population figures unless otherwise indicated.

7. J. Kerr, ed., *The Dictionary of Australian Artists: Painters, Sketchers, Photographers and Engravers to 1870* (Melbourne: Oxford University Press, 1992), pp. 147–49, 329.

8. *Illustrated Journal of Australasia*, 4/21 (March 1858), p. 143.

9. *Cassell's Illustrated Family Paper*, the *Illustrated Melbourne Family News* and the *Australian Home Companion* were quarto-sized, the others were

folio-sized. This latter size was to be the standard size for all subsequent papers. See L. Stuart, *Nineteenth Century Australian Periodicals: An Annotated Bibliography* (Sydney: Hale and Iremonger, 1987), for further information about the papers.

10. Ibid., p. 2.

11. Another example is John Osborne's world-first invention of a commercially viable photolithographic process, developed in 1859 for printing land-sale catalogues more quickly. See Kerr, *Dictionary of Australian Artists*, pp. 597–98.

12. D. Garden, *Victoria: A History* (Melbourne: Nelson, 1984), pp. 75, 80.

13. Ibid., pp. 87–91.

14. A. Lambert, *Nineteenth Century Railway History through the Illustrated London News* (Newton Abbot: David Charles, 1984), pp. 7–8, for circulation figures and impact of railways.

15. Garden, *Victoria: A History*, p. 80.

16. "News-store in the Ballarat Goldfields," *Illustrated London News*, 3 June 1854, p. 503.

17. Stuart, *Nineteenth Century Australian Periodicals*, p. 2.

18. "Introductory Address," *Melbourne Pictorial Times*, 7 July 1855, p. 1.

19. "Principles and Prospects," *Melbourne Pictorial Times*, 14 July 1855, p. 1.

20. C. Lansbury, *Arcady in Australia: The Evocation of Australia in Nineteenth Century English Literature* (Melbourne: Melbourne University Press, 1970), ch. 6, and D. Goodman, *Gold Seeking: Victoria and California in the 1850s* (Sydney: Allen & Unwin, 1994), ch. 4.

21. C. Goodwin, *The Image of Australia: British Perceptions of the Australian Economy from the Eighteenth to the Twentieth Century* (Durham, N.C.: Duke University Press, 1974), pp. 49–51.

22. Goodman, *Gold Seeking*, ch. 5.

23. Ibid., p. 154.

24. Ibid., pp. xvii–xix, 115–18.

25. Advertisement for *Newsletter of Australasia* in *Illustrated Melbourne News*, 23 January 1858, p. 51.

26. *Newsletter of Australasia*, December 1857. A short-lived imitator of the *Newsletter* was *The Polyglot Newsletter: A Summary in English, French, German, and Italian for Transmission to Europe*. Launched in September 1858 and lasting only four issues, its mere founding is indicative of the multicultural nature of gold rush era Victoria.

27. Kerr, *Dictionary of Australian Artists*, pp. 520–21.

28. "Introductory," *Illustrated Adelaide News*, January 1875, p. 2.

29. See G. Davison, *The Rise and Fall of Marvellous Melbourne* (Melbourne: Melbourne University Press, 1978).

30. R. White, *Inventing Australia: Images and Identity, 1688–1980* (Sydney: Allen & Unwin, 1981), pp. 85–88.

31. Jussim, *Visual Communication and the Graphic Arts*, pp. 157–60, for a discussion of the New School of wood engraving.

32. This large-scale publishing project was modeled on *Picturesque America* (1872–1874) and *Picturesque Canada* (1882). Three of the illustrators and a team of engravers from the latter project subsequently came to Australia to produce an Australian version, bringing with them the New School technique.

See A. Moritz, *America the Picturesque in Nineteenth Century Engraving* (New York: New Trend, 1983), pp. 43–44.

33. In January 1887 the weekly *Express*, published in Sydney, became the *Illustrated Express*. It ran until June of the same year. It has not been included in the main text of the chapter because it was a denominational paper directed at a Catholic audience.

34. The *Sydney Mail* is often incorrectly cited as the first illustrated newspaper to produce a halftone image in Australia.

35. In switching to the halftone process, the *Illustrated Australian News* began by experimenting with the photomechanical reproduction of monochrome wash sketches. These gave more tonal contrast in the final halftone print compared to reproductions of photographs that tended to have an overall greyness in appearance. Until folding, line drawings, wash sketches and photographs were all reproduced by the halftone process.

7

Gendered Space and the British Press

Laurel Brake

In late May 1996, readers of the London *Guardian*, a distinguished daily broadsheet, were offered a rare glimpse of the negotiation of the protocol that was to pertain to the television reporting of an inevitable future event, the death of the Queen Mother. So sensitive was the subject, liable to offend the royal family and to expose sources at the BBC, that although the story led the tabloid half of the paper, there was no byline. And revealing as it was of the ideological practices that link the media to the state, the glaring ideologies of gender remained unremarked on and probably unseen. Both the construction of the Queen Mother, who is alleged to occupy the "symbolic position of the Mother of the Nation," and selection by BBC senior executives of the stories deemed appropriate and inappropriate to national mourning are permeated with gendered values. All-male space such as "Have I Got News for You" is to be replaced by "something like BBC2 in around 1974: gardening and music programmes, a reflection of a gentler and more innocent world."[1]

The gendering of the coverage of the Queen Mother's death, which is largely presented as glum and inevitable by the BBC source(s), is confirmed by comparison with the discussion of the television programming for the death of the Duke of Edinburgh. He "is the really interesting one. What would we do if he was killed in a carriage-driving accident tomorrow? There's someone whose reputation and position in national life are complex and very fluid."[2] While it is implied that television might entertain approaching his story, the parallel story about the Queen Mother is viewed as definitely off-limits for the BBC at the time of her death: "The unfortunate thing is," says a senior BBC executive, "that there is a genuine journalistic job to be done on that life: her position and influence within the royal family and so on. And you're not going to get it on television when she goes." "Republicans" it seems "should stock up from the video shop now." So while the *Guardian* piece identifies its subject as "a thermometer of monarchism in Britain," another narrative emerges of gendered reporting and gendered constructions, the "complex and fluid" reputation of the male "non-head of state" and the boring fixity of the female in the analogous position.

This unconsciousness of journalism of its pervasive, even constitutive links with male discourses and cultural values is connected with its intolerance of its own history. As an example, I want to deconstruct the history of the nineteenth-century press in relation to gender as a basis for examining the discourses of gender in *Prospect*, a new British monthly magazine that first appeared in October 1995. History helps!

A glance at the conditions in which the history of the press has been and is being written and the current locations of the history of journalism as a field provide an informative preamble to the specific case. Print journalists in Britain are renowned for their unyielding adherence to experience as an employment criterion; and their dismissal of media studies is at the core of their suspicion of academic education in this connection. If contemporary theory and any nonempirically based knowledge about communication meet with disdain from journalists, the *history* of the press is equally of no interest, a point made recently by Matthew Engel,[3] the *Guardian* man who atypically took leave from his paper to write *Tickle the Public: One Hundred Years of the Popular Press* (Gollancz, 1996). Perhaps it is not a surprising antipathy from a profession to which the word *old* is inevitably pejorative, except insofar as history provides background for the new and topical. This disregard is evident in turn in the construction of both media studies and journalism degree schemes in which the history of journalism seldom figures; the value system of the journalists is replicated in training for journalists of the future.

But the key factor in the genesis of the history of journalism is that, undervalued by its own practitioners and trainers, it is also marginalized by a number of other academic disciplines, such as history, English and bibliography on whose borders journalism loiters, and from which it takes its characteristic forms.[4] The majority of work on journalism history has stemmed from these various borderlands, its very definition hinging on the specific discourse on which it borders. Thus, from journalists and historians have emerged preponderantly factual histories and dictionaries of the press, which foreground evidence and eschew interpretation and theory;[5] from English studies have come textual and cultural histories, now often theorized;[6] while from bibliographers have come the great tools of current-day access to the history of the press—the reference books—which compile and gather information according to the discourses of literature,[7] history[8] and bibliography.[9] Sociologists, like media studies scholars such as the Glasgow Media Group, and practicing journalists normally confine their analyses of print journalism to contemporary titles or problems.

Within English, in Britain, for example, the history of journalism and the treatment of periodicals and newspapers as text are now gradually making their way into the teaching syllabus. Four conferences within twelve months—on journalism and its borders with English—indicate that this is a significant moment in the history of the study of English: It is the formal outing of journalism from a closet of denial, invisibility and contempt that has characterized the relation of literature with journalism, at least since Matthew Arnold's derogation of the new journalism in 1887. Neither journalists, authors nor lecturers have been keen to acknowledge the liaison between journalism and literature, and this continues to be the case. Only recently in the *Times Literary Supplement* (13 October 1995), George Steiner termed the alleged sensationalism of an author under review "journalistic."

This derogation of journalism, *in journals*, by paid literary reviewers whom others might view as journalists—those who write for journals—is commonplace. What has changed is a new visibility accorded to journalism within English (and perhaps in other subjects). University College London's Northcliffe Chair has been held successively in recent years by a journalist (Karl Miller), and by a journalist and scholar (John Sutherland) among whose primary interests is nineteenth-century publishing history; the University of Warwick has recently appointed Jeremy Treglown, former editor of the *Times Literary Supplement* as a professor of English. In addition, the recent and welcome permeability of English as a subject has meant that the rift between authors and journalists, literature and journalism—the separations that George Gissing forcibly chiseled in 1891 in *New Grub Street*—may at least be reassessed. The interdependence of the history of journalism and of literature, of English Literature and the press, could be acknowledged; and courses on cultural production, the book trade and the periodical press could follow, for example, on the quarterlies and the Romantics, serial publication and fiction, and the discourses of literature and journalism. Although specialist scholars and journalists have been addressing these issues for nearly two centuries, it has largely been in *writing* (much of the writing in the press itself), at specialist academic conferences and in the pub, over the *Punch* table and at *Idler* teas, not in the classroom. I strongly suspect that the case of English is not anomalous: The history of journalism is not generally taught in Britain in undergraduate English, history, journalism or media studies courses. We should be clamoring for change in the ways we configure our respective fields of study with respect to journalism.

For my case study on the significance of the history of journalism for understanding present practice, I want to examine the gendered discourses of journalism, first with respect to nineteenth-century journalism, and the relation between our critical practice and readings of texts we treat as literature and as journalism. But I shall keep British contemporary literary weeklies in view, and end with some remarks on *Prospect*, the new monthly that I take to be political journalism and nonliterary. I want to look specifically at the notion of gendered space in the press and in other aspects of the profession of journalism—personnel, cultural values, conditions of work and the definitions and privileging of "news"; and I want to suggest that there is a link between the privileging of news in journalism, the overdetermined strain of hostility in journalism to literature except insofar as it is news[10] and the relative dearth of women as producers and consumers of journalism.

The fortunes of literature and women are closely linked in the nineteenth century in relation to journalism. As monthly magazines, reviews and weeklies came to include current *literature* as opposed to politics, the staple of news, so the incorporation of women in the industry as producers and consumers increased. Margaret Beetham, in her chapter on nineteenth-century women's magazines in *Women's Worlds*,[11] offers an excellent conspectus on the matrix of market and cultural forces that contributed to the representation and involvement of nineteenth-century women in the press of the period. I would argue that not only did the literature of the nineteenth century *make* the periodical press and vastly increase its share of the market to include women and other middle-class readers, but also that the periodical press, with the circulating library, *made* the nineteenth-century novel. Among a multitude of functions of the nineteenth-century journals was their role as one of the two primary distributors of new fiction between the advent of *Blackwood's* in 1817 and the virtual fall of the three-decker system in 1894.

It will come as no surprise to most British readers that a recent study of current British journalists by Anthony Delano and John Henningham[12] summarized in the *Guardian* in 1995[13] finds that 75 percent of British journalists are male. What Ann Leslie wrote in 1966 and Michael Leapman quoted in 1992 in his book *Treacherous Estate* still seems to be largely the case: "Women are basically honoured guests in a masculine fortress. All the standards have been set by men, all the power ultimately rests with them."[14] Moreover, a number of commentators argue that the current culture of daily and weekly newspaper journalism in Britain is still male: Leapman claims that "Women who do succeed tend to do it on the men's terms"[15] and Ann Leslie describes "other Fleet street women" as "the ones who began as ordinary human beings but then became as drunk and foul-mouthed as the men."[16] Robert Darnton, in "Journalism: All the News That Fits We Print," a telling piece from the 1970s,[17] offers a striking structural analysis of the male culture of the newsrooms of two American dailies.

Delano and Henningham also report that only 35 percent of male journalists are under the age of thirty-five (which shows their hold in the industry and on senior positions) while 67 percent of the 25 percent of women journalists are under thirty-five. This youthfulness of women journalists may indicate a recent openness of the profession to women, but it also shows the effect of the glass ceiling, whereby the industry offers a restricted career structure to women, coupled with the incompatibility of working conditions in the profession with family responsibility. However, working conditions do vary significantly; frequency of publication in the nineteenth century, for example, normally not only rigidly separated the genders in journalism, with few if any women working as staff on dailies or weeklies and the great number on monthlies and quarterlies, but also it tended to separate the nascent professional male staff journalist of the dailies from the freelancer writing under pressure for a number of papers and from the gentleman or lady reviewer or author writing more commodiously from home.

This correlation between frequency of publication and gender is still echoed in print journalism: Leapman notes, "Significantly, the first three women editors of nationals were on Sunday papers, where the time pressures are not as great."[18] There is another pressure that is reduced in both evening and Sunday papers, the pressure of news. The space for features and reviews that results can be directly related to two areas of journalism in which women journalists are permitted to congregate and women readers are alleged to. The *gendering* of news as the dominant mode and value of the daily press is implicit in the relative openness of reviewing and features to women journalists. Historically it is explicit. The entry of features and reviews into the British daily press is associated in part with an evening daily, the *Pall Mall Gazette* (from 1865); it was this paper that provoked Matthew Arnold's denunciation of the "new journalism," the late nineteenth-century development that actively recruited women as journalists and readers.[19] The gendered configurations of modern journalism may be delineated more clearly if we look at their ancestry.

It is my view that most if not all space in the nineteenth-century press was gendered; that is, it was either directed at male, female, or "family" readers. Little or no space was gender neutral. The male reader represented the default position; he was the hegemonic addressee of nearly all nineteenth-century dailies, certainly until 1865 and the advent of the *Pall Mall Gazette* that paved the way for the "new journalism," with its "personal" element, its features, its interviews and its avowed incorporation of characteristics from reviews and weeklies, including attention to literature and the arts. Many weeklies were primarily addressed to male readers, such as the *Spectator*, while certain monthly and quarterly reviews, such as the *Edinburgh* and the *Quarterly* in the early part of the century, and the *Nineteenth Century*, which dates from 1877, had periods of apparently exclusive male address. If women readers were invited, the codes were clear—pieces on suffrage or antisuffrage in the *Nineteenth Century*, on literature or on travel. Periodicals for women were positioned as "class" journalism, that is for a special interest group other than the general (i.e., male) reader; "family" periodicals designated those that were suitable for women *and children*, and included Sunday papers such as *Good Words* and the *Cornhill Magazine*.

The *Cornhill*, which was conceived of as a family magazine from the start, had a policy that accorded with their targeted market, the middle-class family. No articles on certain subjects, hereby explicitly gendered, were to appear in its pages; these subjects were politics, religion and philosophy. When Leslie Stephen edited the periodical he placed his various articles on such male and serious subjects elsewhere. One of the primary elements of the success of the *Cornhill* is that it offered, for a shilling, two serial novels per number. This policy of exclusion governed the fiction as well, fiction whose titles are familiar to us all— *Framley Parsonage*, *Lovel the Widower*, *Romola*.

There are several points I want to draw from the example of the *Cornhill*. First, it is a good example of the way the very constituent character of literature by "great authors" such as Trollope, Thackeray and George Eliot is market directed. The apparent demarcation between literature and journalism, art and commerce, is not as rigid as George Steiner implies. Indeed, it is the very fact of the mediated nature of journalism texts, in literary terms the multiple authorship of texts, which so rankles with those in English who adhere to the Romantic or new critical or formalist notions of the autonomy of art, texts and writers. One of the best accounts of the production of the mediated journalism text is Robert Darnton's. His essay specifies four factors—the structure of the newsroom, occupational socialization, standardizing and stereotyping, and secondary reference groups and "the public," the significant element of which is identified as other reporters. Darnton's analysis is over twenty years old, but although its details will have substantially changed, the argument remains; self-censorship, placating the editor, respecting the house policy and writing within the dominant discourses—production is an important determinant of the product in journalism, and a large part of nine-teenth-century fiction did appear in part issue over time or was serial-ized in journals and newspapers.

Second, the *Cornhill*'s construction of women's reading and the na-ture of the family market, stripped of politics in particular, is helpful in understanding the almost exclusive male address prior to the removal of the newspaper tax of most of the dailies, which tended to be given over to political news—domestic, foreign, financial—and comment on it. It is interesting too that not long after *Cornhill*'s 1860 launch, in 1863 when Cox bought the *Queen*, the *Lady's Paper*, he too excluded politics as an unsuitable subject for lady readers. The success of the permeation of these constructions of the women reader market is shown by the continued identification of the mass readership of women *late* in the century with precisely the broad subjects designated for the wealthier classes of women—fashion; domestic concerns including craft, decoration, household management; and leisure activities in-cluding visual art, music and, perhaps above all, fiction and to a lesser degree poetry.

Women of all classes are also positioned ubiquitously as the grateful receivers of advice and/or education. In June 1890 when W. T. Stead published his scheme in the *Review of Reviews* to create "lady journal-ists" who could participate in the journalism of the future, it was poli-tics he designated as the key subject in journalism of which women were ignorant. Requiring them to read the monthly's political articles under the heading "The Progress of the World" as well as the charac-ter sketches, he proposed to examine them and award the winner(s) the cost of an undergraduate degree course at one of the ladies' colleges. While he acknowledges the existence of "many lady journalists," he claims that few "have the ordinary, all-round acquaintance with poli-tics which is expected, as a matter of course, from every man who en-ters a newspaper office."[20] His view of lady readers conforms with the construction of the female readership in the *Cornhill* and the *Queen* in-sofar as he speculates that the "multitude of girls who, but for such a competition, might never have looked in the newspaper for anything but births, marriages, and deaths, the *Court Circular*, and personal gossip."[21]

But of course there were both women in politics in the nineteenth century as well as women journalists and editors. Names in the first category include Josephine Butler, Emily Faithfull, Harriet Martineau, Florence Nightingale, Barbara Bodichon, Helen Taylor, Emily Davies,

Lydia Becker, Frances Power Cobbe. Votes, health, education, property
and marriage law were all political issues around which women organized political campaigns. Theodora Bostick's piece on "The Press and
the Launching of the Women's Suffrage Movement, 1866–1867"[22] documents one example, revealing that the *Queen* along with some of the
usual suspects—the *Fortnightly*, the *Westminster Review* and some unexpected titles such as *Macmillan's Magazine* and the *Contemporary
Review*—supported John Stuart Mill's limited version of women's suffrage or, in *Macmillan's* case, published an article by one of the campaigners. A fact routinely overlooked in the normalized exclusion of
women from politics of the period was that two of the most controversial political novels of the century were written by women in mid- and
late century: Elizabeth Gaskell's *Mary Barton* on Chartism and the
rights of working people, and Mrs. Humphry Ward's *Robert Elsmere* on
the toleration and landscape of religious doubt.

In 1866, out of agitation around the 1867 Reform Act and built on an
earlier magazine from the Langham Place group, came one of the many
women's papers of the century, Jessie Bourcherett's *Englishwoman's
Review*. Evelyn March Phillipps, writing in 1894, singled out Britain
for the diversity as well as the number of its women's newspapers.[23]
Some of these, such as the *Queen*, a weekly published from 1861–1910,
were edited by women, in *Queen's* case Helen Lowe, but many more
were edited by men. Oscar Wilde and Arnold Bennett are two famous
examples, Wilde editing *Women's World*, which he colonized for gay
men as well as new (and aristocratic) women, and Arnold Bennett who
edited *Woman*. Female editors include Mrs. Henry Wood of *Argosy*,
Mary Elizabeth Braddon of *Belgravia* and Emily Faithfull of the
Victorian Magazine. George Eliot made her way as a woman of letters
by among other things sitting herself at one center of the radical middle-
class world, as an editor of the *Westminster Review*; Margaret Oliphant
and Geraldine Jewsbury were similarly embroiled in professional journalism and politics. My point is that the hegemonic view of women, by
and in the mainstream press, excluded women from knowledge of politics and journalism and from participation in them, in the face of (1) a
range of political activity by women, (2) journals for women and (3) a
number of women editors and journalists. Coercive and restrictive, it
defined women as *consumers* in terms of their economic market power,
as purchasers (if indirectly) of clothes, domestic appurtenances, leisure
activities and of health-related products, much of which was advertised
on the wrappers or indeed in the designated editorial matter. Because
women had no political purchasing power, holding neither the right to
vote nor to hold office, the newspaper and periodical press not only excluded them ideologically from most of the newspaper market and a
share of the periodical market for the greater part of the century, but

also positively constructed them as readers in terms of "other" and separate commodity markets. The ideological dedication of the middle
classes to the separation of middle- and upper-class women from the
world of work did similar cultural work. It reinforced the insistence on
the alleged affiliation with leisure and home as purveyed in the periodicals while, from midcentury, writers such as the Brontes and the
journals of the Langham Place group were analyzing and exploring
women's fears of work, the compulsion to work, exploitation at work
and how to survive between jobs and in retirement. Unmarried women,
Gissing's "odd" women, were at issue in several debates in the journals
at different points in the century—"redundant" in the 1860s and "re-
volting" in the 1880s.[24] The ideological denial of politics to women took
some effort to maintain.

Journalism as an industry is implicated in this set of constructions
and exclusions. They are part of *its* history as well as Britain's. The resistance to women at all levels of work in journalism, particularly print
journalism, is plain. Its pervasive and immutable quality is clearly visible week after week in the contents columns of literary weeklies such
as the *Times Literary Supplement* and the *London Review of Books*,
and in the dailies, even in the review pages. In a field in which women
have figured as writers in great numbers for over a century, and as
English lecturers and teachers, women might have been expected to
flourish as reviewers, editors and authors reviewed. But as the survey
sponsored by the Women in Management in Publishing (WIMP!)
showed in 1992, the literary editors, the reviewers and the authors reviewed of the daily and Sunday press were overwhelmingly male.[25] It
was an act of kindness in that survey to exclude the literary weeklies.

In conclusion, I want to look briefly at *Prospect*, a political monthly
that has drawn markedly on journalists associated with two broadsheet dailies, the *Independent* and the *Financial Times*, for its backers
and for its editorial board and staff. If it is staffed with newspapermen,
its periodical ancestry is alleged by two correspondents on the letter
page of the first number to be *Encounter*, the political monthly edited
by Melvin Lasky and backed surreptitiously by the CIA, and it does indeed look backward to the time when politics did not concern women.
Prospect is a modern example of gendered space in a periodical that
does not present itself as a "class" periodical—in this case, a men's
magazine. It reenacts the exclusion of "woman" in a journal that will
"be serious, but never solemn."[26] In its first phase its board of directors
included no women, but the May 1996 inclusion of the deputy editor
made a ratio of ten to one.

Similar proportions characterize the balance of contributors in the
first number, with twenty-one out of its twenty-four contributors being
men. Its deployment of the three women whose work it publishes and its

representation of their work are problematic. A woman economist and editor (Susan Greenberg) has been commissioned to write a short, anecdotal piece on the status of trust in Britain and America; this is risibly titled "The Milkman Theory of Civilisation" and is described on the contents page as "why she decided to marry England." Ann Barr's "Modern Manners" is an even shorter, more amusing piece on a food conference in which cockroaches figure as a delicacy; this item is referred to in the editorial as one of the "small" themes. Sarah Hogg's article "Inside Government" is serious, even solemn, and is the only weighty contribution from a woman writer here. Frederic Raphael writes the one review. It is clear from a sample of subsequent issues of *Prospect* that the male address of the new periodical is maintained in that the dismal representation of women is continued with only the occasional woman contributing to the serious core of the journal, the section of four essays. Nor do women contributors appear regularly, if at all, in the review slots or among the "regulars." Indeed, it is not surprising that a journal so rooted in the culture of the newspaper press in Britain goes on to replicate its male networks and gendered political culture. This is not to say that each issue I have seen does not have a single serious piece by a woman contributor, but rather that the numbers never rise above three or four, and that there is often a direct correlation between the gender of the contributor and the gender of her subject—the family, the queen, feminism, domestic violence—subjects that lie recognizably in the space allocated in the nineteenth century as women's subjects. In this way Fukuyama's subject of "Trust" is gendered by *Prospect* in its headline and description of Greenberg's piece. Clearly there may be a serious gendered subject in trust, but here it is gendered, trivialized and domesticated at Greenberg's expense *by the editing*; her article, if lighthearted in places, is both serious in its autobiography and in its critique of Fukuyama. Who are the editors of *Prospect* wooing and constructing by such editing if not male readers? Where women contributors cover "news," that is, political stories such as Sarah Hogg's "Government Health-Check" (October) or Annie McElvoy's interview with Wolfgang Schauble (November) no such coy titles or descriptors appear. But the minute "women's subjects" appear we have Hilary Burden's piece on women's magazines entitled "The Sex and Shopping Gland" (November), and two of the rare women contributors to the essays section fare no better on non-news subjects: Rosalind Miles' piece on high-achieving women appears on the cover as "Miserable Women" and on the contents page as "The Miserable Regiment of Women" and is described as an investigation of "why Superwoman is sick and tired of 'having to do it all.' Can she find a solution, or at least someone to blame?" Women readers might be forgiven for recoiling from the cliches while male readers may find that they reinforce their deepest fears. Both will be relieved to see that the article itself is quite a different matter. In the April number, Anne Applebaum's piece on the damaging absence of history in Eastern Europe appears on the cover drenched in sexual innuendo as "Post-Communist Blues." The male culture of journalism is so pervasive in *Prospect* that it is almost certainly invisible to the journalists who produce it. But just as in the nineteenth century it became clear that women made up a large proportion of the market potential, so it should be clear to the editors of *Prospect* that to configure news in such a way that excludes or trivializes women as contributors and readers is counterproductive.

This example of the unconscious replication of gendered categories of journalism does I think make the argument for the study of journalism, both in the academy and outside, to include the history of the press. What is normalized and ideological in *Prospect* is clearly discernible in the history of the nineteenth-century press. But the case of *Prospect* does present a challenge to all of us: What would constitute emblems or codes of female address in a middle-class periodical in the present day? And in what ways can "news" be configured differently so as to free it from the constraints of the narrow definitions of the "political," and from the male networks, values and discourses that *still* dominate the cultural formation of journalism?

NOTES

1. Anon., "When Mourning Breaks," *Guardian* (20 May 1996), 3 (tabloid).
2. Ibid.
3. The point was made orally at a media history seminar in March 1996 at the Institute of Historical Research, London.
4. For a recent discussion of this antipathy see Ian Christie, "Lights, Cameras . . . No Action," *Times Higher Education Supplement* (24 May 1996), 16.
5. Examples include Engel's own *Tickle the Public* (London, 1996) and Jeremy Black's *The English Press in the Eighteenth Century* (London, 1987). An exception is Aled Jones' *Press, Politics and Society* (Cardiff, 1995).
6. Examples are Francis Mulhearn's *The Moment of Scrutiny* (London, 1979), Jon Klancher's *The Making of English Reading Audiences, 1790–1832* (Madison: University of Wisconsin Press, 1987), Kathryn Shevelow's *Women and Print Culture* (London, 1989) and Margaret Beetham's *A Magazine of their Own?* (London, 1996). But English in the past has produced a number of monographs focused on allegedly literary newspapers and periodicals that have otherwise foregrounded evidence in much the same way as historians; these include important monographs such as Katherine Mix's *A Study in Yellow* (Lawrence, Kans., 1960).
7. These include the invaluable *Wellesley Index to Victorian Periodicals*, edited by Walter and Esther Houghton, and latterly Jean Slingerland, Alvin Sullivan's *British Literary Magazines* and John North's *Waterloo Directory*, as well as Rosemary VanArsdel's and J. Don Vann's guides to the Victorian

periodical for MLAA. But Sullivan's attempt to impose the twentieth-century concept of 'literary magazine' on the nineteenth-century press is uneasy and problematic, and the Houghtons excluded poetry and reviews from the listings of contents in the early volumes of the *Wellesley Index*. Sheila and Henry Rosenberg's work for the *New Cambridge Bibliography of English Literature (NCBEL)* on the press comprised a rare example of cooperation of literature with history.

8. See D. Griffiths' *The Encyclopedia of the British Press, 1422–1992* (London, 1992), for example, an analogue in its way to Sullivan's *British Literary Magazines*.

9. See the successive bibliographies, *The Nineteenth-Century Periodical Press in Britain. A Bibliography of Modern Studies*, which cover the years 1901 to 1987; 1901–1971 was edited by Lionel Madden and Diana Dixon (1975, 1976) and 1972–1987 (*VPR*, 1992) by Larry K. Uffelman with assistance from Lionel Madden and Diana Dixon.

10. The *Times* of the early and mid-nineteenth century only published reviews of books when Parliament was not in session.

11. R. Ballaster, M. Beetham, E. Frazer and S. Hebron, *Women's Worlds* (London, 1991).

12. Anthony Delano and John Henningham, *The Survey Report* (London, 1995).

13. Anthony Delano and John Henningham, "Hacks: Read All About 'Em," *Guardian* (16 October 1995), 14–15 (tabloid).

14. Michael Leapman, *Treacherous Estate* (London, 1992), p. 36.

15. Ibid., p. 37.

16. Ibid.

17. Robert Darnton, "Journalism: All the News That Fits We Print," *The Kiss of Lamourette* (London, 1990), pp. 60–93.

18. Leapman, *Treacherous Estate*, p. 37.

19. For W. T. Stead's and others' bids for women readers and journalists see L. Brake, "The Old Journalism and the New," in *Papers for the Millions*, ed. Joel Wiener (Westport, Conn., 1988), pp. 1–24.

20. [W. T. Stead], "Women and the Study of Contemporary History," *Review of Reviews*, I (June 1890): 470–71.

21. Ibid., 471.

22. T. Bostick, "The Press and the Launching of the Women's Suffrage Movement, 1866–1867," *Victorian Periodicals Newsletter*, 13 (Winter 1980): 125–31.

23. Evelyn March Phillipps, "Women's Newspapers," *Fortnightly Review*, 56 (November 1894): 661–70.

24. For "redundant" (i.e., unmarried) women see [W. Greg] "Why Are Women Redundant?", *National Review*, 14 (April 1862): 434–60 and for daughters in revolt see B. Crackanthorpe, "The Revolt of the Daughters," *Nineteenth Century*, 34, 35 (1894): 23–31, 424–29.

25. Joanna Luke and Diane Stratton, *Investigation into the Representation of Women Authors and Reviewers on the Book Pages of Quality and Midmarket Newspapers* (Hertfordshire: West Herts College, 1992).

26. David Goodhart, "Editorial," *Prospect* (October 1995): 1.

8

Toward a Cultural Critique of Victorian Periodicals

Mark W. Turner

Over the past several years in studying the serialization of novels in the 1860s, I have continually been aware of the need to provide a methodological framework for my study of periodical literature. In trying to formulate a theoretical model for reading Victorian magazines, I have been building on work that has been ongoing for several decades in a developing interdisciplinary field. In 1971, Michael Wolff "charted the golden stream" of Victorian periodicals and argued that the usefulness of magazines and newspapers is in the ways nineteenth-century society is reflected,[1] but over the past twenty years, scholarship has gradually refined this early conceptualization of the field. A number of scholars of the newspaper and periodical press have brought to the field theoretical questions about the archive and our methodologies in studying it. The ways we work with the archive no longer necessarily mean that we regard periodical literature as merely reflecting society. For example, studying Victorian periodicals helps bring into focus the ways cultural products circulate and accumulate meanings within a social system, and it is within such studies of material culture and the nineteenth-century media that I locate my own interests in the field. Here, I wish to indicate some of the ways that thinking about and applying critical theory has helped to open up the study of Victorian periodical literature.

While ambitious archival research has enormously enriched and grounded the study of Victorian periodicals—the *Wellesley Index* and

Waterloo projects, most obviously—less critical analysis of the archive has followed than might be expected, and recently a number of scholars have argued for the need to produce theoretically based methodological projects for studying Victorian periodicals. Lyn Pykett maintains that any number of theoretical practices (structural, poststructural, Marxist, feminist, psychoanalytic) provide ways of interpreting the empirical studies already amassed.[2] In a special issue of *Victorian Periodicals Review* in 1989, the guest editors argue that valuable as archival work is (and it is undeniably important), the entire textual base can never be known, and they, too, indicate a number of theoretical possibilities for studying the periodical press.[3] One problem is that bibliographic work can only present a partial representation of the field of study. John Sutherland estimates that there were about 3,500 Victorian novelists, and believes that "some bio-bibliographical profile (dates of birth, death, career details, marital status, total number of novels published) can be readily retrieved for about 1,200 Victorian novelists." But by far, most Victorian novelists have "sunk forever without a trace."[4] Still, what we do recover can only expand our knowledge of periodicals and the ways in which literature is produced, distributed and consumed. Furthermore, biobibliographical research and critical examination of the archive are *not* exclusive or opposed, but rather complementary and interrelated.

I have assumed a number of theoretical positions in studying Victorian serials, largely informed by poststructural theories of textuality. While poststructural critiques are common in many areas of English studies, the field of periodical studies has generally resisted attempts to theorize the press, and only recently has substantial theoretical work on periodicals appeared.[5] Within the interdisciplinary field of study, comprised of scholars from a range of parent disciplines, debates about the use of textual and cultural theories are lively. It is to this debate that I hope my work here will contribute.

PERIODICALS AND PLURALISM

Periodicals, by nature collectives of different voices, require that some notion of plurality be accepted in critical interpretation. A broad concept of intertextuality has been useful to me in understanding how cultural discourses intersect with discourses in serials, either in specific serial parts or more widely in public discourses. Relating the intertextuality to periodical literature problematizes traditional approaches in my parent field of English, not least because the centrality of the book and the author as the foci for research is called into question. It has not been until relatively recently that the early twentieth-century work of Mikhail Bakhtin has been discovered by literary critics. His theories of the ways language(s) operate within and between texts have underpinned my readings of periodicals. In *The Dialogic Imagination*, Bakhtin's notion of social heteroglossia is articulated in his discussion of the dialogic form of the novel. Bakhtin's translators have defined heteroglossia in the following way:

At any given time, in any given place, there will be a set of conditions—social, historical, meterological, physiological—that will insure that a word uttered in that place and at that time will have a meaning different than it would have under any other conditions; all utterances are heteroglot in that they are functions of a matrix of forces practically impossible to recoup, and therefore impossible to resolve.[6]

The principle of heteroglossia insists that every text is in dialogue with any number of other texts, posing a severe challenge to formalist and some structuralist criticism that focuses on the single text in a vacuum. Bakhtin asserts that,

The living utterance, having taken meaning and shape at a particular historical moment in a socially specific environment, cannot fail to brush up against thousands of living dialogic threads, woven by socio-ideological consciousness around the given object of an utterance; it cannot fail to become an active participant in social dialogue. After all, the utterance arises out of this dialogue as a continuation of it and as a rejoinder to it—it does not approach the object from the sidelines.[7]

The single utterance, then, leads inevitably to a whole network of other utterances; the single voice is always already polyglot. Bakhtin finds the ultimate expression of heteroglossia in the novel in which any number of languages or discourses intersect, but he contends that "the dialogic orientation of discourse is a phenomenon that is, of course, a property of *any* discourse."[8] One result of heteroglossia is that the text opens up to any number of possible meanings: "Between the word and its object, between the word and the speaking subject, there exists an elastic environment of other, alien words about the same object, the same theme, and this is an environment that it is often difficult to penetrate."[9] The sense of excitement in the "tension-filled interaction" of texts is what has appealed to literary critics, especially of the novel, in recent years.[10] Bakhtin virtually celebrates cacophony and dissonance, which had been important as tenets of poststructural criticism in literary studies.

In the mid-1960s, Julia Kristeva, following Bakhtin, coined the term "intertextuality" referring to the ways texts or discourses or languages intersect:

each work (text) is an intersection of words (texts) where at least one other word (text) can be read. In Bakhtin's work, these two axes, which he calls *dialogue* and *ambivalence*, are not clearly distinguished. Yet, what appears as a lack of rigour is in fact an insight first introduced into literary theory by Bakhtin: any text is constructed as a mosaic of quotations; any text is the absorption and transformation of another. The notion of *intertextuality* replaces that of intersubjectivity, and poetic language is read as at least *double*.[11]

Kristeva's rearticulation of Bakhtin became important especially for Marxist critics in the 1960s and 1970s because of "the politically subversive nature of celebrating dialogism/intertextuality." "Kristevan intertextuality suggests, in line with marxist sociology, that meaning is not *given* nor produced by a transcendental ego. Indeed the transcendental ego is itself an effect *produced* in a social context."[12] Traditional categories in formalist and stylistic criticism are challenged by the assumption that literature is "a segment of social discourse stratified into numerous contending ideological dimensions: the text is part of the social text, an arena of struggle."[13] Meaning, then, requires interpretation of discourses, not merely the comprehension of inherent textual structures and forms. Intertextuality does not require us exclusively to find sources, to identify allusions, to discover influences on writers. If the purpose of intertextual readings is to provide possible (not final) discursive readings, then the concept of "the intertext is not a real and causative source but a theoretical construct formed by and serving the purposes of a reading."[14]

My assertion that intertextuality operates at the site of periodical literature is further buttressed theoretically by Roland Barthes' *S/Z*, which demonstrates how a multiplicity of readings and meanings intersect within a given text. His conceptualization of the text as plural, layered with multiple meanings, is crucial for the way I understand serials within periodicals. In a section on "interpretation," Barthes asks us to

posit the image of a triumphant plural, unimpoverished by any constraint of representation (of imitation). In this ideal text, the networks are many and interact, without any one of them being able to surpass the rest; this text is a galaxy of signifiers, not a structure of signifieds; it has no beginning; it is reversible; we gain access to it by several entrances, none of which can be authoritatively declared to be the main one; the codes it mobilizes extend *as far as the eye can reach*, they are indeterminable (meaning here is never subject to a principle of determination, unless by throwing dice); the systems of meaning can take over this absolutely plural text, but their number is never closed, based as it is on the infinity of language.[15]

There are a number of positions here that illustrate important principles of poststructural thinking: a refusal to accept the structural

Saussurian linguistic binary (signifier/signified); a refusal to define the "beginning" or origins of a text; an assertion that texts are plural, bursting with competing and perhaps contradictory discourses; a contention that texts are intersected by other texts; a declaration that texts are infinite in their meanings.[16] Such assertions seem ideally suited for a study of Victorian periodicals for several reasons. For example, as indicated above, periodicals are by their very nature multi-textual, or plural. Periodical texts have no single originating author (although there is an editor function), but rather a number of authors whose identities may or may not be known. Furthermore, periodicals are seemingly infinite in time: daily, weekly, monthly, quarterly or annually—the periodical text continually proceeds, containing a pre-history and projecting futurity (this is especially significant in serialization).[17] Finally, periodicals present numerous ways of reading: one can start in the middle, at the end, wherever, and not ever finish the periodical; other literary commodities such as the book, conversely, present generally one way of reading, cover to cover, in which we all participate similarly. In this sense, reading periodicals can be liberating, presenting as they do the freedom for the reader to roam, to wander textually—a pleasure of the periodical text.

Barthes' notion of the text as a methodological field[18] is also fertile in considering periodicals. In his conception, a distinction is made between the *work*, something like a fixed object as in a book, and the *text*, a limitless field of meanings and interpretations:

> The Text is plural. Which is not simply to say that it has several meanings, but that it accomplishes the very plural of meaning: an *irreducible* (and not merely an acceptable) plural. The Text is not a coexistence of meanings but a passage, an overcrossing; thus it answers not to an interpretation, even a liberal one, but to an explosion, a dissemination.[19]

Barthes' theory of plurality challenges us to consider the numerous (indeed, apparently endless) ways in which texts can be read. Periodicals are particularly suited for such a conceptualization because everything about a periodical resists traditional definitions and categories of genre and authorship. Periodicals are unruly and difficult to pin down for critics partly because of the choices we must make in delimiting what constitutes the text, or the unit of study: Is it the single issue, a volume, an entire run? Barthes' notion of plurality is complemented by an understanding generally of Jacques Derrida's deconstructive theory. Barbara Johnson, introducing Derrida's *Dissemination*, explains that "the deconstruction of a text does not proceed by random doubt or generalized scepticism, but by the careful teasing out of warring forces of signification *within the text itself*. If anything is destroyed in a deconstructive reading, it is not meaning but the claim to unequivocal domination of one mode of signifying over another."[20] In reading periodicals, one focus might be to tease out potential significations of different discourses from a pluralist text, but not to present these as the final readings of the texts.

The inherent playfulness of Derrida's writing and his deconstructive practice has led some deconstructive critics to focus on Derrida's "dizzy, exuberant side."[21] And what many critics object to is the lack of discipline in some deconstructive practice; if it is all about textual play, then why bother? Derrida's most recent work, *Spectres of Marx* (1994), is an attempt to merge (perhaps to make peace between?) Marxist thinking and deconstruction, but that mediation constructs a ghostly, nonmaterial version of Marxism. Certainly, a worry for materialist criticism is that both Barthes' and Derrida's seemingly rule-less practices lead one away from cultural specificity. How is social change accommodated and identified in a boundless textuality? How are shifts in material culture registered? Where, in short, is the politics? Raymond Williams worries that in accepting blindly a multiplicity of writing, "the generalizing and connecting impulse is so strong that we lose sight of real specificities and distinctions of practice," and other Marxist critics reiterate Williams' concerns.[22] However, plurality need not necessarily remove the text from cultural, public discourse. The plurality of the text does not exist apart from history, but within it.

Michel Foucault provides a useful intervention in thinking about the relation between plurality and materiality because of the way he discusses discourses around particular institutions such as the hospital and the prison. Foucault historicizes discourses allowing for multiple circulating discourses anchored in history.[23] The link between institutions and discourse provides a common ground between the plural intertext and culture. Vincent Leitch argues that "another name for differance is *instituting*. 'There is nothing outside the text' means there is no escaping institutions."[24] Following Foucault, Leitch contends that "we can theorize 'literature' as a social category of discourse variously defined in different places and different times with varying interests and outcomes."[25] Language is constrained by institutions. In writing about periodicals, it is useful to move freely from textual criticism to material criticism in what might be seen as theoretical eclecticism; however, such turns allow for the cultural location of discourse, which bridges the gap between materialism and poststructural plurality.

MAGAZINES IN THE 1860S: A CASE IN POINT

In studying serial fiction in the mid-nineteenth century, the sorts of institutions that I identify as significant include formations such as the men's club, the home and the circulating library. Let me briefly indicate some examples of what I mean. Something that runs throughout a number of middle-class periodicals in the 1860s is the cultural formation of the men's club, which impinges upon the construction of contents within the periodicals. The club, of course, demarcates gendered boundaries founded upon the exclusion of women from an all-male space. This construction of gendered space, I would argue, is often upheld within the formation of the periodicals largely run by networks of male publishers and editors.[26] What is striking is the similarity of the social configuration in a number of periodicals founded in the mid-nineteenth century, around the time of the great middle-class magazine boom of the 1860s. *Macmillan's*, for example, founded in 1859, originated in the weekly gatherings of literary men at the firm's Covent Garden offices, during which young journalists would rub shoulders with more renowned writers such as Alfred Tennyson and Charles Kingsley. These weekly gatherings became known as the "Tobacco Parliament," a name that fuses male pleasure (smoking) with the ultimate men's club (Parliament).[27] The cosy male network can also be seen in magazines as various as *Punch* (founded in 1842) and the *Fortnightly Review* (founded in 1865).[28]

Other magazines used a similarly male framework in conceiving their magazines. When the shilling monthly *Cornhill* was founded in 1860 with Thackeray, perhaps the most eminent living novelist, as editor, the magazine's early circulation figures became legendary with sales of up to 120,000 copies of the first issue. In an open letter describing the tone of the new magazine, which Thackeray sent out to potential contributors, he writes:

If our friends have good manners, a good education, and write in good English, the company, I am sure, will be all the better pleased; and the guests, whatever their rank, age, sex be, will be glad to be addressed by the well-educated gentlemen and women. . . . There are points on which agreement is impossible, and on these we need not touch. At our social table, we shall suppose the ladies and children always present; we shall not set up rival politicians by the ears; we shall listen to every guest who has an apt word to say; and, I hope, induces clergymen of various denominations to say grace in their turn.[29]

There is a lot to be said about this passage—for example the way in which Thackeray wishes to construct his new magazine as noncontroversial. But I want particularly to point to two things. First, the magazine is intended to be open to a range of middle-class contributors with seemingly catholic tastes. Thackeray wants *Cornhill* to be an open table at which any reader would feel comfortable to dine. However, as it turned out, *Cornhill* was not at all the diverse forum Thackeray imagined. A glance at the *Wellesley Index* indicates the frequency with which *Cornhill* relied on a core of mostly male contributors in its early years. Thackeray's announcement of variety in the open letter to contributors was never realized, at least not in the range of contributors. While the fiction is written by both men and women, nonfiction is almost exclusively dominated by middle-class professional men, such as Fitzjames Stephen. This gendered dimension of the nonfiction was perhaps augmented by the well-known monthly dinners to which *Cornhill* contributors were invited. As with *Macmillan's*, business and leisure overlap and the closeness of the male network can be seen to impinge on the ideological outlook of the magazines.

The second thing I wish to point out in the passage from Thackeray's letter is the way the presence of women and children regulate the contents of the magazine. Thackeray, in effect, rules out the overt discussion of traditionally male subjects such as religion and politics, although both of these discourses creep into the fiction and nonfiction in disguise. *Cornhill*, by its insistence on the presence of women and children, was defining the middle-class *family* magazine, with something for everyone. *Cornhill* was a periodical that could equally be read at the club, in the study and in the family parlor. Thackeray uses the institution of the family to construct the contents, and he exercised his powers of censorship accordingly.[30] Choosing *Cornhill* contributions to suit a female audience, the editors were defining the magazine according to gender, and the exclusion of politics and religion was, in a sense, an emasculation. Although many articles published were specifically aimed at men and written within a male discourse, none approached a serious discussion of theological or political ideas controversial to the reader in the way the heavy quarterly reviews (the *Quarterly*, the *Edinburgh*, the *Westminster*) or even a monthly like *Blackwood's* might. *Cornhill*, the most successful of the new shilling monthlies in the early 1860s, participated in creating a periodical literature—the middle-class family shilling magazine—demarcated by gendered boundaries.

The definition of family reading would lead one also to consider how the institution of the circulating library contributed in the construction of middle-class periodicals. *Cornhill* was destined for the reading room at Mudie's and the other circulating libraries where most readers obtained their fiction. As the head of the largest circulating library, Charles Mudie was the overriding figure of importance in considering the morality of a work of fiction. As Guinivere Griest asserts, "what Mudie thought good became more and more important as his library flourished and expanded."[31] As it happened, Mudie rarely censored fiction, although the threat was always present. More common was self-censorship exercised by the writers themselves,[32] but I think it is reasonable to assume that middle-class magazine editors like Thackeray were mindful of crossing an unstated line with the circulating libraries. Certainly by the mid-1880s, a backlash against what was seen as repression by the libraries had begun, led by the banned novelist George Moore: "The librarian rules the roost; he crows, and every chanticleer pitches his note in the same key. He, not the ladies and gentlemen who place their names on the title-pages, is the author of modern English fiction."[33] Moore goes on to argue that by the 1880s, fiction had become too feminized, and, of course, much of the fiction that Mudie carried and that Moore attacks first appeared as serials in magazines. For a publisher to realize a profit on a new triple-decker novel, it had to sell large numbers to the circulating libraries, and publishers depended on the libraries to buy the three expensive volumes before the cheap editions were published. Prior serialization in magazines served as advance advertising for the fiction; however, serialized novels destined for the libraries had to adhere to Mudie's moral code. Businessmen like Mudie, at least indirectly, influenced the contents of serialized novels in middle-class family periodicals aimed at circulating-library readers.

That the circulating library, the family and the men's club overlap as institutions constructing the contents of periodicals—for example, in the way gender is an important factor in all three—we can perhaps already see. What I would argue is that readings of the periodicals generally need to take into account the discourses around institutions that determine how the text is constructed. Furthermore, the ways in which these constructions of periodical literature intersect with ideological discourses circulating in public would yield one fruitful approach to studying periodicals. Such an approach would merge poststructural concerns with the discourses of institutions with historical and contextual readings of periodical and literary culture broadly. It would theorize the reading of the periodical while anchoring it culturally.

THE LIMITS OF GENRE

In considering the periodical as text, notions of genre in traditional literary studies seem unhelpful. How can periodicals be classified generically? What is most obvious about the form of Victorian magazines is that in terms of genre, they are often hybrid: a mix of serial fiction, short stories, poetry, illustrations, travel articles and other forms of nonfiction. In a discipline (English studies) that has often relied heavily on studying a taxonomy of genre, the periodical has no place, hence the tendency to take contributions from the periodical without attention to the periodical itself—to study a specific contribution as a political article, as a short story, as a travel article, and so forth. Ultimately, one result of this method has been to study the novel as a book but not as a serial. Foucault, in the *Archaeology of Knowledge*,

automatically decenters traditional literary studies (which have privileged novels as books) by opening up the category of literature to interdisciplinary and more encompassing methodological approaches. "The
frontiers of the book," Foucault writes, "are never clear-cut: beyond the
title, the first lines, and the last full stop, beyond its internal configuration and its autonomous form, it is caught up in a system of references to other books, other texts, other sentences: it is a node within a
network. . . . The book is not simply the object that one hold in one's
hands."[34] Foucault has, in a sense, redefined the book by placing it in a
potentially endlessly referential cultural formation. And, interestingly,
his description of the book could also be that of a periodical contribution: A text that exists even physically within a system of other sentences, other texts, other periodicals. One of Foucault's challenges is to
conceptualize literary studies without predetermined notions of genre
that are also linked to physical form.

Raymond Williams argues that theories of genre impose rules that
limit our understanding of how texts operate within a sociocultural context. He asserts that to presume that "there are still things a novel 'can'
or 'cannot' do" amounts to "the reduction of classification to absurdity."[35]
More significant for cultural studies is a recognition of the historical
specificity of forms: For example, how does form in the nineteenth century determine cultural valuing? Categories of genre lose significance in
poststructural thinking because often generic forms overlap and coexist (most obviously in the periodical text); if one accepts a notion of the
plural intertext, rigid generic boundaries break down.

The interrogation of genre is also related to questions of authority in
texts.[36] The authority of the author has often been used to determine
possible readings of texts. In debates about the role of the author, from
the New Critics to Barthes and Foucault in the late 1960s, notions of the
author as an individual intervening and controlling the text have been
profoundly reconsidered. In magazines, of course, there is no single author, so to look to an author as the producer of meaning is often not an
option. Mid–nineteenth-century periodical authorship is collective, and
its contributors are often anonymous. At midcentury, the vast majority
of periodicals were not signed (the *Fortnightly Review* in 1865 went
some way to challenging this convention) so anonymous writing—the
absence of the author—is at the center of mid-Victorian periodical texts.
Constructing the presence of the "author" is an act of remapping and
needs to be refigured.

What needs far more consideration is how the author function is perhaps replaced by an editor function in periodical literature, and this we
can see in *Saint Paul Magazine* (1867–1874), initially edited by Anthony Trollope who largely controlled the political bias of the magazine
and who published two serials, several articles and short fiction in the

magazine during his tenure. From October 1869 to May 1870, Trollope published a series of short stories entitled "An Editor's Tales," stories recounting the difficulties encountered by a gentle and benign magazine editor in dealing with mostly untalented contributors. The series was published anonymously in *Saint Pauls*, and then as a signed one-volume book in May 1870. Trollope was clearly playing with a slippage of identity—he was a well-known editor-novelist, publishing his own stories anonymously in his own magazine.

When the stories were published in book form, there was no indication that they were initially published in a magazine, let alone Trollope's own magazine. What we have are two cultural products, two literary commodities, that use differently and playfully the positioning of the originator-creator, the author. In *Saint Pauls*, it is Trollope's status as editor—a plural, even fragmented identity—that readers might connect to the stories; in the book, it is Trollope's role as author that was intended to sell the volume. In "An Editor's Tales" (the series) and *An Editor's Tales* (the volume), we see a negotiation of authority—that of the editor and that of the author—to attach different values to each cultural product, but there is room for ambiguity in identifying the author-editor. Certainly, some reviewers (for example, the *Illustrated London News*) linked the series directly to Trollope the editor, and subsequent critics and biographers have unproblematically read Trollope's own life into the stories. But Trollope tries to distance himself from the fictional editor through his particular title, "an" editor, not "the" editor, and he seems to be playing with the possible uncertainty of who the ultimate authority figure behind the stories really is: Trollope the fiction writer or Trollope the magazine editor. The point surely is that these two identities blur, merge and complicate our responses to the stories, so that there is no final, original source of authority for the tales.

But there are other ways in which authority for texts can be discussed. Pierre Bourdieu, for example, starts from the premise that even individual authors do not inherently maintain authority over their own texts. "Who creates the 'creator'?" Bourdieu asks. The shift in emphasis becomes determining "what authorizes the author, what creates the authority with which authors authorize."[37] This is a question that also arises in considering a novelist such as Trollope, who attempted to forge a second literary identity by publishing two serials anonymously in *Blackwood's Magazine* in the mid-1860s. In November 1865, just four months after Trollope had argued for signed journalism in the pages of the *Fortnightly Review*, he began writing *Nina Balatka*, which he hoped to publish anonymously. It was an interesting experiment, since the popular novelist was attempting to test his own salability as a brand name. Were his novels continually selling well on their own merit, or simply because they were written by the circulating library giant "Anthony Trollope"? The question of authorship here becomes one of image in an increasingly competitive and mass culture with a greatly expanding periodical press as a primary medium for popular literature. Neither *Nina Balatka* nor the second anonymous serial, *Linda Tressel*, sold well, but the publisher (Blackwood, who was not his usual publisher) was willing to humor Trollope in his experiment, perhaps hoping that he might bring a genuine, signed Trollope novel to the firm in the future.

Bourdieu has addressed the relationship between literary and artistic figures and publishers and galleries that helps us to theorize the periodicals market in the mid-nineteenth century. For Bourdieu, the accumulation of "symbolic capital" is one of the functions of cultural vendors: " 'Symbolic capital' is to be understood as economic or political capital that is disavowed, misrecognized and thereby recognized, hence legitimate, a 'credit' which, under certain conditions, and always in the long run, guarantees 'economic' profits."[38] A publisher might endorse an author as "symbolic capital" rather than as "economic capital" because the author brings status to the publisher "when the only usable, effective capital is the (mis)recognized, legitimate capital called 'prestige' or 'authority', the economic capital that cultural undertakings generally require cannot secure the specific profits by the field—not the 'economic' profits they always imply—unless it is reconverted into symbolic capital."[39] In short, the authority of the author is not the only source of value for a literary text, for without the cultural apparatus linked to the author—such as publisher and distributor—the author's name is largely valueless.

At the time Trollope's two anonymous serials were published in *Blackwood's Magazine*, he was a consecrated popular author in the serials market. Although the publisher Blackwood seemed aware that the experiment would probably not pay off (we see this in some of Blackwood's letters), he was perhaps hopeful that the "author of Nina Balatka" might just catch on. Although the book did not sell well, the authorship was talked about to some extent. The publisher's primary interest may have been in his ability to consecrate a second literary identity for Trollope, based on the buzz around the author's identity. In Bourdieu's terms, it is in this struggle to consecrate authors that value is actually found, not in individual persons, single institutions, publications or personalities: this is what constitutes the "field of cultural production" and it is within this field that the terms of value and authority are negotiated.

In reading Victorian periodicals, I believe it is helpful to merge a number of strands of recent poststructuralist and Marxist criticism in order to understand how studying literature within a cultural framework of institutions and material conditions opens up new readings of serial fiction especially. I assume that each periodical presents a distinct cultural formation, with its own particularities, within a general field of literature and culture. Linking discourses within the periodical texts to other cultural texts assumes that intertextuality operates within the textual field of methodology. Finally, I think it important to accept that readings of periodical texts are available but not definitive. Generally, I am most anxious to question why it is that periodical literature has been largely ignored in English studies and how it is that we might study periodicals in creative and productive ways. Underlining my work is a call to examine why particular forms of Victorian literature (especially popular forms) remain a neglected fields of research.

NOTES

1. Michael Wolff, "Charting the Golden Stream: Thoughts on a Directory of Victorian Periodicals," *Victorian Periodicals Newsletter* no. 13 (1971): 23–38.

2. Lyn Pykett, "Reading the Periodical Press: Text and Context," in *Investigating Victorian Journalism*, ed. Laurel Brake, Aled Jones and Lionel Madden (London: Macmillan, 1990), 3–18.

3. Laurel Brake and Anne Humpherys, "Critical Theory and Periodical Research," *Victorian Periodicals Review* 12:3 (Fall 1989): 94–95.

4. John Sutherland, *Victorian Fiction: Writers, Publishers, Readers* (London: Macmillan, 1995), 152, 153.

5. See A. J. Parry, "The Intellectuals and the Middle Class Periodical Press: Theory, Method and Case Study," *Journal of Newspaper and Periodical History* 4:3 (Autumn 1988): 18–32; Ros Ballaster, Margaret Beetham, Elizabeth Frazer and Sandra Hebron, *Women's Worlds: Ideology, Femininity and the Woman's Magazine* (London: Macmillan, 1991); Aled Gruffyd Jones, *Press, Politics and Society: A History of Journalism in Wales* (Cardiff, UK: University of Wales Press, 1993); the special issue of *Victorian Periodicals Review*, ed. Brake and Humpherys; and Laurel Brake, *Subjugated Knowledges: Journalism, Gender and Literature in the Nineteenth Century* (London: Macmillan, 1994).

6. M. M. Bakhtin, *The Dialogic Imagination*, ed. Michael Holquist, trans. Caryl Emerson and Michael Holquist (Austin: University of Texas Press, 1981), 428. There is a glossary of Bakhtin's terms at the back of the book.

7. Ibid., 277.

8. Ibid., 279.

9. Ibid., 276.

10. Ibid., 279. Bakhtin champions the novel as dialogic, but argues that poetry is monologic and restrictive, an assertion with which I do not agree.

11. Julia Kristeva, "Word, Dialogue and Novel," (1966) in *The Kristeva Reader*, ed. Toril Moi (London: Basil Blackwell, 1986), 37.

12. Michael Worton and Judith Still, eds., *Intertextuality: Theories and Practices* (Manchester: Manchester University Press, 1990), "Introduction," 17.

13. Vincent B. Leitch, *Cultural Criticism, Literary Theory, Poststructuralism* (New York: Columbia University Press, 1992), 56.

14. John Frow, "Intertextuality and Ontology," in *Intertextuality: Theories and Practices*, ed. Worton and Still, 46.

15. Roland Barthes, *S/Z: An Essay*, trans. Richard Miller (1974; reprinted New York: Hill and Wang, Noonday Press, 1993), 6.

16. See Leitch, *Cultural Criticism*, xiii. For an introduction to poststructural thinking, see also Robert Young, ed., *Untying the Text: A Post-Structuralist Reader* (Boston: Routledge & Kegan Paul, 1981).

17. See Linda Hughes and Michael Lund, *The Victorian Serial* (Charlottesville: University Press of Virginia, 1991).

18. See Roland Barthes, "From Work To Text," in *Image Music Text*, trans. Stephen Heath (London: Fontana Press, 1977), especially 156–57.

19. Ibid., 159.

20. Barbara Johnson, "Translator's Introduction" to Jacques Derrida, *Dissemination* (1972; reprinted London: Athlone Press, 1981), xiv.

21. Christopher Norris, *Deconstruction: Theory and Practice* (rev. ed., London and New York: Routledge, 1991), 91. Norris is especially thinking of applications of Derrida by the Yale critics (excepting de Man).

22. Raymond Williams, *Marxism and Literature* (1977; reprinted Oxford: Oxford University Press, 1992), 145. Norris writes that Terry Eagleton has "recognized more clearly that an open-ended free play of rhetorical transcoding—with the ideal of an infinitely 'plural' text—is resistant to the purposes of Marxist criticism," *Deconstruction*, 79.

23. Edward Said follows this methodology broadly in *Orientalism* (1978; reprinted London: Penguin Books, 1991).

24. Leitch, *Cultural Criticism*, 144.

25. Ibid., 57.

26. Certainly, the presence of women in periodicals in the 1860s was prominent and there were, increasingly, many women editing magazines (such as Mary Braddon and Mrs. Henry Wood). However, I would maintain that the capital behind the industry was still largely men's, not women's.

27. Charles Morgan, *The House of Macmillan (1843–1943)* (London: Macmillan, 1943), 50.

28. For a discussion of the male configuration of the *Fortnightly*, see Mark W. Turner, "Hybrid Journalism: Women in the Liberal *Fortnightly*," in Kate Campbell, ed., *Reading Journalism* (Keele: Keele University Press, forthcoming).

29. Gordon N. Ray, ed., *The Letters and Private Papers of William Makepeace Thackeray* (London: Oxford University Press, 1946), 161.

30. Elizabeth Barrett Browning, Anthony Trollope and John Ruskin, for example, all fell afoul of Thackeray's code of morality.

31. Guinivere Griest, *Mudie's Circulating Library and the Victorian Novel* (Bloomington: University of Indiana Press, 1970), 35. See also Nicholas Hiley on Mudie's and censorship: " 'Can't You Find Me Something Nasty?': Libraries and Literary Censorship in Britain from the 1890s to the 1910s," in *Censorship and the Control of Print in England and France 1600–1910*, ed. Robin Myers and Michael Harris (Winchester, UK: St. Paul's Bibliographies, 1992), 123–47.

32. See Donald Thomas, *A Long Time Burning: The History of Literary Censorship in England* (London: Routledge & Kegan Paul, 1969), 239.

33. George Moore, *Literature at Nurse, or Circulating Morals* (London: Vizetelly and Co., 1885), 20. This pamphlet is a slightly revised form of an article that appeared in the *Pall Mall Gazette*.

34. Michel Foucault, *The Archaeology of Knowledge*, trans. A. M. Sheridan Smith (1972; reprint, London: Routledge, 1991), 23.

35. Williams, *Marxism and Literature*, 181.

36. See Leitch, *Cultural Criticism*, 73: "What poststructuralism does, then, is to question the assured status and authority ascribed to discursive genres, not their existence nor their necessity."

37. Pierre Bourdieu, *The Field of Cultural Production* (Cambridge: Polity Press, 1993), 76, 77.

38. Ibid., 75.

39. Ibid.

9

Tokens of Antiquity: The Newspaper Press and the Shaping of National Identity in Wales, 1870–1900[1]

Tom O'Malley, Stuart Allan and Andrew Thompson

The most to be said of this town [*Brecon*], is what indeed I have said of many places in Wales, (viz.) that it is very ancient, and indeed to mention it here for all the rest, there are more tokens of antiquity to be seen everywhere in Wales than in any particular part of England. . . . The stories of Vortigern and Roger of Mortimer, are in every old woman's mouth here.[2]

When Daniel Defoe published the second volume of his *Tour* in 1725, he described Wales as a country with a past that stretched beyond the Roman occupation.[3] Wales then, like today, was an "imagined community" with its collective traditions informed by popular memory and embedded in symbols, rituals and customs.[4] During the eighteenth and early nineteenth centuries, Welsh intellectuals continuously reinvented this past in order to produce a portrait of Welsh history characterized by continuity, distinctiveness and romance.[5] By the end of the nineteenth century, however, this emphasis on the idyllic antiquity of Wales had been directly challenged by a new generation of Nonconformist, Liberal intellectuals and politicians. As D. Gareth Evans writes: "In the 1850s and 1860s there occurred a massive cultural and political shift to a 'Nonconformist Nation', and the Welsh were encouraged to forget their past with its passion for poetry, legend and history. The new emphases were on practical knowledge, industriousness, progress, the language of success, and the Victorian ethos of self-improvement."[6] It is this idea of a shift in the prevailing definitions of Welshness that we intend to explore through a critical discussion of the newspaper press.

Historical accounts of Wales in this period tend to focus on how a combination of industrialization, the growth of nonconformity and electoral reform fused to produce a political current that engendered a new sense of Welsh national identity. This emergent form of identity is said to have found its expression in both the ascendancy of the Liberal Party in Welsh politics after 1868 and, furthermore, in attempts to refashion the contours of a national mythology. Significantly, many of these same accounts recurrently accord to the press in Wales a pivotal role in the public articulation of what is, and what is not, the essence of Welshness.

This chapter's exploratory examination of the links between these wider processes and the press in Wales suggests that several of the conceptual presuppositions underpinning these accounts need to be reconsidered. We will argue that the press, in a society in which a variety of different nationalist projects sought to define what it meant to be Welsh, tended to prioritize local definitions of Welshness. Accordingly, its news and editorial coverage displayed diversity rather than uniformity in the ways that it represented "the Welsh nation," both with regard to its position within the formalized dictates of political culture, as well as in its informal negotiation via the politics of everyday life. This chapter thus aims to intervene in current historical debates by outlining the basis for an alternative account of the role of the press in the public rearticulation of elite and popular conceptions of Welshness in the final decades of that century.

Our discussion will assume the following form. After detailing several aspects of recent Welsh historiography, we offer a brief overview of the economic, social and political context of the press in this period. We argue that the widely held view that Welsh political culture at that time was dominated by a Liberal, Nonconformist conception of the nation requires substantive qualification. We then proceed to show how a consideration of the dynamics of national identity calls into question the thesis that there was a unitary, authentically traditional definition of Welshness in circulation across the public sphere. We then provide an illustration of how these dynamics operate by examining a range of editorial leaders published in the *Western Mail* and the *South Wales Daily News*, two major mass circulation daily newspapers published in South Wales.

WALES, THE NATION AND THE PRESS

There are several prominent strands in Welsh historiography that interpret nineteenth-century history through a nationalist prism. Studies undertaken by Kenneth Morgan, John Davies and D. Gareth

Evans, respectively, provide commentaries that, with different degrees of emphasis, stress how the social and economic changes in nineteenth-century Wales contributed to the growth of nationalism and national identity in the last decades of the century.[7] John Davies has commented how:

With the striking exception of the Calvinistic Methodist denomination, there were virtually no specifically Welsh organizations in 1850, and few people would have defended the notion that Wales was an entity comparable with England, Ireland or Scotland. By 1914 Wales had a national university, library and museum; in a number of sports—rugby, in particular—it had a national team; there was some degree of administrative devolution and a tentative tradition of specifically Welsh legislation had been established. Although it was still considered that the United Kingdom represented the union of three kingdoms, it was increasingly acknowledged that it contained four nations.

Davies has also observed that "national consciousness became more intense as the railways undermined the age-old isolation of the communities of Wales."[8] Kenneth Morgan has similarly stressed the importance of situating Welsh national identity within the context of national UK politics. He has, for instance, interpreted the careers of two of the most prominent Welsh Liberal MPs of these years, Tom Ellis and Lloyd George as politicians who "redefined the national identity with permanent results."[9]

Gwyn Williams has sought to emphasize how, in his view, "Wales has always been a patchwork of cultures."[10] Moreover, he contends: "What has come to be thought of as 'traditional', Nonconformist, Welsh-speaking, radical Wales in particular, that Wales which created so many of the characteristic Welsh institutions, notably the educational, was in some sense a by-product of . . . industrialisation, in other senses a reaction against it."[11] Accordingly, given that there is a question mark over the view that places nationalism and national identity at the center of political developments in late nineteenth-century Wales, it follows that there must be another question mark over the relationship between the newspaper press and these processes.

The importance of the press in accounts of Welsh social and political development has often been acknowledged by commentators.[12] Although there is a growing literature concerned with the history of the press in Wales, frequently there is a tendency in synoptic accounts of Welsh history to view the press as a source of evidence for material on political history. Kenneth Morgan has noted how the newspaper press in Wales "is a vital aid in understanding the structure and essence of the Liberal movement." In particular, the *South Wales Daily News* is, in his view, "an invaluable source for historians, a unique commentary on the bourgeois elite, Conservative as well as Liberal, who dominated the civic life of Cardiff at its greatest period of expansion."[13]

Recurrently it is the case that when the press in nineteenth-century Wales is made the subject of discussion, attention focuses on its contribution to social and political life. D. Gareth Evans, for example, contends that the formation of public opinion on the question of public health is directly linked to "the diffusion of the printed word, by magazines, denominational journals and by the voluminous literary output of the "eisteddfodau." He maintains that: "The appearance of national newspapers such as *The Times* and the *Daily Mail*, as well as the local provincials, the *Swansea and Glamorgan Herald*, *The Cambrian* and *The Merthyr Guardian*, stretched the mental capacities and broadened the experiences of the working communities." More specifically, he claims that Nonconformist journalists in the middle of the century, along with preachers and Radical politicians, were instrumental in transforming "the history of Wales . . . into Nonconformist and radical propaganda" and later played a key role in promoting the growth and diffusion of the eisteddfodau.[14]

Of particular interest here, however, is the role of the press in the formation of national identity. In the 1960s, R. D. Rees argued that the press in South Wales, in the first half of the century, "served to render articulate that emerging sense of national self-awareness that came to dominate the cultural and later political life of Wales."[15] John Davies has argued that it was through the Welsh-language periodical press "that the Welsh people received their political education."[16] Kenneth Morgan has linked the growth of a "sense of national identity" in Wales after 1850 with "the explosive growth of a powerful vernacular political press." He has also argued that the *Cymru Fydd* (Young Wales) nationalist movement of the 1880s and 1890s "found widespread support in the popular press."[17]

In the most sustained investigation of the Welsh press to date, Aled Jones has sought to render problematic the ostensible links between the press and the public projection of nationalist discourse. He observes that in nineteenth-century Wales:

In addition to being self-consciously partisan agents on the cutting edge of social conflicts, in a less formal way journalists were also actors in a more consensual process of change in Welsh popular culture. The popularization by the press of literary forms, from poetry to the novel, its extending news coverage, its reviews, women's sections and sports pages, engendered an inclusive sense of community that carried with it a sense of nationality.

He sees journalists "of all kinds actively participating in a general political process" in a society where "assumptions regarding the social power of journalism went largely unquestioned" and where "the anxieties and manoeuvring of rival religious and political forces indicate that the effects of the press on leadership groups was considerable." He also considers that in spite of divisions in Welsh society, "a more inclusive sense of community was engendered through the dissemination of popular literature and a growing consciousness of Wales as a nation."[18]

Clearly, then, there is a diverse range of accounts that attribute to the press a central role in the promotion of Welsh nationalism and, at the same time, a pervasive sense of national identity. Nevertheless, and rather surprisingly, very little attention has been directed to the task of elucidating how this complex ideological work of determination might have been accomplished by the press. It is with this concern in mind that we will examine a selection of texts from the *Western Mail* and *South Wales Daily News* that address the issue of national identity. We shall argue that neither of these dailies were capable of projecting a unified picture of national identity to their readers. Conflict, rather than consensus, was the order of the day on this issue. Far from standing "outside" of the events that they reported on, these dailies need to be seen as being involved in the overall shaping of the public sphere, in general, and the ideological representation of nationalist discourse, in particular. It is this perspective that we develop in this chapter. Here we wish to stress that the effectivity of these representations should not be reduced to a matter of direct, unmediated influence on newspaper readers; rather, the press was only one of many diverse institutions seeking to articulate a preferred definition of Welsh national identity in opposition to the alternative definitions in circulation at that time.

A TIME OF CHANGE AND CONFLICT

The history of Wales in the nineteenth century is usually told as a story of rapid, dynamic and disruptive change. After 1800, the economic structure of Welsh society was increasingly shaped by the effects of industrialization based, initially, on iron and tin, and later on coal and steel production. The population of Wales and Monmouthshire grew from about 700,000 in 1811 to about 2 million in 1901. Accompanying this expansion was a shift in population movement from the Welsh countryside to the new urban centers like Cardiff, Merthyr Tydfil and Swansea. Cardiff, the largest city in Wales, saw its population rise from 1,800 in 1801 to 33,000 in 1861, and by 1901 it had reached 164,000.[19] This brought with it problems of poverty, bad housing and unsanitary conditions for the bulk of the working population.[20]

In linguistic terms, Wales was divided between the literate and the illiterate, on the one hand, and by the Welsh speakers and the English speakers, on the other. In spite of a good deal of voluntary activity in the establishment of schools, it was estimated that by midcentury 45 percent of men and 70 percent of women were unable to write their own names.[21] In 1891, 54.4 percent of the population spoke Welsh, while approximately 30 percent spoke only Welsh.[22] These social divisions were further compounded by the often difficult geographical features of the country. Distributing a national press under these circumstances, never mind constructing a unified national audience, proved all but impossible in Wales in the nineteenth century.

To the extent that there were unifying factors, foremost among them were the railways and religious opposition to the Anglican Church in Wales. Turning first to the railways, a large part of the Welsh rail system was in place between 1858 and 1868. This made communications within Wales and between Wales and England much easier. It allowed Welsh newspapers to reach wider audiences, a potentially unifying factor, yet it also accelerated the speed with which newspapers produced in England could circulate in Wales.[23] Second, as Wales was transformed demographically, industrially and spatially, so it came under the influence of Nonconformity. The 1851 census showed that the Nonconformists (Baptists, Independents, Quakers, Unitarians) had become the dominant religious group in Wales, with the Anglican Church in Wales well behind.[24] The strength of these sects rested on the ways in which chapels, led by Welsh people, serviced the local cultural, political, social and spiritual needs of their communities. According to Matthew Cragoe:

By 1868, all nonconformist and dissenting denominations in Wales shared one view of politics . . . Nineteenth-century Wales was a "nation of nonconformists". . . . Nonconformity also formed the basis of the distinctively "Welsh" political identity which emerged in the years after 1868, finding expression first in support of Gladstonian Liberalism, and later in the nationalist programme of *Cymru Fydd* ("Young Wales").[25]

Overlaying these developments was the campaign for the extension of the franchise. The Reform Acts of 1832, 1867, and 1884 expanded the number of Welsh parliamentary seats and, gradually, enfranchised increasing numbers of males as the century wore on. The political response after the 1850s to this combination of social deprivation, cultural diversity and an expanding electorate was not to be located in the emergence of a strong, independent, separatist nationalist grouping (as occurred in Ireland). Instead, these factors culminated in the growth of the Welsh arm of the English Liberal Party. The 1868 election returned twenty-three Liberals and ten Tories; by 1885 the Liberals dominated Welsh representation with thirty seats, fourteen of which were held by Nonconformists.[26]

The idea that late nineteenth-century Wales was a nation of Non-conformist Liberals, and as such was increasingly allied to a rapidly cohering sense of national identity, is in need of careful qualification. Nonconformity was not a homogeonous religious movement; rather, it was made up of different religious sects. Although these sects united around several key national issues during this period, it is, arguably, the case that they were equally concerned with their own local issues and spiritual separateness, as the sheer number and diversity of their journals indicates. In addition, Nonconformists and members of the Anglican Church in Wales never constituted a majority of the Welsh population. In 1903, out of a population of 2,012,917 people, only 744,760 were classified as church attendees. Over 50 percent of the population, it would seem, did not attend church.[27]

Furthermore, a range of factors point to the social, geographical and political divisions within Nonconformity. In general, Nonconformist congregations were dominated by the social influence of farmers, rather than by agricultural laborers. Moreover, it would appear that the political influence of Nonconformist preachers was not as great in the southern, urban industrial belt as it was in the rural areas. During the 1868 general election, evidence emerged of a concerted attempt by preachers to intimidate Nonconformist communities into voting Tory and not Liberal. The fact that this "moral coercion" existed testifies to the absence of political homogeneity among Nonconformist congregations in this election year.[28] A number of prominent Methodist clergymen in the early nineteenth century, such as John Elias and Christmas Evans, were opposed to the involvement of the Nonconformist clergy in the political arena.[29] Given these divisions, it is hardly surprising that Nonconformity failed to project a coherent sense of national identity.

Despite the existence of an aggressive and effective Nonconformist political machine, by the closing decades of the nineteenth century the idealized conception of a unified, classless, Nonconformist "Welsh nation" was being openly rejected by sections of the working population in favor of a more locally grounded conception of Welshness. Merfyn Jones, for example, points out that in late nineteenth-century Gwynedd the lack of popular support for a Welsh nationalist movement in the communities, which grew up around the slate quarries, can be partly explained in that conflicts tended to remain at the local level.[30] Moreover, in the industrial centers of South Wales, the experiences of living and working in the conditions thrown up by rapid industrialization resulted, as Gwyn Williams argues, in "a growing radicalisation of working people which was increasingly finding the politics of what was presented as Welshness irrelevant."[31]

Glanmor Williams has commented on the absence of any sustained demand for an "autonomous Welsh nation-state" in the mid-nineteenth century, explaining that while "the Welsh" were not "ignorant of the kind of nationalist aspirations that existed in Europe and Ireland . . . they applauded their radicalism not their nationalism. The radicalism they regarded as being relevant to their own aspirations, the nationalism they did not."[32] Conflicts over what was Wales certainly found sharp political expression in one of the most important political vehicles for nationalist aspirations, the Welsh Liberal Party. The divisions between the North Wales and South Wales Liberal Federations over the issue of home rule, specifically the refusal of the latter to merge, as the former had, with the *Cymru Fydd* League, illustrated that fundamental changes had taken place in Wales. *Cymru Fydd* was not a separatist nationalist movement; rather, it sought to generate for Wales a greater degree of independence *within* an imperial framework. However, at the famous 1896 public clash in Newport between Lloyd George and delegates from the South Wales Liberal Federation, it was evident that the concept of "Wales" that the North Wales Federation was articulating was unacceptable to their fellow Liberals in South Wales. Gwyn Williams quotes one delegate attending that meeting as stating that Cardiff "would never submit 'to the domination of Welsh ideas.' "[33]

Overall, then, it is apparent even from this brief sketch that the growth of a Nonconformist, Liberal-led nationalism cannot be regarded as a defining feature of Welsh history in this period. As we have seen, the social developments associated with the absence of either a strong extraparliamentary or parliamentary nationalist current after 1868, the fact that over 50 percent of the population by 1903 did not attend Church, the divisions within the political outlook of Nonconformists and the need to account for the role of the emerging working classes in these processes, make this assertion difficult to sustain.[34] The last quarter of the nineteenth century has often been conceived of as representing, in the words of one historian, a "national renaissance,"[35] and in the words of another, a "cultural awakening."[36] Nevertheless, and in contrast with Kenneth Morgan's assertion that "by the 1880's . . . the concepts of Wales and Welshness were beginning to assume a more coherent form,"[37] we would maintain that there were so many competing claims to represent "Wales" and "Welshness" in late nineteenth-century Wales that any sense of coherence is impossible to discern.

In cultural terms, these concepts of Wales and Welshness have been linked to the reshaping of popular myths about Welsh history. As noted above, D. G. Evans argues that by the middle of the nineteenth century the Welsh were being actively encouraged to forget their past. According to Prys Morgan, this involved dispelling the "spirits and phantoms of remote centuries of Welsh history which had so entertained and inspired the previous generations" and welcoming, in turn, the arrival of "fresh myth-makers and creators of traditions, those of radical and

non-conformist Wales."[38] Given that, following Morgan, the "old way of
life [had] decayed and disappeared, [and] the past was very often tat-
tered and threadbare," it is perhaps not surprising that new forms of
mythology were required. A national mythology is characterized, in
part, by cultural constructions of the past, that is, by selective reap-
propriations of "national history" fashioned in such a way as to create
a shared sense of community and belonging. Still, in our view, the public negotiation of this larger collective identity will be, by definition,
fraught with uncertainty and ambiguity; it is a contradictory process
that is itself embedded in relations of power and resistance. As we intend to show, both the *Western Mail* and the *South Wales Daily News*
were sites of ideological contestation over what should constitute a
Welsh national identity. More specifically, a close reading of these
newspapers reveals that there was a vigorous conflict over discourses
of "memory" taking place, and that each of these discourses sought to
define the reality of Welshness in the present by mobilizing their preferred narratives of the past to advantage.

Accordingly, in attempting to elucidate the role of the newspaper
press in the discursive struggle over national identity in the late nineteenth century, it is the politicization of popular memories of "the past"
in the name of "history" or "tradition" that clearly needs to be centered
in our investigation. Our discussion thus turns in the next section to
address the institutional specificity of the press in this process. We
seek to highlight a series of dynamics that acted to shape the rearticulation of national identities across the public field. We shall argue that
the specific role of the press tends to be oversimplified in debates about
the rise of Welsh nationalism.

THE WELSH PRESS: LOCALISM AND DIVERSITY

Aled Jones' highly informative account of the Welsh newspaper press
in the nineteenth century presents a range of important insights of direct relevance to our discussion here. Specifically, the press was culturally diverse, linguistically divided and, in general, locally based and
distributed. Even the emergence of a mass circulation daily press in
Cardiff after 1869 does little to modify this situation. The complex
forces at work in Wales after 1800 provided the framework for the
growth of the press. Jones has pointed out that: "Rapid population
growth, urbanization, the repeal of the 'Taxes on Knowledge' the introduction of improved printing technology and commercialisation of production all provided key contexts for the development of the press in
Wales, but the single most important contribution to the growth of the
mass newspaper markets was made by the railways."[39] By the end of
the century, reading newspapers had "become a deeply engrained social

habit that cut across class, language and regional differences."[40] But although reading newspapers may have become increasingly popular as the century progressed, the geographical circulation of the various titles was restricted, for the most part, to the local level.

The earliest newspapers in South Wales during the first half of the century were intensely local in their focus. They were small-scale and "earned their owners a modest profit at best."[41] Throughout the century, this localism dominated the Welsh press. According to Aled Jones, all the newspapers "were local in the sense that they were associated with specific places or communities of belief."[42] This makes it hard to speak convincingly about a uniform national press promoting national sentiment during the nineteenth century. In addition, this national press was, from the start, locked in battle with the English press. In South Wales, before the 1860s, "English prints predominated, and had the better chance of survival. . . . There was no daily newspaper until 1861, when the *Cambrian Daily Leader* began." This strong English presence in the Welsh market continued throughout the century and accelerated into the next. As late as 1892, David Davies noted the heavy dependence of the Welsh press on English journalists: "In Wales the leading papers are still compelled to recruit their literary staffs chiefly across the border, and . . . until a few years ago, a Welshman was a rarity on the Welsh daily press."[43]

Not only was the Welsh newspaper press localized and subject to competition from English newspapers, the range of titles was limited, as was the circulation. There were approximately forty publications in South Wales between 1804 and 1855. No newspaper printed in Welsh lasted very long and the "weekly sales of most of them . . . were counted in hundreds, and their net revenues from sales were proportionately small." In 1831, there were three stamped newspapers in South Wales, in 1835 there were five, in 1844 there were nine, in 1850 there were eleven and in 1854 there were twelve.[44] The period of the most dramatic enhancement in the overall number of titles occurred in the 1870s and continued up until World War I. There were 37 titles in 1861, 69 in 1876, 101 in 1891 and 136 by 1911. These figures, however, included local editions of chain newspapers, so the number of discrete newspaper enterprises was smaller than these figures would initially appear to suggest. The most rapid growth in titles occurred in the heavily industrialized county of Glamorgan, partially as a result of the dramatic growth in the size of that county's population.[45]

Until the advent of the railways, the geographical spread of each newspaper was restricted by poor roads, with distribution often conducted through local agents and by postal subscription. This improved after the 1870s. One estimate puts readership per copy at a factor of seven to eight in the countryside and upward of thirty in the towns. In the 1850s, the circulation of some of the Cardiff and Swansea titles was between 1,000 and 1,500 copies. There have been unverified estimates that by 1886 there were around 120,000 copies of Welsh-language newspapers printed a week. Nevertheless, before the advent of the railways and the mass circulation daily press of the later decades, the readership of these early titles was relatively small. Throughout the century, then, the circulation of most journals remained predominantly local.[46]

This marked localism corresponds in interesting ways with the political diversity of the press. *The Cambrian*, Wales's first weekly newspaper, founded in 1804, reflected the Whiggish views of a group of Swansea entrepreneurs, while the *North Wales Chronicle* (1807) and the *Carmarthan Journal* (1810) were advocates of Tory positions.[47] Cobbett's *Political Register* had circulated in Merthyr, and the Chartists had established two newspapers in Wales, *The Merthyr Free Press* (1840) and *Udgorn Cymru* (1840–1842). Their own UK title, the *Northern Star*, circulated in South Wales toward the end of the 1840s. The other major type of newspaper was produced by the denominational press, although these newspapers echoed the sectarian divisions and different outlooks of the various groups that together made up Nonconformity in Wales. These journals united to condemn commonly perceived injustices, such as the 1834 Poor Law Amendment Act and, later, in the 1880s, landlordism and the Anglican Church in Wales.[48] In addition, this diversity in the political outlook of the various titles was articulated through different linguistic media, as by midcentury there was a well-established Welsh-language press.[49] The press in Wales was thus diverse in geographical, linguistic, political and religious terms.[50]

Nonetheless, in spite of this diversity, historical accounts have tended to portray the press as being responsible for the articulation of a uniformly "national" agenda. This attribution of a functionalist role to the press may be partly explained by the fact that key figures in Welsh political life and journalism during the nineteenth century often chose to represent the press in this manner. For Liberal politicians keen to promote their cause, there were important advantages to be gained by cultivating the support of members of the press. By according to the press a dynamic purpose in the governance of Welsh society, such politicians were simply recognizing that journalists and editors "had most to gain from the proposition that the press wielded great power and influence."[51]

Henry Richard, the prominent Nonconformist MP, argued in 1888 that mid-Victorian journalists had helped "to leaven the public mind, and to give rise to a vague feeling of dissatisfaction, among at least some of the leaders of the people at the somewhat ignoble position which Wales occupied in our political system."[52] The journalist John Hughes, writing in the same year, asserted that the English language Liberal press, both Welsh and English, "has not made Wales less national; it has fortified our nationality, and at the same time enlarged Welsh vision."[53] In 1891, the Liberal politician T. E. Ellis told the editor of the *South Wales Daily Star* that "it is our new writers which are bringing to the minds of the Welsh people that they have a past and are a nation . . . to bring this about Editor, should be your work."[54] Four years later, the editor of *Y Genedly Gymreig* (*The Welsh Nation*) declared that his newspaper had to "defend the interests of Nonconformity, and to teach the principle of Liberalism and Nationalism."[55] Moreover, by 1888, Welsh Tory opponents of Nonconformity and disestablishment had become concerned about the extent of the political agitation in the Welsh-language press, arguing that it was "advocating and getting up a cry for a species of Home Rule for Wales."[56]

Both Nonconformist politicians and journalists were thus committed to promoting the cause of their respective institutions. This is not to suggest, however, that all Welsh newspapers were expressly interested in advancing an explicitly nationalist politic. As one writer in the *Western Mail* put it in 1885: "A good deal of the literature of the Welsh newspapers consists of biographical sketches of departed worthies, and the personal experiences of men and things, written in very slipshod fashion."[57] It is open to question whether or not those newspapers that did identify with a nationalist agenda were formulating a coherent program for its realization, or rather were expressing their own particular versions of national identity and solutions to Wales' problems. On these contentious questions, not all of the newspapers in this period would appear to have delineated a particularly clear or consistent position. Nor, of course, were they always successful publications. In 1889, the new editor of the overtly nationalist *Cymru Fydd*, R. H. Morgan, contended that the title had become "too narrow in scope and too rancorous and censorious." Two years later, it had ceased publication.[58]

Attempts to operate a nationalist newspaper in South Wales met with little success, as in the case of the failed Barry *Star* and the Swansea *Daily Post*.[59] When the nationalist Liberal MP, Tom Ellis, accepted a post in Gladstone's government in 1892, a move that provoked a great deal of debate in nationalist circles, there followed a range of responses from the Welsh press, in turn critical, noncommittal and supportive.[60] Needless to say, declarations regarding how nationalist the Welsh press was in the last three decades of the century are contingent upon the definition of nationalism being employed. Indeed, as our discussion of the *Western Mail* and the *South Wales Daily News* will demonstrate, the newspaper press played a far more complex role in relation to the issue of national identity than some of the more orthodox formulations we have cited would appear to suggest.

THE *WESTERN MAIL* AND THE *SOUTH WALES DAILY NEWS*

By the late nineteenth century, Cardiff was the nexus for a range of significant changes that were unfolding in Wales. A rapid expansion in its population followed the development of the valley coalfields. As the franchise became extended and the conflict over land and disestablishment intensified, the two major political parties, the Conservatives and the Liberals, were involved in the creation of the first mass circulation, English-language daily press in Wales. Both the *Western Mail* and the *South Wales Daily News* played an active part in the cultural politics of Cardiff during the last quarter of the century. Their respective treatments of the issue of national identity is, of course, only one dimension of their involvement in such politics, but it will be the subject of our exploration here.[61]

Both of these newspapers were written in English, although they also continued with the established practice of bilingual journalism; by the 1880s, these titles were regularly running items in the Welsh language. Changes in patterns of migration into Glamorgan in the closing decades of the century had resulted in a decline in the number of Welsh speakers.[62] For most of the century, there was no consensus among politicians or journalists that being Welsh meant being competent in the Welsh language. The use of English in these papers clearly reflected the nature of the market they targeted. In addition, two of the key figures in the early history of the newspapers were not Welsh, a fact reflecting a common experience of cross-border movement by journalists and printers, in both directions, during the nineteenth century. David Duncan, who founded the *South Wales Daily News*, came from Perth in Scotland. Lascelles Carr, the founding subeditor and later editor (1869–1901) of the *Western Mail*, came from Yorkshire via Liverpool.[63]

The two newspapers were primarily directed toward serving the needs of the burgeoning commercial classes of Cardiff and South Wales. At a cost of 1d each per day, and with an expansive layout and detailed articles, the newspapers assumed a readership that was privileged with regard to personal capital and leisure time. Joanne Cayford has argued that the *Western Mail*, for much of its first thirty years, was "responding to a recognised political constituency, but this was essentially a small network which had a strong Conservative element—the financiers, the stockbrokers, the 'gentlemen' of Cardiff."[64]

Indeed, the origins of the *Western Mail* were directly linked to an attempt to bolster support for the Conservative Party. Earlier in the century, a number of printers and journalists had been involved in the setting up of "a supportive press" for that party. In Merthyr, the second Marquis of Bute secretly funded the *Merthyr Guardian*, which circulated in Cardiff. Eventually it was merged with the pro-Tory, *Monmouthshire Advertiser*.[65] In 1852, the Butes' traditional hold over their Cardiff seat was broken when the Unitarian Walter Coffin won the seat. This development reflected a general electoral trend throughout Wales, one that marked the beginning of the ascendancy of the Liberal Party. In that year, only eleven of twenty-nine MPs from Wales were Liberal, yet by 1857 the Liberal MPs were in the majority. The 1868 election saw twenty-two Liberals and eight Conservatives returned (by 1880, the Liberals had gained an additional six seats at the expense of the Tories). It was this political shift that provided the impetus for the establishment of the *Western Mail*. In the November 1868 election, "the Bute estates costly attempt to regain the seat was unavailing; the failure was attributed to the lack of a local Conservative paper, and as a result the *Western Mail* was launched on 1 May 1869." It was the third Marquis of Bute who provided the capital for the launch, his decision having been prompted by the desire to provide a counter to "the publicity enjoyed by Cardiff Liberals through the agency of the *Cardiff Times*."[66] Bute, who in 1868 converted to Catholicism, was a substantial contributor to Tory funds and was alleged, by 1873, to have spent £30,000 on the *Western Mail*.[67] In 1869 it sold 6,000 copies and by 1871 it was selling 11,667 per day.[68]

In spite of its pro-Tory politics, the *Western Mail* proved remarkably successful in "anchoring itself firmly, even in Liberal South Wales." It was frequently defined as "the scourge of Welsh nationalist and socialist movements." The newspaper was staunchly anti-Liberal and "persistently and confidently styled itself as Wales' 'national' newspaper." Indeed, by 1873, Henry Richard was urging his constituents to ban it from their homes.[69] However, the availability of the newspaper throughout Wales, particularly in the north of the country, was severely restricted by poor north-south communications.[70] Even though it was explicitly anti-Liberal and antinationalist, it was "an effective newspaper, much more lively than its local Liberal rival, the *South Wales Daily News*."[71]

Joanne Cayford has noted the paradox of the success of a Tory newspaper in a Liberal stronghold. While pointing out that the reasons why Welsh people read the *Western Mail* "remain unclear," she nevertheless suggests that the key to understanding its success was its commercial role rather than its political position: "The paper capitalised on its status as a title which had the advantages of being local in its production and national in appeal." This "national appeal," as we have noted, did not extend to support for nationalist politics. In this period, the *Western Mail* appears to stand out as an opponent of nationalism. A closer examination of it and the *South Wales Daily News* in the context we have provided, however, suggests that its position on the national issue may have been more pronounced than other newspapers, but that it was not alone in failing to sing a clear nationalist tune in these years.[72]

The foundation of the *South Wales Daily News* reflected a long and sustained involvement by Liberals in the launching, buying and subsidizing of newspapers in the nineteenth century.[73] When David Duncan, proprietor of the *Cardiff Times*, launched the *South Wales Daily News* in 1872, the newspaper was, from the first, locked into conflict with local Conservative Party interests. Emerging as a response to Tory influence in Wales, the *South Wales Daily News* remained an ally of Liberalism until it was taken over by the *Western Mail* in 1928.[74]

In 1891, Duncan, in an application for a Westminster lobby ticket, asserted that: "The *South Wales Daily News* . . . is of a national character, so far as Wales is concerned."[75] As with nationalist politics more broadly in Wales, the form of nationalism being articulated by the *South Wales Daily News* was firmly embedded within a Liberal framework. However, the *South Wales Daily News* was never as successful in terms of its circulation as the *Western Mail*. According to Kenneth Morgan, the reason for this was that it was less fun to read than its rival, and because it "gave little prominence to cultural or educational affairs." The *South Wales Daily News*, he suggests, was "basically an honest paper, if dull."[76]

Out of Cardiff, then, came two daily newspapers that were responding to a number of interrelated developments: the changing political environment following population growth, urbanization and electoral reform; the opportunities for a mass-market daily press presented by the growth of large conurbations; local political battles between Tory and Liberal forces; and debates about the place of Wales in the UK's political system.

EMPIRE, PARTY, LOCALISM AND IDENTITY

Our examination of leaders published in the *Western Mail* and the *South Wales Daily News* during January 1885 provides us with further evidence regarding the respective roles these two newspapers played in nationalist politics.

Turning first to the stylistic differences between the dailies, it is apparent that the *Western Mail* was organizing its leaders around a structure that, to modern eyes, mixes the concepts of the headline, the index to contents, and the long editorial. Beneath the newspaper's banner, there were up to nine short summary items (which we have called short leaders), followed by up to three, but more typically two, longer articles, or long leaders. Stylistically, this arguably made it easier to read than the *South Wales Daily News*, for which all leading items assumed the form of long editorials.

Beginning with the *Western Mail*, we examined all the leaders during January 1885.[77] In total, 203 topics were addressed in both long and short leaders. More specifically, the majority of the leaders (ranked here in order of prominence) dealt with issues of national, UK-centered politics and individual deaths, as well as matters relating to the British Empire, crime, transport accidents and industrial news. If we examine the long leaders on their own, of which there were forty-three, the largest share was devoted to national, UK-centered politics, followed by those on the empire, on cultural issues and on education.[78]

In general, leaders in the *Western Mail* during this month operated at three levels: the imperial or international level, the national, UK level and the local, at times parochial, level. Recurrently it was the case that within the newspaper political discussion followed the contours of wider debates taking place in Westminster and, indeed, throughout the imperial context. As the totals suggest, it did engage with Welsh political topics, but in quite specific ways, such as reporting on the redistribution of parliamentary seats in South Wales, and on Cardiff's public health and education. The *Western Mail* did not give a high status to issues related to Welsh national identity in either a positive or a negative sense during this period. Although it dealt with issues of national identity and nationalism, the coverage was infrequent and, as far as its leaders were concerned, without any substantive analysis or critique. If there is an encompassing theme in these leaders, it is the Liberal versus Tory political conflict, a dynamic that was defined by an extensive array of issues in which nationalism and national identity figured only occasionally.

Of the forty leaders in the *South Wales Daily News* in January 1885, about one-third were on national UK politics, and the rest on issues such as trade and poverty framed in a national UK context, on empire, on local political issues and on the redistribution of parliamentary seats. It touched on the Welsh Sunday Closing Act, cultural issues and religion, all of which had a distinctive Welsh dimension. Still, through the prominence it gave to issues in its leader columns, this daily situated itself as a Liberal, imperial publication.

The *Western Mail*, in spite of its reputation as a scourge of nationalism, routinely projected a sense of Welshness, albeit within an imperial context. It recognized the existence of a distinctive Welsh tradition (to be defined primarily in relation to that of the English) while simultaneously indicating that there were open questions regarding its precise nature. For example, in March 1874, a reply to an attack on the "Druidical System" was printed that admitted there was a debate to be had over the nature of the Welsh past:

Another instalment of the elaborate and extended reply of MYFYR MOR-GANWG to the attacks made upon the Druidical system, by "John Jones, of Observatory Cottage" is published in our columns this morning. The general position assumed by the Arch-Druid appears to be that all "the Oriental Christianities" were corruptions of "the pure and primitive Christianity of the Stone Circles," and in the present letter the writer particularises certain points in proof of this startling contention.[79]

Arguably, by using the word *startling* in relation to one of the positions, the *Western Mail* was exercising a degree of skepticism, albeit in a manner that allowed space for a debate about the authority of Welsh traditions. In another example, one that similarly speaks to the role of the past in Welsh society, the leader is partly mocking the persistence of certain traditions, and yet asserts that they are of little consequence: "Perhaps there is no nation more thoroughly superstitious than the Welsh, and yet there are no people to whom it is less harmful. Tradition has haunted every nook and cranny of the Principality, and filled it with the ghosts of the glorious past."[80]

There is, then, a degree of ambiguity with respect to the treatment of "the glorious past" within the *Western Mail*. It is humorously invoked, for the context of this piece is an ironic commentary on popular almanacs, but it is accorded popular saliency. It is a past held at a respectful, if sometimes amused, distance. Equally the *Western Mail* could stress the nature of Welshness in a less ironic, more integrative sense, emphasizing the degree to which the Welsh were acquiescent to the demands of the United Kingdom and its empire. In the words of an editorial leader published in the *Western Mail* on 1 July 1885:

It should be remembered that the Welsh are not the creatures of yesterday, or that the accidental outward complexion of affairs at a given moment is to be accepted as the interpretation of their true character. . . . The Welsh people make no pretences—save in the matter of harmony and song—to be above their neighbours; but if they are taken at their depth they may be pronounced as loyal and as patriotic as their fellow-subjects throughout the length and breadth of the land. They take the gifts the gods have given them without a murmur. They are convinced that they, even by their quiescence, assist in welding the kingdom in one grand whole.[81]

The newspaper also invoked the recent past to discredit its Liberal opponents' claims to be the true guardians of Cardiff's civic interests. In so doing it inflected the political debate in terms of local rather than nationalist concerns. When Lascelles Carr campaigned for a seat on Cardiff Council in 1888, his address focused on the divisions between the Liberals and the Tories in the city. He deliberately accentuated recent Liberal involvement in the establishment of the rival Barry docks in order to question their credentials for the good government of Cardiff. At the meeting where Carr made this comparison, one of his supporters, Mr. Ensor, stressed the past in a different sense. He saw the recent past in terms of rapid change within an imperial context, for since "his first recollection of Cardiff some 34 years ago, it had progressed into one of the very first municipalities in the United Empire."[82]

When one of the Liberal MPs for Cardiff resigned in 1888, the *Western Mail* again invoked the recent past—in this case the 1880 general election—to demonstrate the dismal effects on Merthyr of what it deemed to be a demagogic campaign waged by dissenting ministers during the election. It used the opportunity to attack the other MP, Henry Richard, and to call into question his definition of nationalism by putting it in inverted commas and comparing it to cheap jewelry— or pinchbeck: "His politics and his 'nationalism' are pinchbeck both, and were he to resign there would be considerable rejoicing even in his own camp."[83] This is a dispute over whether the term *nationalism* can be used to describe Richard's politics, a term that the Liberals, by implication, cannot lay proper claim to in this context. It is also a criticism of both his and, again by implication, the Liberal conception of nationalism as cheap, populist and tawdry. It is, finally, an invocation of nationalism to abuse a Liberal MP—as such, it is a dispute of the here and now, of the impending local political struggle rather than over the nature of national identity.

Our preliminary survey would suggest, therefore, that the *Western Mail* did not prioritize issues of the Welsh nation in the areas we examined. Instead, its focus was on the politics of the local, of party and of empire. The evidence is of a slightly detached, mildly critical view of a Welsh identity linked to Druidic traditions and to the role of the past in Welsh culture, coupled with an aggressive assertion of the need to protect the interests of Cardiff and South Wales within an imperial context. The critique of Liberal nationalism is done within this context and, as such, lays claim to the existence of other ways of defining Welsh identity.

In sharp contrast to the *Western Mail*, which had opposed the emergence of a nationalist movement in Wales, the *South Wales Daily News* had assumed a far more sympathetic position. This is not to suggest, however, that in riding this current of nationalism, the latter newspaper provided uncritical support for a nationalist politic. The newspaper did not, from our evidence at least, articulate a unified sense of what it was to be Welsh. Sir Edward Reed, the Liberal MP for Cardiff, asserted in a letter published in the newspaper in 1891 that " 'the great commercial and cosmopolitan town of Cardiff,' with a population of 150,000, could not be severed from its economic relations with the industrial areas of England."[84] In 1894, the editor of the *South Wales Daily News* reprimanded its London correspondent for taking the side of four Liberal MPs who resigned the Whip over the Liberal government's failure to support Welsh Disestablishment. Moreover, in 1898, Cardiff Liberals and this newspaper united in opposition to plans to give equal weight to all constituencies on Lloyd George's proposed Welsh National Liberal Council.[85]

Still, our evidence suggests that the *South Wales Daily News* did seek to address the popular significance of history for the "Welsh nation" in a more sustained manner than did the *Western Mail*. In 1885, for example, we see frequent references to the idea that there is a distinctive Welsh nation, one defined by its past. Yet at the same time, this past needs to be rewritten and disentangled from myth. The *South Wales Daily News* implicitly accepts that there is a contest over what it was to be Welsh. In welcoming the setting up of a cultural body, the Cambrian Society, it hoped that this new institution would be non-party-political and nondenominational in spirit:

The well-educated Welshman can do a great more towards collecting and collating facts and legends bearing upon history or the language of his people than an uneducated man could possibly do. . . . Educated people will demand that history shall be genuine, not spurious; that it will be fact not fable. Those who have either ignorantly or knowingly palmed off mere legends for facts will soon find their proper place. Wales has a history, a history to be proud of, and though, like all other old countries, its history has, to a considerable extent, got mixed up with doubtful tales, there is still a plentiful store of genuine records which the Cambrian Society may recover, and set forth in such a form as to reach all classes, and make even the bewildered Englishman understand that the Welsh are no more a barbarous or a curious people than any other modern nation.[86]

This passage invokes the past in relation to a present characterized by modernity, thereby asserting that a new Wales will be characterized by a new attitude to its past. National fables and doubtful tales are to be dispensed with in favor of the collation of historical facts. The newspaper projects a pride in Welshness, linking the acquisition of a "genuine" history to the establishment of a modern nation coequal with that of the English people. Significantly, though, this is a discursive reinflection defined in terms of regional identity, not separatism. The past, and in a sense the linked conception of Welsh nationhood, is being used to endorse the underlying tenets of modernity: The past needs to be rewritten to better serve the interests of progress.

Earlier in the same month, the newspaper evoked a different sense of the past. This conception was much more diffuse and, it might be said, mystical:

The deerstalker's theory is that a country like ours should be let to the highest bidders, and that the people, when found to be inconvenient, should be politely informed that the land of their birth, the country endeared to them by the memory of their fathers, is to be converted into a playground and that they must therefore go elsewhere, find new homes, and commence a new history . . . the practical working man will never be such an idiot as to be persuaded that a transaction like this is capable of justification on economical or any other grounds.[87]

Here the past and the nation are allowed to strike a more emotive resonance. The past is actualized in a form of national memory that is used to connect the current issue of poverty with a history of emigration. In this context, "memory" is not the same as the modern, carefully collated accurate history called for a week later, but is instead framed in territorial terms. It is invoked in a positive (if sexist) sense as a means of transmitting a bond to the land from father to son. The past supports an emotional, and yet "practical" response to the exigency of poverty; it is reinflected in a manner that makes explicit its class specificity, its implications for national identity are seen to be overdetermined by economic imperatives. To enforce emigration through the improper management of the consequences of a depression in trade would be to deprive people not only of their home but also a part of themselves — their history. Here the past is employed in an appeal to social justice, the ideological purchase of which depends on a shared sense of place, of "the country endeared to them by the memory of their fathers."

The past, as represented on the pages of the *South Wales Daily News*, is similarly employed in accounts of contemporary political developments, just as it was in the *Western Mail*. In 1887, the former daily invoked the past to discredit the claims of the peerage to having a legitimate Welsh connection.[88] Similarly, it figures in the contrast the newspaper draws between the reverence landowners had for the antiquity of their legal right to land with that of the poor who, if not dealt with immediately, will act in a manner showing that they "have less reverence for antiquity."[89] On religious issues, the disputes between the Nonconformists and the Anglican Church in Wales were reported in terms suggesting that the former, by virtue of their historical role in establishing chapels throughout the country, had a greater claim to being the church of the nation. This was in comparison with the Anglicans who worshipped in cathedrals, and thus were alleged to be, by implication, culturally distinct from the Welsh people.[90]

Also in this period, Lord Bute was attacked in the *South Wales Daily News* for rewriting the history of Scottish religion and attacking the Nonconformist tradition in that country: "Lord Bute gets the credit of being well versed in the history of Wales and the Welsh. Let us hope that his claim to this distinction rests upon a stronger basis than his claim to be an historian in matters connected with his fatherland."[91] The past, in this discussion, is used to render problematic local political relations in Cardiff in ways that reaffirm a certain sense of tradition. Bute was a dominant Tory figure in that city, a Scotsman and a Catholic in a land with many dissenters, and an open critic of the Protestant Reformation in Scotland. His alleged misuse of history is constituted as sufficient grounds to discredit him, for he was objectionable in the eyes of this newspaper for reasons of party, of nation and of religion—not just for national reasons. Once again, then, the right to define the "true essence" of the past and of the nation, is a site of struggle. As was the case with other leaders in the *South Wales Daily News*, the past was invoked in order to situate local topics in a larger, national matrix of political issues. Far from being used to construct a new identity for the Welsh nation, contending definitions of the past provided a basis on which these different voices sought to fight out local claims to political legitimacy within the context of the United Kingdom and the empire.

CONCLUSION

The evidence we have drawn from this preliminary investigation clearly calls into question what is often an easy association made by historians between the nineteenth-century press in Wales and the promotion of a uniform sense of nation or national identity. The diverse range of political voices in the newspapers under scrutiny ensured that the notion of the Welsh past was mobilized in ways that met the rhetorical needs of an extensive range of contradictory objectives. Accordingly, we could find little evidence to suggest that there was a dominant definition of the past in discussions of national identity nor that there was a coherent sense of Welsh national identity embedded in the texts under consideration. Both papers projected images of the Welsh past and present, each laying claim, in different contexts, to particular images of Welsh identity. In terms of their mode of address, these Cardiff-based newspapers sought to reaffirm national UK and imperial interests by devoting to them most of their attention; local issues, especially the lives, deaths and crimes of local figures, were recurrently reported against this national backdrop. The key division between the two newspapers is one of party politics, not the politics of Welsh national identity.

To close, we would argue that the newspaper press, far from being positioned outside of the political processes it sought to report on, played an integral part in the formation of a local politics of Welsh national identity.[92] Our evidence indicates that these processes of national identity formation were much more diverse and contested in their articulation than has perhaps hitherto been thought. Both the *Western Mail* and the *South Wales Daily News* projected a range of different perspectives on Welsh history and politics that, from the vantage point of today, are not easily categorized as pro- or antinationalist. Each daily gave priority to the idea of Wales as a part of the empire and, in turn, fought over the nature of the Welsh (but Westminster-based) politics that should shape that polity. Hence in our view it is important that we explore the involvement in the press of those social groups that, at that time, were seen to be authorized keepers of the national past and the "genuine facts" of its history. Wales was undergoing dramatic change in this period, but the complex and contradictory effectivity of the press in these transformations needs further analysis and critique. However, as we have argued, it was not involved in a wider process of imposing a dominant definition of Welsh national identity, nor in the elimination of "tokens of antiquity" from popular memory.

NOTES

1. We would like to thank Chris Evans and Patrick Hagopian for commenting on an earlier draft of this chapter. The authors received support in preparing this chapter from the Regional Research Programme of the University of Glamorgan.

2. D. Defoe, *A Tour through the Whole Island of Great Britain*, ed. Pat Rogers (London: Penguin, 1971), p. 376. Vortigern was a British leader of the fifth century, while Mortimer was the Earl of March (1287–1330), ibid., pp. 377 and 705. Volume II of the *Tour*, from which the description of Wales is taken, was first published in 1725.

3. Ibid., pp. 376–89.

4. For a discussion of national identity see B. Anderson, *Imagined Communities: Reflections on the Origins and Spread of Nationalism*, 2nd ed. (London: Verso, 1991). On the cultural politics of identity formation, see S. Hall, "The Question of Cultural Identity," in *Modernity and Its Futures*, ed. S. Hall, D. Held and T. McGrew (Cambridge: Polity, 1992). The role of social memory in processes of national identity is explored in J. Fentress and C. Wickham, *Social Memory* (Oxford: Blackwell, 1992); D. Thelen, "Memory and American History," *The Journal of American History*, 75, no. 4 (1989): 1117–29. See also M. Foucault, "Film and Popular Memory," *Foucault Live* (New York: Semiotext(e), 1989) and discussions of popular memory in R. Johnson, G. McLennan, B. Schwartz and D. Sutton, eds., *Making Histories: Studies in History-Writing and Politics* (London: Hutchinson, 1982).

5. Prys Morgan, "From a Death to a View: The Hunt for the Welsh Past in the Romantic Period," in *The Invention of Tradition*, ed. E. Hobsbawm and T. Ranger (Cambridge: Cambridge University Press, 1988), pp. 43–100.

6. D. Gareth Evans, *A History of Wales 1815–1906* (Cardiff: University of Wales Press, 1989), p. 127.

7. K. O. Morgan, *Rebirth of a Nation: Wales 1880–1980* (Oxford: Oxford University Press; Cardiff: University of Wales Press, 1981); J. Davies, *A History of Wales* (London: Penguin, 1993); Evans, *A History of Wales*.

8. Davies, *A History of Wales*, pp. 398–99, 410.

9. K. O. Morgan, "Tom Ellis versus Lloyd George: the Fractured Consciousness of Fin-de siècle Wales," in *Politics and Society in Wales; 1840–1922. Essays in Honour of Ieuan Gwynedd Jones*, ed. G. H. Jenkins and J. Beverley Smith (Cardiff: University of Wales Press, 1988), p. 111.

10. G. A. Williams, "When Was Wales," *The Welsh and Their History* (London: Croom Helm, 1982), p. 198.

11. G. A. Williams, "Imperial South Wales," *The Welsh and Their History* (London: Croom Helm, 1982), p. 182.

12. A number of these accounts are cited in Aled Jones, *Press, Politics and Society: A History of Journalism in Wales* (Cardiff: University of Wales Press, 1993), p. 3.

13. Morgan, *Rebirth*, pp. 49–51. Although published before Aled Jones' study, Morgan's discussion of the press exemplifies a long tradition of historical writing that has often treated the press as a relatively unproblematic institution, thereby displacing questions regarding its larger ideological effectivity. For comments on how this practice has become a consistent feature of the historiography of the seventeenth century, see T. O'Malley, "Religion and the Newspaper Press, 1660–1685: A Study of the *London Gazette*," in *The Press in English Society from the Seventeenth to Nineteenth Centuries*, ed. M. Harris and A. Lee (London and Toronto: Associated Universities Press, 1986), pp. 27–28.

14. Evans, *A History of Wales*, pp. 52, 222, 224, 228. See, also, Davies, *A History of Wales*, p. 505.

15. R. D. Rees, "South Wales and Monmouthshire Newspaper under the Stamp Acts," *Welsh History Review*, vol. 1 (1961–1963): 301.

16. Davies, *A History of Wales*, p. 350.

17. Morgan, "Tom Ellis," p. 93; K. O. Morgan, *The Welsh in British Politics*, 3rd ed. (Cardiff: University of Wales Press, 1991), p. 105. See also Gwyn Williams' comments on this topic in his "Imperial South Wales," *The Welsh*, pp. 171–72.

18. Jones, *Press, Politics and Society*, pp. 153, 141, 176, 178.

19. Ibid., p. 91.

20. Evans, *A History of Wales*, pp. 1–3, 41–42, 59, 70 on the poor living conditions, overcrowding and the inadequate sanitation and medical provision.

21. Jones, *Press, Politics and Society*, p. 93; Evans, *A History of Wales*, p. 124.

22. Jones, *Press, Politics and Society*, p. 92.

23. Evans, *A History of Wales*, p. 191; Jones, *Press, Politics and Society*, pp. 108–10.

24. Evans, *A History of Wales*, p. 220.

25. M. Cragoe, "Conscience or Coercion? Clerical Influence at the General Election of 1868 in Wales," *Past and Present*, no. 149 (1995): 143–44 n. 20, 145, 146.

26. Evans, *A History of Wales*, pp. 282–84, 292, 302–4.

27. These comments are based on a reading of Jones, *Press, Politics and Society*, Evans, *A History of Wales*, and Morgan, *Rebirth*. Attendance statistics based on Morgan, *Wales in British Politics*, p. 83, Appendix B, p. 316.

28. Cragoe, "Conscience and Coercion?" pp. 149, 153 n. 62, 155ff.

29. P. Jenkins points out that "Elias, the 'Pope of Anglesey,' was . . . determined that the new church would not share the common trend of Welsh dissent to produce theological liberals and political radicals"; see P. Jenkins, *A History of Modern Wales 1536–1990* (London: Longman, 1992).

30. Merfyn Jones, *The North Wales Quarrymen, 1874–1922* (Cardiff: University of Wales Press, 1981).

31. G. A. Williams, *When Was Wales?* (London: Penguin, 1985), p. 230.

32. Glanmor Williams, *Religion, Language, and Nationality in Wales* (Cardiff: University of Wales Press, 1979), p. 143.

33. Williams, *When Was Wales?*, p. 231.

34. See K. O. Morgan's *Rebirth of a Nation: Wales 1880–1980*.

35. Ibid., p. 94.

36. Evans, *A History of Wales*, p. 316.

37. Morgan, *Rebirth*, p. 4.

38. Evans, *A History of Wales*, p. 127; Morgan, "From a Death to a View," pp. 98, 100.

39. Jones, *Press, Politics and Society*, p. 107.

40. Ibid., p. 90.

41. Rees, "South Wales," p. 320.

42. Jones, *Press, Politics and Society*, p. 6.

43. Rees, "South Wales," p. 304; Jones, *Press, Politics and Society*, p. 5; D. Davies, "The Eisteddfod as a Drag upon National Progress," *The Welsh Review*, no. 2 (December 1891): 126.

44. Rees, "South Wales," pp. 301, 304, 319.

45. Jones, *Press, Politics and Society*, pp. 94–95.

46. Ibid., pp. 94–104.

47. Davies, *A History of Wales*, p. 358.

48. Evans, *A History of Wales*, pp. 141, 208, 221ff; Cragoe, "Conscience or Coercion," pp. 150, 151 n. 50. They were not always united in outlook.

49. Davies, *A History of Wales*, p. 416. Welsh language papers were not exclusive in their attitude to language. They were desperately eager to attract English advertisements. Jones, *Press, Politics and Society*, p. 69.

50. Evans, *A History of Wales*, pp. 133, 171; Davies, *A History of Wales*, p. 378. Chartist leaders in Wales also read the London *Times*. Evans, *A History of Wales*, p. 145; further evidence of this diversity is in R. D. Rees, "Glamorgan Newspapers Under The Stamp Acts," *Morgannwg*, vol. 111 (1959): 61–94.

51. Jones, *Press, Politics and Society*, p. 156.

52. Ibid., p. 161.

53. Ibid., p. 199.

54. Ibid., p. 156.

55. Ibid., p. 157.

56. Ibid., p. 172.

57. Gwyliedydd, "Spirit of the Welsh Press," *Western Mail* [hereafter *WM*], 12 Jan. 1885.

58. Morgan, *Wales in British Politics*, p. 110 n. 2.

59. Ibid., p. 110.

60. Ibid., p. 121 n. 4.

61. We acknowledge the limited nature of our illustration. A more systematic study would need to, first, situate these two newspapers in relation to their competitors, especially those published in the Welsh language, and, second, expand the period of news coverage under scrutiny here. For these and other reasons, we make no larger claims regarding the representative status of our illustration.

62. Morgan, *Wales in British Politics*, Appendix A, p. 315, which shows that by 1911 nearly 50 percent of the population of Glamorgan only spoke English.

63. Evans, *A History of Wales*, p. 241; Jones, *Press, Politics and Society*, p. 178.

64. J. Cayford, "The Western Mail, 1869–1914: The Politics and Management of a Provincial Newspaper" (Ph.D. thesis, University of Wales, 1992), p. 414.

65. Jones, *Press, Politics and Society*, p. 125; Rees, "South Wales," p. 313.

66. Davies, *A History of Wales*, pp. 428, 432; Jones, *Press, Politics and Society*, p. l66; Cayford, *The Western Mail*, p. 53.

67. A. Jones, "Trade Unions and the Press: Journalism and the Red Dragon Revolt of 1874," *Welsh History Review*, vol. 12, no. 2 (1984): 212 n. 65; L. Brown, *Victorian News and Newspapers* (Oxford: Clarendon Press, 1985), p. 70.

68. Brown, *Victorian News*, p. 53; Jones, *Press, Politics and Society*, p. 97.

69. Morgan, *Rebirth*, p. 57; J. Cayford, "The National Newspaper of Wales?" *Planet: The Welsh Internationalist*, no. 98 (April/May 1993): 57.

70. Davies, *A History of Wales*, p. 466; Cayford, "The National Newspaper," pp. 57, 62.

71. Morgan, *Rebirth*, pp. 45–46.

72. Cayford, *The Western Mail*, pp. 1, 8, 415.

73. Jones, *Press, Politics and Society*, pp. 130, 134.

74. Cayford, "The National Newspaper," p. 58; Jones, *Press, Politics and Society*, pp. 129–30.

75. Jones, *Press, Politics and Society*, pp. 153–54.

76. Morgan, *Rebirth*, p. 51.

77. We consulted copies of both papers at Cardiff public library. Copies of the *Western Mail* (*WM*) January 1 and 3 were incomplete and so do not figure in our analysis of leaders. We devised the categories based upon our interpretation of the main topic of the item.

78. These categories are indicative of the relative prominence of the different topics: The precise demarcation between topics is not as sharp or clear-cut as these figures might otherwise imply. The same holds true for our comparison with the *South Wales Daily News* below. Furthermore, given the obvious conceptual and methodological problems associated with treating newspapers as proxies for public opinion, we make no such claims in this regard.

79. *WM*, 10 March 1874.

80. "Popular Superstitions," *WM*, 7 Jan. 1885.

81. *WM*, 1 July 1885.

82. "Cardiff Municipal Bye-Election," *WM*, 11 Jan. 1888.

83. "What Are the Merthyr Folk Going to Do?" *WM*, 8 Feb. 1888.

84. "Letter," *South Wales Daily News* (hereafter *SWDN*), 17 March 1891, cited in Morgan, *Wales in British Politics*, p. 110.

85. Morgan, *Wales in British Politics*, pp. 145, 170–71.

86. "New Cambrian Society," *SWDN*, 15 Jan. 1885.

87. "An Artisan's View of Depression in Trade," *SWDN*, 8 Jan. 1885.

88. "Our Welsh Aristocracy," *SWDN*, 8 July 1887.

89. "Wages Depression and Poverty," *SWDN*, 31 Jan. 1885.

90. "The Dean of Spiritual Enthusiasm," *SWDN*, 8 Jan. 1885.

91. "Lord Bute and John Knox," *SWDN*, 24 Jan. 1885.

92. See also Jones, *Press, Politics and Society*, pp. 141, 176

III

The Twentieth Century

America's Press-Radio Rivalry: Circulation Managers and Newspaper Boys during the Depression

Todd Alexander Postol

Although the image of the American paper boy on his route is known to everyone, little has been written on the history of twentieth-century newspaper carriers or the industry in which they worked. This chapter attempts to recover part of that lost history by examining a familiar event, the press-radio "war" of the early 1930s, through the eyes of the nation's newspaper circulation managers. Drawing on the rich internal records of the International Circulation Managers' Association (ICMA), I argue that competition from commercial broadcasting played an important role in the creation of the middle-class American newspaper boy. Fighting to regain lost media market share, managers during the Depression countered the growing influence of broadcasting by reinventing daily newspaper delivery service. Central to this process was the effort to train millions of middle-class schoolchildren to inexpensive market newspaper subscriptions.[1]

In discussing the impact of broadcasting on daily newspaper publishing, historians have typically focused on the reactions of publishers and print journalists. Given the power and prestige of these two groups, this orientation seems reasonable.[2] But the industry's fight with radio was not waged solely in boardrooms or editorial offices; it was also fought in living rooms where individual consumers made private decisions that ultimately transformed the way news was gathered and distributed in the United States. By concentrating on the actions of media leaders and ignoring larger patterns of consumption, scholars have missed one of the most significant consequences of the press-radio conflict of the 1930s.

From the perspective of publishers and journalists, the newspaper industry clearly lost the intermedia war. Within a decade broadcasting ended print domination of daily news reporting and established a solid advertising base for future growth. Yet this defeat, if it was a defeat, was hardly total and is not supported by newspaper sales and subscription numbers. Well before lean times ended, newspapers won back all the readers lost during the dark, early years of the Depression. This remarkable achievement was accomplished, in substantial measure, by newspaper circulation managers, who were more deeply involved in the day-to-day struggle to preserve readership and subscription revenues than either publishers or journalists.

SUBSCRIPTION MARKETING BEFORE THE ADVENT OF RADIO

While newspapers had long waged spectacular circulation battles to boost street sales, the industry was slow to develop marketing strategies targeted specifically for home readership. Prior to the turn of the century, papers occasionally took on help to secure subscribers, but augmenting long-term consumption "beyond a normal growth," a circulation manager recalled in 1925, "was considered beneath the dignity of the publishers or owners."[3] The industry did not consistently begin recruiting subscription accounts until the Progressive era, and men, rather than boys, were the central figures in its initial solicitation campaigns.

Circulation chiefs at the *Indianapolis News* were among the earliest to promote aggressive subscription marketing. The paper's salesmanship program was first used in 1913 with adult solicitors to stimulate demand for rural readership; within a generation its recommendations would be adopted by dailies across the United States to attract non-rural, residential readers serviced by juvenile carriers. Guidelines drawn up by the *News* informed solicitors that the primary requisite for success was to "know your business thoroughly." Solicitors were to study the paper, learn what features it offered and know what proportion of the paper was devoted to news and what to advertising. In tacit recognition that the clientele for news was growing to include diverse elements of the community, the paper advised solicitors to emphasize that the *News* offered the area's fullest sports, market and farm coverage, in addition to running a large classified section. Solicitors were told to carry identification, obtain subscriptions honestly and never to lose their tempers.[4]

This endorsement for trained men was tinged with irony. At the very time solicitors were being pushed to become salesmen, urban managers were beginning to complain of the high cost and inefficiency of using men to garner new readers. The growth of residential areas in and around cities compressed delivery routes, making them much more accessible to cheaper juvenile labor. Hiring adults to canvass a neighborhood no longer made economic sense. As one manager observed at the 1917 ICMA convention, solicitors rushed to get the easy customers and left the hard cases for the route carrier. It was better "to encourage carriers to get ALL the subscriptions."[5]

Over the next decade circulation departments began embracing the idea of using boys to be company salesmen. Some papers merely furnished a set of written rules. In 1922 the *Chattanooga News* issued a list for its boys, reminding them that in order to be real salesmen they had to "dress neat and tidy," and "take your hat off when a lady appears at the door." Other papers went further, actually training minors to sell. The *St. Paul Dispatch and Pioneer Press*, for example, founded a "Carrier School of Instruction" where boys were "drilled in the method of presenting arguments for getting new subscribers" while the *Terre Haute Star* was "careful to teach all carriers the art of salesmanship and good business methods."[6]

As impressive as these training programs were, they were still the result of individual managers' decisions. It took a long time for the industry as a whole to move away from adult solicitors and formulate a comprehensive strategy for employing boys as salesmen. A meeting of circulation managers in 1922, for example, revealed deep divisions as to which approach was best. Some relied on boys exclusively; others used carrier and solicitor crews composed entirely of adults. J. J. Lynch of the *Cleveland Press* preferred juvenile carriers because "the quality of business secured by the boy is much better." Carrier boys were "much more economical, as subscribers secured through this method ought not to cost one-tenth as much as subscribers secured by canvassers." Ray S. South, of the *Birmingham (Alabama) News*, disagreed. He was satisfied with an adults-only system. Regular delivery of the paper was handled by men carriers; when the *News* wanted to spur readership, South sent district personnel out to customers' homes. Even the president of the ICMA admitted that "in St. Louis we have carrier men. We do not have carrier boys and in recent years . . . very little has been done to encourage boys to get subscriptions."[7]

Throughout the 1920s sales programs lurched forward in fits and starts. During this period many papers benefited from an expanding urban economy to enjoy record levels of circulation. With metropolitan readership increasing, managers saw no reason to experiment with untested personnel policies. Interest in juvenile salesmanship accordingly tapered off. At the 1927 ICMA meeting, circulation men debated whether carrier training was becoming more effective or losing its punch. The next year, *Editor & Publisher* stated "no epoch-making ideas for gaining circulation" were recorded at the association's convention. Yet circulation managers were, in fact, starting to show renewed passion for instructing youngsters. With unintentional prescience, the journal noted that "deepest interest was evinced in the training of carrier boys as salesmen."[8]

NEWSPAPERS AND RADIO: THE EARLY YEARS

The rise of radio directly stimulated this interest. Commercial broadcasting was the catalyst that prompted managers to decisively turn away from adult solicitors and accelerate training programs for juveniles; indeed, it led many circulation managers to implement extensive personnel selection procedures for the first time to identify the best available boys for sales instruction. With limited financial resources at their command, and under continual pressure to maintain healthy readership, circulation managers fought back using what they had—carrier forces composed of juvenile workers.

Until this point newspapers in the United States faced few exterior threats. Even the appearance of a popular periodical press following the Civil War had failed to shake the industry. Broadcast programming during the 1920s dramatically altered this situation. Radio quickly became a serious commercial rival to daily newspaper publishing. In 1923, 400,000 households in America had radio sets; by 1930 that number had soared to nearly 14 million.[9] Magazines lagged far behind newspapers in reporting the latest news; radio was instantaneous. It had the potential to cut into paid circulation in a way that periodicals did not, compelling publishers to slash the rates they charged advertisers. Radio could lure even the most loyal subscriber away from the pages of the local paper. Money that previously would have been earmarked for newspaper advertising could now be used to buy radio time instead.

This was not anticipated by circulation managers during the first years of broadcasting. Managers initially reacted with enthusiasm to "wireless telephone," deeming that readers' interest in the craze spurred newspaper growth.[10] Radio sets were constantly improving and everywhere new stations were being established; the place to keep up with all the latest changes was the local newspaper. Circulation men went so far as to encourage radio ownership as an inducement to get boys to sell subscriptions. In 1921 the *Chicago Tribune* launched a popular sales campaign using bicycles as prizes for its most productive carriers. Other papers soon ran bicycle campaigns of their own. The following year radios became the rewards of choice. Newspapers in Chicago, Los Angeles and Indianapolis printed advertisements enticing youngsters to earn a receiving set by selling subscriptions. The new toy seemed to open up worlds of adventure to children. There was only one difficulty: radio was so novel, boys hardly understood what it was. "The radio campaign had to be carried on a little different than the bicycle," commented Sidney D. Long of the *Wichita Eagle*. "Every boy knew all about a bicycle. While with the radio it was necessary to educate and enthuse him at the same time." Newspapers went out of their way to tell youngsters how rewarding a radio could be: "Oh boy! What fun! Just rig up the aerial in your back yard—call in Skinny and the gang— and then the fun begins. Music, baseball scores, speeches, 'n everything."[11] As managers were using radio as a promotional attraction, publishers were also seeking to cash in on radio's popularity by acquiring in-house broadcasting stations.

For much of the decade there was reason to suppose radio helped, rather than hurt, newspaper circulation. Even after stations began regularly reporting the news (thereby killing the tradition in the newspaper industry of printing extra editions to cover late-breaking events) circulation managers tended to view radio positively. A. L. Parker of the *Los Angeles Times* felt one-line radio bulletins whetted the interest of listeners for "the complete story of the event, and only the newspaper can give this."[12] Managers treated radio favorably because they did not yet see it as a threat to the advertising lifeblood of daily newspaper publishing. Like most of their contemporaries, they considered broadcasting to be an exciting but economically marginal fad.

Media expert J. George Frederick probably spoke for a majority of circulators when he wrote in 1925 that "radio is not and never will be a 'big' advertising medium for it cannot do real selling work." Frederick made a strong case against broadcast advertising. Unlike type, radio spots rarely blended in with what came before or after. Listeners would no more welcome interruptions in a program than theatergoers would appreciate a man walking on stage between the acts of a play to sell automobile tires. Printed ads formed only a portion of a paper's content; broadcast ads dominated the radio waves when they were being aired. They occurred suddenly, catching listeners when they were unprepared and possibly unwilling to hear the sponsor's message. Stations also could not target their commercials; they simply beamed to whoever happened to be tuned in at the moment.

Getting and keeping the attention of the consumer, Frederick saw, was the real problem. Radio advertisers who treated their listeners as sober, intelligent buyers projected a stuffy image over the airwaves. The only way radio advertising could win the ear of the American public was to employ verbal and audio gimmickry. But modern shoppers did not accept, as their parents had, the inflated claims of disreputable advertisers. By reducing "*advertising to innuendo*; to delicate little hints, clever tricks, and sheer *name-consciousness*" broadcasting antagonized the very people it wanted to impress.[13]

As it turned out, Frederick overestimated the aesthetic sensibilities of audiences and underestimated the allure of free entertainment. Consumers were willing to put up with a few ads in return for their favorite programs. They did not mind occasional messages any more than readers resented having to flip past advertising copy to get to the second half of an article. The public knew radio could sell, and when advertising agencies devised snappy commercials, listeners rapidly became customers. Newspapers and radio would eventually each secure definable advertising areas, but at the close of the 1920s it was unclear which markets were destined to belong to whom.[14]

COMPETITION AND DEPRESSION: TRAINING JUVENILES TO SELL

Economic depression in the early 1930s brought the simmering conflict to a boil. Following the crash of Wall Street, advertising revenue declined sooner and more radically for newspapers than for radio. Between 1929 and 1933, newspaper ad revenue decreased by nearly half; radio advertising did not begin to fall off until 1934.[15] In February 1933, L. J. Hoffmann, circulation manager of the *St. Louis Star-Times*, gave a speech before the Midwest Circulation Managers' Association. "It is very strange," he said, that radio's challenge to newspapers "is going on practically unabated." Radio was no longer a toy or novelty; it was becoming "a definite menace" to newspapers. During the 1932 presidential election, CBS had gotten a jump on the nation's publishers by airing live election returns throughout the night. By the time readers received their papers the next morning, the news that Roosevelt had won was hardly news at all. With more and more stations broadening coverage, newspapers were losing their exclusive control of reporting the day's events. Of course papers could not stop stations from recounting the news, but they were under no obligation to assist in their own demise by printing radio program announcements for their readers. "Radio and the newspaper industry are in a serious fight," Hoffmann concluded, "and the newspaper industry is getting the worst of it."[16]

Large, well-capitalized publishers moved to check the advance of broadcasting by purchasing or establishing stations of their own. If radio did not flourish, their newspapers would continue to function as before. If radio grew, their operations would grow along with it. In any case, they stood to gain. The real losers in the contest between print

and broadcasting were independent publishers who relied upon newspaper advertising to survive, and circulation managers, who were expected to keep newspaper sales high without exercising much power to
affect the outcome of events. The best that circulation men could expect
was a return to the status quo, where newspapers vied among themselves for a community's attention; the worst was increased competition for a shrinking share of the advertising market.

One might have expected circulation managers at independent newspapers to take the lead in promoting juvenile sales training as a foil to
broadcasting. But managers who worked for multimedia firms (that is,
enterprises engaged both in printing a newspaper and operating a
broadcasting station) were more familiar with radio, and it was they
who formed a coherent salesmanship movement. These men toiled on
the front line of the print-radio war, in situations of extreme occupational stress. The career of Harold Hough, circulation manager at the
Fort Worth Star-Telegram, illustrates the contradictory economic demands that managers faced during the Depression. Hough was, first
and foremost, a newspaper man. In speaking to fellow circulators he offered consolation to those fighting a losing battle with radio. "We find
ourselves confronted with the cold fact that the article we have been exclusively selling and distributing all our lives," he told managers in
1935, "is now being delivered to our customers faster than we can get it
there, and that article, as you well know, is *news*." Hough knew just
how powerful a medium broadcasting was, for the publisher of the
Star-Telegram also owned a broadcasting station that provided detailed news coverage. The publisher believed his station was so important that he selected seasoned leadership to oversee its operations. The
station's manager was . . . Hough! "During the day my job is to try to
sell the news, and during the night I am working to give away the stuff
I have been trying so hard all day to sell. I am riding the fence, and,
brother, the rail is getting pretty sharp." Hough fretted over serving
two masters, but finally resolved, "It's a problem for the editors."[17]

In truth, the commercial threat of radio offered no obvious solution. As
late as 1938, managers were striving to neutralize the implications of radio and recover their lost share of the media market. Circulation men
were annoyed with broadcasting, manager George H. Mitchell remarked
that year, because it "has taken away so much advertising revenue that
publishers everywhere have been looking for some new mine to tap, some
way to make up this great loss to radio." Responding to radio was a difficult assignment, for managers had no way to match the speed with which
it brought the news into people's homes. Mitchell feared technological ad-
vancements would soon make the situation even worse. Stations were experimenting with "facsimile transmission, a system of providing home
newspapers by radio." The day was not distant when customers might

wake up in the morning to find a fresh copy of the evening's news neatly printed beside their personal facsimile receiver.

This novelty was still in the planning stages, but the threat of television, Mitchell observed, already existed. Radio listeners longed to see the people and events that were described over the air. Television, which displayed live, moving images, could inflict far more damage on newspaper readership than radio. It was already a success in Britain (viewers within a 50-mile radius of London had recently watched the English Derby), and as soon as the mechanics were perfected American networks would "be right in there with both feet." Mitchell felt newspapers needed to meet these new challenges head-on. 'This is too big a fight to lose," he said. He suggested running more photos in newspapers and thought publishers should band together in negotiating ad policies with multimedia conglomerates.[18]

These were worthwhile prescriptions, but they offered little to managers who were struggling to ensure the solvency of their papers. Managers adopted several broad strategies to boost industry revenues. First, they argued that retail prices for their product were artificially low in relation to other goods. Many papers had kept the same price for years; when publishers did raise prices, income more than covered any drop in readership. Within a short time customers accepted the higher price and lost readers returned, making the price change doubly advantageous to newspapers. Managers also pushed for higher wholesale rates to distributors, news outlets and carriers. Since there were few opportunities for paid work open to boys under sixteen, juvenile carriers had few options but to absorb the price hike. Here and there adult middlemen refused the new rate, but all wholesalers depended on a steady flow of papers, and when newspapers instituted revisions they were obliged to go along with the new pricing structures.[19]

A third strategy for enhanced revenues existed: Sell more papers. This was an exquisitely simple objective to express, and an extraordinarily difficult one for managers to achieve. With daily newspaper advertising on the decline after 1930, publishers cut promotional budgets, depriving managers of the ability to mount the kinds of highly publicized solicitation campaigns they had relied on in the past. In many cases departmental personnel consisted of a staff of district managers and a large force of carrier boys recruited from local sales areas. The possibilities for profit that these boys represented was too great for cash-strapped managers to ignore. "During this present business depression," J. C. VanBenthem of the *San Francisco News* said in 1931, "it is to the advantage of all of us to operate as economically as possible. One sure way of accomplishing this is with more intensified work among our carrier boys." A well-trained carrier organization, together with a good newspaper, was the best hedge against declining revenue.

VanBenthem estimated that over 90 percent of his fellow managers preferred using minors to adults. However, this may have been overstating the proportion of managers who favored boys over men. In a comprehensive ICMA survey conducted the following year, one-third of the 919 managers who were contacted indicated they still used solicitors to increase city readership. But there is little doubt that the trend toward using boys to sell, which began after World War I, gained momentum during the 1930s.[20]

Attempting to stave off radio with reduced funds, managers abandoned the costly "professional door bell ringer" in ever greater numbers.[21] "I have conferred with many circulators in the past year," I. Isenberg of the *Jersey City Journal* announced in the fall of 1933 "and find that they are all turning to the carrier boy for new business. They are fully convinced that the carrier boy is the one who produces the best business at the least possible cost." The next year circulation head Don R. Davis of the *Birmingham (AL) News* told how newspapers had profited from juvenile workers. "Through the proper development of the boy carrier, many publishers have, during the past four years, saved many thousands of dollars that would have been paid out to solicitors." By carefully selecting appropriate candidates for sales training, newspapers were enjoying cost-effective, dependable service in spite of the depressed state of the American economy.[22]

CONCLUSION

Managers understood the appeal of a polite boy at the door and recognized that radio, for all its influence, never actually came face-to-face with the listener. In the hands of the right youngster a newspaper was a compelling sales prop, capable of being held, opened and exhibited. Unlike radio, which existed only in sound, it was "real."[23] From a promotional standpoint, print enjoyed a distinct advantage. Each day circulation men were given the opportunity to interact with readers through the daily ritual of delivering the news. Carriers handled customers' concerns quickly and efficiently; they also served as a newspaper's unofficial field representatives, reporting to managers and their subordinates what they learned on their routes. Seen in this context, training boys to engage the consumer on a house-by-house basis was the least expensive, most flexible answer to broadcasting. This insight vitalized the industry and explains why the concept of salesmanship, which managers had been flirting with on and off for fifteen years, did not finally become a national phenomenon until the early 1930s.

Through a range of instructional activities, including carrier sales schools, group training sessions and annual sales conventions, circulation managers prepared boys to market subscriptions to the general public. Radio alone did not lead to the enactment of these programs. Other factors, such as the emergence of a discrete culture of consumption during the interwar period and the aggressive promotional policies of the ICMA, played a critical part in the construction of salesmanship in newspaper home delivery. And not all managers believed radio was undermining their profession—some were ambiguous as to the ramifications of broadcasting, others believed that the two media could peacefully coexist. But many felt radio posed a serious threat, and this shared conviction provided a strong impetus for change.

By the latter part of the decade, the unbending fiscal logic of juvenile labor would convince circulation managers of the necessity of elevating schoolchildren to a position of prominence in the industry. In contrast to other contemporary trends that faded away when the economy recovered, carrier training programs left a lasting imprint on newspaper circulation. Newspaper boys would continue to market subscriptions long after prosperity returned and publishers recouped revenues lost in the wake of Black Tuesday. Motivated by the need to address intermedia competition during the Depression, circulation managers laid the groundwork for a unique, enduring alliance between newspapers and middle-class childhood in the United States.

NOTES

1. Boys had carried the news to readers since the dawn of printing in America, but papers did not begin to systematically train juveniles to market subscriptions until the Depression years. This training distinguishes twentieth-century route service from earlier forms of delivery work. For overviews of children in newspaper distribution see Alfred McClung Lee, *The Daily Newspaper in America: The Evolution of a Social Instrument* (New York: Macmillan Company, 1937), 287–300; William J. Thorn and Mary Pat Pfeil, *Newspaper Circulation: Marketing the News* (New York: Longman, 1987), 35–54 and David E. Whisnant, "Selling the Gospel News, or: The Strange Career of Jimmy Brown the Newsboy," *Journal of Social History* 5 (Spring 1972): 269–309.

Any discussion of carrier sales training must begin with the reports, talks, papers and annual proceedings generated by the ICMA. Founded in 1898 as the National Association Managers of Newspaper Circulation, the association served as the sole professional organization for circulation managers for most of this century. During the early to mid-1930s it had approximately eight hundred members in the United States and Canada. The ICMA was merged out of existence in 1992 when it, and six other organizations, formed the Newspaper Association of America. A brief review of the ICMA's history is provided in *ICMA Update* (June 1992): 1.

2. On the role of publishers in the debate see Edwin Emery, *History of the American Newspaper Publishers' Association* (Minneapolis: University of Minnesota Press, 1950) and George E. Lott, Jr., "The Press-Radio War of the 1930s," *Journal of Broadcasting* XIV: 3 (Summer 1970).

Print journalists are discussed in Gwenyth Jackaway, "America's Press-Radio War of the 1930s: A Case Study in Battles Between Old and New Media," *Historical Journal of Film, Radio and Television* 14: 3 (1994). A more complete treatment appears in Jackaway, "The Press-Radio War, 1924–1937: A Battle to Defend the Professional, Institutional and Political Power of the Press" (Ph.D. diss., University of Pennsylvania, 1992). For a discussion of broadcast industry policies during this period see Robert McChesney, *Telecommunications, Mass Media, and Democracy: The Battle for the Control of US Broadcasting, 1928–1935* (New York: Oxford University Press, 1993).

3. Royal W. Weller, "Evolution of the Newspaper Circulation Department," talk before the Inter-State Circulation Managers' Association, Wilmington, Delaware, September 15, 1925. Reproduced in *The Official Bulletin of the International Circulation Managers' Association* (September 1925): 8. Hereafter referred to as *ICMA Bulletin*. The ICMA was composed of subordinate regional bodies, including the Inter-State Circulation Managers' Association, which hosted meetings and special events throughout the year.

4. William R. Scott, *Scientific Circulation Management for Newspapers* (New York: Ronald Press Company, 1915), 280–90.

5. *Proceedings of the Nineteenth Annual Convention of the International Circulation Managers' Association* (1917): 120. Hereafter referred to as *ICMA Annual*.

6. "Makes Salesmen Carriers," in *ICMA Bulletin* (September 1922): 20; "School of Instruction Teaches Carriers How To Manage Their Routes In Business-like Fashion," *ICMA Bulletin* (November 1925): 30; *ICMA Annual* (Twenty-Eighth/1926): 35.

7. *ICMA Annual* (Twenty-Fourth/1922): 50, 54, 51.

8. "Promotion Through Carrier Organization," *ICMA Annual* (Twenty-Ninth/1927): 41–48; "Quality Circulation Stressed By I.C.M.A.," *Editor & Publisher*, June 23, 1928: 9.

9. *Historical Statistics of the United States: Colonial Times to 1970* (Washington, D.C.: U.S. Bureau of the Census, 1975), 796.

10. The phrase "wireless telephone" appears in an advertisement for radio handbooks featured in *ICMA Bulletin* (May 1922): 5.

11. "Radio, Bikes and Pogo-Sticks Prizes for Boy Circulation Getters," *Editor & Publisher*, June 10, 1922: 56.

12. "Service Newspapers Give Model for Other Business," *ICMA Bulletin* (September 1927): 4.

13. J. George Frederick, "Unable to Tell Sales Story, Radio is Doomed As Advertising Aid," *Editor & Publisher*, June 13, 1925: 3.

Early radio advertising is situated in a broader context in Stephen Fox, *The Mirror Makers: A History of American Advertising and Its Creators* (New York: William Morrow, 1984), 150.

14. This stability lasted until the advent of television, when advertising boundaries would again be redrawn.

15. Frank Luther Mott, *American Journalism: A History of Newspapers in the United States Through 260 Years: 1690 to 1950*, rev. ed. (New York: Macmillan Company, 1956), 675, 679.

16. "Hoffmann Calls Radio Menace to Newspapers in Bristling Paper Read at Midwest Meeting," *ICMA Bulletin* (March 1933): 19–22. The 1932 election is discussed in Edward Bliss Jr., *Now the News: The Story of Broadcast Journalism* (New York: Columbia University Press, 1991), 40–41.

17. Hough is quoted in *Editor & Publisher*, June 22, 1935: 10.

18. George H. Mitchell, "Radio's Position in the Eyes of the Circulation Manager," *ICMA Annual* (Fortieth/1938): 99–102.

19. On raising retail prices see Russell Stokley, "Effect of Price Raise on Circulation," in *ICMA Annual* (Thirty-Sixth/1934): 35–42. Frank Newell of the *Toledo Blade* argued that declining revenue left papers with no choice but to hike wholesale rates. See *Editor & Publisher*, June 24, 1933: 9–10.

20. J. C. VanBenthem, "Promotion Through Carrier Organization," paper read at the California Circulation Managers' Association, Santa Barbara, Autumn 1931. Reproduced in *ICMA Bulletin* (November 1931): 12. The survey results are presented in *ICMA Annual* (Thirty-Fourth/1932): 65. Of course, many of the papers employing solicitors may also have used juvenile carriers to sell.

21. This derogatory term for adult solicitors appeared in a talk given by Alton H. Adams before the New York Circulation Managers' Association in Utica in late 1930. See "Building Carrier Morale," reprinted in *ICMA Bulletin* (November 1930): 26.

22. "Best Plan Hour," paper read to the Interstate Circulation Managers' Association. Reprinted in *ICMA Bulletin* (January 1934): 16; *American Newspaper Publishers' Association Bulletin*, April 16, 1934: 186.

23. Or, as a popular saying went, "You can't wrap a fish with radio."

Trial by Fire:
Newspaper Coverage of the
Nuremberg Proceedings

Jessica C. E. Gienow-Hecht

During the 1991 Gulf War, Western journalists and politicians rallied behind the idea of charging Iraqi President Saddam Hussein with international war crimes. German foreign minister Hans-Dietrich Genscher noted the similarities between Iraqi atrocities and those of Nazi war criminals tried in Nuremberg after World War II. Amnesty International denounced Saddam's violation of international law and his annihilation of the Kurds, calling for an international tribunal to prevent further bloodshed. Even U.S. President Bush considered international legal action along the lines of Nuremberg. With this measure he hoped to condemn the Iraqi conflagration and prevent further mass murders. Half a decade later, the international community again invoked the Nuremberg proceedings when condemning crimes against humanity in the course of the Bosnian-Serbian conflict.

In both cases, the supporters of an international trial ignored the underlying purpose of the International Court in 1945/46. The Nuremberg trial formed part of a larger reeducation program that the Allies envisioned for the reconstruction of Germany in their effort to transform the defeated country into a member of modern Western civilization. Today, nobody considers the reeducation of the Iraqi, Bosnian or Serbian people in order to prevent further battles in the Middle East and Eastern Europe. None of the contemporary cases reflects the idealism on the part of the judges nor the clear-cut division between judges and defendants present in 1945. Current calls for international tribunals for vague "crimes against humanity" and "war crimes" reflect a spirit of vengeance untethered to education or enlightenment.

A closer look at selected commentators on the Nuremberg proceedings reveals why this trial does not provide us with an example for future international trials. This study investigates a tool of reeducation that the U.S. military government in Germany (OMGUS) used when, for the first time in history, a victorious nation set out to reform its defeated opponent. The American newspaper *Neue Zeitung*, published in Munich, Frankfurt/Main and Berlin between 1945 and 1955, appeared with the explicit purpose of "reeducating" the German population in the U.S. zone.[1] Officially the paper was designed as a propaganda tool to familiarize the defeated people with American political values and viewpoints. The editors, however, maintained enough room for their German readers' arguments, which were often markedly adverse to Allied opinions, and even criticized the proceedings of the International Court. They displayed a sense of optimism and faith in their reeducational endeavor that is completely absent in contemporary media.

My key intention in examining the *Neue Zeitung*'s coverage of the proceedings is to retrace how the editors tried to bring the Nuremberg trial to public attention, which standpoint they took in their attempt to reconcile OMGUS' policy with their readers' individual opinions and how the population responded to their efforts. Analyzing the editors' method and argument, the first part of my chapter summarizes the background of the trial. Part two evaluates the reaction of the German people to the trial reflected in letters to the editor, public opinion polls and articles written by guest writers. The final section discusses the results of the editors' efforts and attempts to explain why their mission to reeducate and to inform ultimately failed.

SIDELIGHTS FROM NUREMBERG

> War, pogrom, kidnapping, holocaust and torture are sitting here in the dock. They are present as invisible giants right beside the defendants. We will hold the responsible accountable—but will that be a successful enterprise? Moreover: it must . . . be a successful enterprise . . . in any future case.[2]

On November 20, 1945, in the name of the four victorious powers of World War II, Sir Geoffrey Lawrence opened the first of 403 public sessions of the trial against major Nazi war criminals before the International Military Tribunal in Nuremberg, Germany.[3] During the following ten months, prosecutors from the United States, the Soviet

Union, Great Britain and France charged and tried twenty-three leading members of the German National Socialist Party who were statesmen and army officers of the Third Reich.[4] The court also tried various para-military and political organizations that had served the Nazi system: the SS, the SA, the Gestapo-SD, the Reich Cabinet, the High Command of the Armed Forces and the Leadership Corps of the Nazi Party.[5]

The charge was based on the so-called "conspiracy/criminal organi-zation plan"[6] that had been developed according to the hitherto rather vague principles of international law.[7] It accused defendants of four war crimes: the common plan of conspiracy, the crimes against peace, war crimes and crimes against humanity.[8] "The real complaining party at your bar is Civilization," the American chief prosecutor Robert H. Jackson adjured in his opening statement. "Civilization asks whether law is so laggard as to be utterly helpless to deal with crimes of this magnitude by criminals of this order of importance. It does not expect that you can make war impossible. It does expect that your juridical ac-tion will put the forces of International Law, its precepts, its prohibi-tions and, most of all, its sanctions, on the side of peace."[9]

The attorneys of the defense did not devalue the prosecution's charges. They contended that no penalty could be imposed if no law ex-isted prohibiting an act (*nulla poena sine lege*). Since the charges brought forth at Nuremberg had never been explicitly condemned be-fore by any international authority, the lawyers argued, the defendants could not be accused of having violated a law.[10]

One hundred witnesses testified, hundreds of documents were ex-amined and testimonies bearing thousands of signatures were pre-sented to the tribunal.[11] On September 30 and October 1, 1946, the judges announced the verdict: twelve death penalties, three sentences of life imprisonment, four sentences of imprisonment between ten and twenty years and three acquittals. The judges rejected the idea of *nulla poena sine lege* and declared "an attacker must know that he is doing wrong, and so far from it being unjust to punish him, it would be unjust if his wrongs were allowed to go unpunished."[12] They deemed aggres-sive war a crime per se. All participants in the preparation of aggres-sive war received an indictment of guilty.

From the beginning, OMGUS used Nuremberg as a tool for the Germans' recognition of their guilt and their reeducation. In 1945 the United States was pursuing a "policy of austerity" in Germany that or-dered harsh and merciless treatment of the local population. One of the most heatedly debated issues was the notion of "collective guilt," which deemed not only selected individuals but all German citizens guilty of the Nazi atrocities. According to a number of U.S. observers, the Germans had to recognize this "collective guilt" in order to establish a democracy.[13] A major instrument for this was the Information Control

Division (ICD), a subdivision of the War Department responsible for the German media system's reconstruction. The coverage of the Nuremberg trial as a shining example of denazification, ICD members hoped, would convince Germans of the necessity to root out all traces of Nazism. Confronting them with their catastrophic past would result in a broad moral and political reorientation erasing German militarism for all time.[14] U.S. authorities thus reconstructed and employed the moribund German media system to disseminate democratic ideas.

The *Neue Zeitung* began publication on October 18, 1945, one month before the trial began. Six to eight pages in length, it appeared twice a week and reached a circulation of 2.5 million,[15] eventually reaching all four zones and Berlin. The leading staff consisted of German-Jewish émigrés who had left the country in the 1930s and returned with the Allied Psychological Warfare Division during the final stages of the war in order to help reconstruct the German media. "Americanized" Germans could more knowingly address and engage the German population.[16] "The Neue Zeitung will be a factor in demonstrating to the German people the necessity of the tasks which lie ahead of them," General Dwight D. Eisenhower, Chief of Staff Supreme Allied Commander, wrote in the paper's first issue. "For all civilized nations on this earth, aggression is immoral; the Germans, however, have to be educated to this self-evident truth."[17]

Eisenhower's straightforward speech reflected a missionary zeal that many Germans found untenable. They appreciated the significance of the Nuremberg trial but did not grasp its legal basis nor could they identify with any of the parties represented. The presence of the victors as judges in Nuremberg repudiated the Allies' claim that they had no interest in punishing the entire German nation. It defied the notion that the lawyers in Nuremberg would be acting also on behalf of the German population.[18]

The editors of the *Neue Zeitung* recognized and addressed the Germans' suspicion. While U.S. authorities such as ICD chief General Robert McClure claimed that "the Germans do not need to develop their own view—the Germans have to be told," Hungarian-born editor Hans Habe respected his readers as civilized and intelligent people. He intended to reconcile both cultures by discussing the trial's implications and by inspiring a dialogue both among Germans and between Germans and Americans.[19]

The journalists started out with a campaign comprised of regular reports on the front page, a sequence of features titled "Nuremberg gallery," biographies of various participants, opinion polls, frequent editorials and a number of articles in the style section. Dry reports of the court proceedings were enhanced with essays on the human side of the trial. These included elaborate accounts of the various illnesses that the defendants all suddenly developed, their daily conduct in the court-room, as well as personal portrayals of defense counselors, prosecutors and judges.

The detailed coverage of daily events at Nuremberg formed a strik-ing contrast to the reporting of most German newspapers at this time, most of which devoted the bulk of their reports to local and regional events, but paid little attention to international affairs.[20] The *Neue Zeitung*'s reprint of many documents presented at Nuremberg, regular follow-up reviews of even the most minor decisions made by the court and the frequent repetition of previous court decisions were designed to keep Germans up-to-date. Sensational headlines captured readers' at-tention: "Gas Chambers and Operetta Music: The Auschwitz Trap," "They Made Soap of Human Bodies" or "The Man Who Never Regrets: For 13 Hours Göring Speaks on His Own Behalf."[21]

The significance of Nuremberg for the future of Germany and the prospect of international law formed a priority in the *Neue Zeitung*. The trial, Habe argued, would convince the world that not all Germans had been National Socialists. Not Germany, but National Socialism and its supporters were on trial.[22] Aligned with chief prosecutor Jackson's the-ory of two different Germanies, one good, one bad, the editors saw the significance of Nuremberg in the promotion of the "good" Germany. "The National Socialists attempted to identify with Germany and Germany with themselves," the paper wrote in November 1945. "Only after the iron curtain over Germany was lifted, did America have an opportunity to see whether there were really 'two kinds of Germany.' "[23]

Next on the editors' list stood Nuremberg's promotion of a democra-tic legal system in contrast to Hitler's manipulation of the courts. One report, for example, juxtaposed Jackson's cross-examination of Her-mann Göring with the examination techniques of Nazi prosecutor Robert Freisler who tried the conspirators of July 1944.[24] The treat-ment of a defendant as a dignified human being, the readiness to give this person a chance to defend himself and the exhaustive examination of evidence served as a model of democratic proceedings that Germans should adapt for the future: "What happens today in Germany seems to be unique for a defeated nation," the paper wrote in February 1946. "Germans are being informed by order that they cannot be deprived of their property and their freedom without a regular trial."[25]

Moreover, Nuremberg would send two important messages to the world. First, "a criminal policy which is deliberately aimed at genocide is finally given the definition it deserves: it is a common crime that is as punishable as any other crime." This dispute would institute a new law.[26] Second, Nuremberg would create a device to prevent coming wars if the community of nations came to an agreement about how to legally punish aggressive war and mass murder.[27] In order to achieve these goals, however, Nuremberg had to clarify the issue of culpability in Nazi Germany: Who was guilty?[28]

The question of guilt formed the bulk of the *Neue Zeitung*'s trial coverage. "[H]ow large is the ignorance on the part of the Germans concerning the German war crime," the editors asked quoting a Swiss newspaper on October 21, 1945. In any case "the German people will have to pay the bill for the Second World War for which its government is responsible."[29] This line reflected the *Neue Zeitung*'s standpoint on Germany's culpability for the next several months. It echoed Jackson's rejection of collective guilt in his opening speech on November 22 in which he stated that "crimes are always committed only by individuals."[30]

The *Neue Zeitung* published an analysis of Jackson's speech written by the American journalist Louis Lochner. Lochner noted that the prosecution differentiated between Nazi criminals and the German people and that one could not make Germans exclusively responsible. The international community had helped prepare the way for a situation "where the German people could easily become the victim of delusion and the National Socialist conspiracy."[31] Lochner urged the world to distinguish between the active guilt of collaboration and the passive guilt of nonresistance.

Another commentary titled "Guilt and Debt" explained Germany's collective liability in a metaphorical way: "If I had a brother who had deprived somebody of his property and someone came and said I was guilty, then this would be an unjust charge. But if somebody said because I was the thief's brother I should help to return the stolen good or its material value to the person that has been robbed, I would answer without any hesitation: 'I will do so.' I would have to reject the guilt but not the debt."[32] Germans had to foot the bill for the Nazi Reich not because they had actively participated in the genocide but because they were Germans; they were not *guilty* but *responsible*. This formula became essential to the editors' attempt to bridge the mutual suspicion between their German readers and the Allies.

Nonetheless writers of the *Neue Zeitung* familiarized readers with many different arguments. They quoted French prosecutor Charles Dubost's claim that Germans were a nation of latecomers who had only entered the circle of civilized people in the year A.D. 800 but had never really replaced their inherent inclination for tyranny with modern virtue.[33] The Germans "proved to be particularly weak when confronted with the demons due to their incredible instability," Swiss psychiatrist Carl G. Jung concluded according to the *Neue Zeitung*. "For the psychologist the question of collective guilt is a fact . . . and it will be one of the most important tasks of therapy to make the Germans acknowledge this guilt.[34] Yet the editors' comments consistently reflected their disapproval of the concept of "collective guilt."[35]

One of the most intriguing questions arising, from the complex problem of active and passive guilt was the issue of military obedience. At Nuremberg, defendant Wilhelm Keitel argued that German soldiers who had been bound by oath to the Führer could not be charged for nonresistance.[36] Even U.S. lawyers and soldiers criticized the court's decision that implied that every army man should evaluate the morality of each order before acting on it. Officials in the War Department wondered aloud what would have happened to them if they had not been on the victorious side. Yet the *Neue Zeitung* disagreed because "the actions for which he [*the soldier, J.G.*] now has to stand up before his judges have nothing in common with honor but are a result of just the opposite, namely the neglect of duty."[37]

GERMAN REACTIONS

As the trial progressed the *Neue Zeitung* shifted focus from the question of guilt and responsibility to the Germans' awareness of it. The editors urged their readers to confront the trial and their past. Germany's leading role as promotor of science, ethics and culture had given way to moral decay, disregard of human values and a totalitarian regime. In order to "digest" this past, the Nuremberg proceedings needed to generate a critical discussion about the Nazi crimes among the German people. "If you want," one editor marveled in March 1946, "Nuremberg will lay the foundation for a new foreign policy but only if the Germans are willing to learn from their errors of the past."[38]

For a time it appeared as if at least some German readers responded to American expectations. In numerous letters to the editor, readers commented on the Nuremberg trial, expressing confusion over their current political status and concerns about their future in the international arena. On the issue of collective guilt, readers articulated a variety of views. Many claimed to have lived through a twelve-year-long nightmare of unconfirmed suspicions of Nazi atrocities. "Did the individual German know for sure whether the piece of soap he used did not contain some remainders of the victims?" reader Martin Meier asked. "Or whether the bread he ate was not made of grain grown on the artificial fertilizer produced from these innocent dead people?"[39] Other letters did not grant leniency for protests of ignorance. Reader Paul Distelbarth urged his fellow countrymen to accept their responsibility as a necessary first step to a new beginning: "Every act of guilt must be followed by repentence, otherwise . . . it will poison your entire life until one day, the abscess bursts open. The abscess Hitler originated in the fact that the German people did not accept their culpability after World War I but denied it."[40]

"Such letters," editor Habe observed in a general evaluation of these writings, "are, far beyond their actual content, messengers of better times that grow out of thought—just as the National Socialist epoch grew out of thoughtlessness."[41] Habe supported public discussion by offering space for all opinions on his "Free for all" page, even if writers sought to justify Germany's turn to Hitler. "Don't you see that it was the defeated people of World War I who in all their desperation subscribed to a regime of terror?" Alfons Reuß asked on February 4, 1946. "This was done by nations who had lost their most precious good. . . . Is it any wonder, then, that under these circumstances the belief in sheer power becomes so attractive?"[42]

Most letters to the editor approved of the trial in general but criticized the actual proceedings. An opinion poll taken by the *Neue Zeitung* in February 1946 revealed that many readers had difficulties understanding the legitimacy of an international court in which victors tried to defeat losers judicially after having subjugated them militarily. Anglo-Saxon law that formed the basis for the trial remained a mystery to French, Russian and German lawyers trained in the continental school.[43] German lawyers doubted the legality of the trial because there existed no clause in international law that would justify Nuremberg.[44] The Kellogg-Briand Pact of 1928 condemned the crimes with which the defendants were charged but did not prescribe any method of punishment.

Moreover, lawyers practicing in the United States came to the Germans' defense, doubting that any war could be judged as a crime at all. They rejected the idea of an *ex post facto law* and pointed to the war guilt committed by the United States, including Hiroshima.[45] The *Neue Zeitung*, conversely, echoed Jackson's opinion that aggressive war had been recognized as a war crime before the Nazis came to power.[46]

Some Germans complained that Nuremberg came too late and called for the trial's speedy conclusion.[47] The editors of the *Neue Zeitung*, conversely, believed that much time was needed to find and convict the truly guilty and to discern the criminals' guilt judicially: "The trials did not come too late, they could only have come too early. Delay means thoroughness, postponement means conscience."[48]

One of the most often heard complaints was the charge that the only Germans who were allowed to participate in the trial were the defense counsels.[49] If it was true, as the American prosecutor had said, that the trial was held on behalf of the German nation, why then did nobody accuse the twenty-three defendants of the harm they had done to the German people? "It would be only logical and an act of justice to those Germans who have fought such a desperate and sacrificing combat against fascism," the *Neue Presse* wrote in March 1946, "if this Göring would also be convicted for his arson by a German prosecutor and in the name of the German people."[50] Why was there no German prosecutor? Why were Germans not permitted to sit among the audience?

Some critics even demanded that at least one of the judges should be a German because the defendants should not only be charged with their crimes against other nations but also with their manipulation of the German people.[51]

Habe initially attempted to soothe those complaints by relating that many of the journalists attending Nuremberg came from the newly re-constructed German press. The German news reporter, however, could not replace the German judge. Habe thus invoked a metaphor stating that the German defense counsels "professionally fight for the advantage of their clients and yet with their own personality they represent the 'other' Germany."[52] This argument must have struck every reader as extremely inappropriate—particularly since the defense counsels found themselves almost excluded from the German law community very soon after the trial's end.[53] But the *Neue Zeitung*'s increasingly ambiguous view was not the only reason for the subsequent rapid decline of readers' curiosity in Nuremberg. Discussions over survival problems, food shortages, general daily hardships and local politics gradually replaced concerns regarding Nuremberg.

The growing indifference toward the proceedings by the German people in turn elicited the international community's scorn, which now accused Germans of denying their past and their stake in Nuremberg. Travelling across Germany, the dean of a British cathedral observed that Germans were too occupied with their current hardships to ponder their recent past.[54] Meanwhile, the *New York Times* discerned that "one should think that the Nuremberg Trial takes place somewhere far away from Nuremberg, farther away even than from New York where the interest runs incomparably much deeper."[55]

The confrontation with the Nazi atrocities led many Germans into either denial or apathy. In February 1946, prosecuting attorneys presented the documentary "*Die Todesmühlen*" (The Mills of Death) that exposed the Holocaust of Nazi concentration camps in the Nuremberg courtroom. The film subsequently played in movie theaters throughout Germany. Most viewers showed no reaction or interpreted it as American propaganda. Why did people presume that this was not their concern, the *Neue Zeitung* asked. "Would it have been better not to confront them with reality? Did they not want to know the truth?"[56]

The question remained not only whether the German people were actively or passively guilty but why they were not willing to confront this problem. In February 1946, the editors investigated the widespread apathy among their readers. The foremost reason, they found, was pure emotional exhaustion. Said a young actress: "Our feelings, overly stressed by the sorrows of the war, are burnt out. We need a break."[57] After six years of war, immense material and personal loss, it was difficult to confront the sudden, shocking revelation that all hardships had not only been useless, but had even served a horrible end. One should have given people some time to recover, said a factory owner from Munich, rather than overwhelm them immediately with the whole bulk of evidence. "It is like after a long period of illness or after a heavy blow," said a neurologist. "You say: In order to recover, you may not look backwards but you must forget, look to the future and make a new start. But you can only make a new start when you have finished something else first."[58] Young people in particular refused to engage in the debate. When asked to write their impressions of the Nuremberg trial, students of the University of Aachen countered that such an assignment lay beneath their dignity.[59]

Ultimately the editors' interest declined with the curiosity of their readers. In early spring 1946, Habe recalled his star reporter from the trial and restricted coverage to pure news reporting from Nuremberg. Editorials diminished and became focused on daily events or sarcastic observations rather than on the trial's larger implications. Letters to the editor concerning Nuremberg soon disappeared altogether.

This development roused the scorn of the international press. OMGUS blamed the *Neue Zeitung* for covering the trials insufficiently.[60] But since U.S. officials overall exercised little pressure on their press delegates in 1945–46, the journalists of the *Neue Zeitung* continued to shape their paper according to their own dictates.

Even during the final weeks of the trial, in fall 1946, the *Neue Zeitung* only marginally revived its reporting of the proceedings. It refrained from commenting on the final statements despite some of the defendants' pleas that almost compelled journalistic reflection.[61] The editors instead restricted themselves with cynical remarks on the defendants' behavior: "What poorer account could they give of themselves than claiming 'to have never entered a concentration camp?' "[62]

Toward the very end of the proceedings in 1946, the editors revived their earlier zeal. They devoted the entire issue of October 2, 1946, to the trial, after the tribunal had announced the final verdict. News reporting, commentaries of the foreign press and, for the first time in several months, a long editorial that underscored once again the significance of the trial dominated that day's copy.[63] The most important significance of Nuremberg, the editors concluded, was its warning to the world that genocide would henceforth be punished with the death penalty. Furthermore, Nuremberg provided Germany's path back into the circle of civilized nations. "The fundamental horror that man feels for death, no matter who actually dies, is such a human standard. Its use was prohibited in Nazi Germany because such a standard confirms the link from one human being to the other."[64]

A wave of popular disapproval in Germany after the announcement of the verdict may have accounted for the editors' renewed interest.

After months of silence, apathy or denial, Germans began to discuss the trial in newspapers, at work and in political assemblies. Leaders in the British and the American zones demanded the immediate arrest of the acquitted in order to try them before a German court. They encouraged locals to press their respective state governments into legal action. In Berlin, 250,000 workers struck in protest against the verdict and threatened to lynch those who the court had not sentenced to death.[65] In a way, these reactions seemed to contradict the Germans' initial resistance to the proceedings. Yet the manner in which people manifested their scorn against the acquittals and their threat to take action themselves, pointed to the same urge they had displayed before: They wanted to forget Nazism. Once Americans had seemed suspect because of their rigor during the proceedings. Now they were distrusted for their laxity.

Yet the editors of the *Neue Zeitung* welcomed this sudden popular unrest as a "good sign" for the future of German democracy. Finally the people did what the journalists had tried to inspire before. They spoke up, they took a stand in the trial, they participated in the international debate in a way that extended beyond the editors' expectations. "Even if the proceedings and the judgment of Nuremberg had no other consequence than this one, it would turn the trials into a path-breaking event in German history."[66]

CONCLUSION

As my study shows, the Information Control Division founded the *Neue Zeitung* with the explicit purpose of reeducating German postwar society in the U.S. zone and of confronting it with its guilt. The Nuremberg trial was supposed to act as a catalyst for that enterprise. An analysis of the articles relating to Nuremberg demonstrates that the editors initially centered their coverage on two major issues: the debate over German war guilt; and the significance of the Nuremberg trial for Germany and the international community. Both themes formed the core of U.S. officials' vision for a new postwar world order: a non-aggressive, democratic Germany and an intentionally accepted standard of ethics that would facilitate a peaceful world order.

Yet, at the same time, ICD members were lackadaisical in the implementation of their policy. American officials in the State and War Departments failed to supply their proconsuls in Germany with clear-cut orders, which in turn led to a widespread confusion over U.S. goals among the latter. Because of that, ICD officials allowed their "explicit" purpose to become diluted. In this vacuum of power, the editors of the *Neue Zeitung*—most of whom were not American-born—came to enjoy great autonomy and editorial freedom.[67]

Habe and his staff realized that in order to "popularize" the Nuremberg trial they had to address the Germans' unstated grievances. In doing so, they made a unique effort to reach the German population but were only partially successful. The reason for this lay not only in their readers' peculiar interpretation of the trial but in the Allies' persistent disregard of German viewpoints as well.

The editors echoed Jackson's opinion that a new jurisdiction, as well as a method to predict and to avert future wars, would open a new era in world history. They also departed from the widespread notion of German collective guilt. They judiciously considered the appropriateness of the proceedings. They debated the distinction between those who were actively guilty and those who were passively liable. They never contradicted the official American standpoint, as represented by chief prosecutor Jackson, but expressed criticism "through the back door" via letters to the editor, opinion polls and guest articles.

The reaction of the Germans, in turn, was characterized by skepticism, then suspicion and, finally, apathy. Some denied any guilt, claiming not to have actively participated in the genocide and thus abandoning the scheme of collective responsibility altogether. Others admitted some liability but cited overwhelming state control for their inability to resist. Few Germans acknowledged the idea of collective responsibility.

Readers of the *Neue Zeitung* in particular doubted the legality of the trial. While most acknowledged the need for a war crime trial, they did not agree with the deliberations at Nuremberg. Many could never abide the conversion of the victorious powers into neutral judges on a tribunal that admitted no German lawyer. The fact that the German people themselves were not given a voice as prosecutors on the tribunal alienated many readers. Feeling themselves as losers on all grounds, abused by their former regime and despised by the victors, most Germans eventually retreated into undiluted passivity.

The editors of the *Neue Zeitung* initially misread German apathy for German disinterest. What seemed to be a lukewarm response was in reality disguised anger. When the journalists came to doubt the efficacy of publicizing the trial to stimulate reeducation and consequently ceased to prioritize Nuremberg, they misinterpreted their readers' stoicism as passivity. Germans were actually outraged at their former leaders for having wrecked the country. Most people regarded the sentences as too lenient.

Ultimately the original mission to publicize the Nuremberg trial and to disseminate the idea of collective responsibility of the editors was successful only to a limited extent. Their campaign backfired when Germans began to view themselves not as collectively responsible but as collectively victimized. This frustrated the editors' effort to mitigate

mutual suspicions between occupiers and civilians, as well as to reconcile American official occupation policy with German postwar perspectives. Unable to resolve the dilemma between their function as a tool of
reeducation on the one hand, and their desire to listen to the native
population on the other, the journalists eventually reacted similarly to
their German readers—furious over their own helplessness they retreated into a passivity that was really a veiled vehemence.[68]

Those who cite Nuremberg today as a model for contemporary war
crime trials should remember that a unique conglomeration of historical events allowed for such a trial. In 1945 there were victors and
vanquished. American lawyers who dominated the proceedings still believed that mental reeducation, regardless of the costs of such an enterprise, could change men and nations. No contemporary case aligns
with this historical constellation and idealism.

NOTES

1. Norbert Frei, "Die Presse," in *Die Bundesrepublik Deutschland*, vol III,
Kultur, ed. Wolfgang Benz (Frankfurt a. M.: Fischer Taschenbuch Verlag,
1989), 274–76; Hans Habe, *Im Jahre Null. Ein Beitrag zur Geschichte der
deutschen Presse* (Munich: Verlag Kurt Desch GmbH, 1966), 27, 87; Heinz-
Dietrich Fischer, *Reeducations- und Pressepolitik unter britischem Besatz-
ungsstatus* (Dusseldorf: Droste Verlag, 1978), 22.

2. Erich Kästner, "Streiflichter aus Nürnberg," *Neue Zeitung*, München
(henceforth quoted as *NZ*), Nov. 23, 1945, Feuilleton.

3. The trial led by the International Military Tribunal opened up a whole
series of other trials that subsequently took place in Nuremberg. Klaus-Jörg
Ruhl, *Die Besatzer und die Deutschen. Amerikanische Zone 1945–1948* (Düsseldorf: Droste verlag, 1980), 137. Bradley F. Smith, *Reaching Judgment at Nuremberg* (New York: Basic Books, 1963), xiii.

4. Of the twenty-three accused, only twenty-one men were present to hear
the final verdict. Robert Ley, chief of all Nazi organizations since 1937, founder of
the "Labor Front" and the leisure organization "Strength through Joy" committed suicide in his prison cell on October 25, 1945. Martin Bormann, head of the
party chancellery since 1941, could not be found after the German capitulation.
In 1973, a West German court officially pronounced him dead. Ann Tusa and
John Tusa, *The Nuremberg Trial* (New York: Atheneum, 1984), 40–41, 134, 494.

5. Comprising roughly 2 million members, those organizations were dealt
with as abstract entities.

6. American influences shaped the proceedings as well as the rhetoric at
Nuremberg. The London Charter ratified by the four powers in the summer of
1945, which laid down the actual trial system, was merely a reflection of a plan
created almost exclusively in Washington, D.C., by a group of American officials.
Bradley F. Smith, *The Road to Nuremberg* (New York: Basic Books, 1981), 4.

7. International law condemned the disregard of humanity and the
planned breach of international peace. In the Kellogg-Briand Pact of 1928

Belgium, Germany, France, Great Britain and her Commonwealth, Ireland, Italy, Japan, Poland, Czechoslovakia and the United States agreed to renounce war as an instrument of national policy and to solve all international disputes by peaceful means. The signers condemned aggressive war as a crime, but declared a self-defensive war to be a legal means for upholding national sovereignty. By 1938 nearly fifty more states had signed this treaty. It later formed the core of the charges against Nazi Germany brought forth at Nuremberg. William J. Bosch, *Judgment on Nuremberg: American Attitudes Toward the Major German War-Crime Trials* (Chapel Hill: University of North Carolina Press, 1970), 4ff.

8. Eugene C. Gerhart, *America's Advocate: Robert H. Jackson* (Indianapolis, New York: The Bobbs-Merrill Company, 1958), 355.

9. R. Falk, G. Kolko and Robert J. Lifton, *Crimes of War: A Legal, Political-Documentary and Psychological Inquiry into the Responsibility of Leaders, Citizens, and Soldiers for Criminal Acts in Wars* (New York: Random House, 1971), 87.

10. Wilbourn E. Benton and Georg Grimm, *Nuremberg: German Views of the War Trials* (Dallas: Southern Methodist University Press, 1955), 54.

11. Ibid., xiii.

12. See further excerpts of the judgment's text in J. M. Sweeney, C. T. Oliver and N. E. Leech, *Cases and Materials on the International Legal System* (Mineola, N.Y.: The Foundation Press, Inc., 1973), 694–707.

13. Joint Chiefs of Staff directive 1067 gave harsh instructions to U.S. officials ordering the denazification, decentralization, democratization and demilitarization of Germany. Douglas Botting, *From the Ruins of the Reich* (New York: Crown Publishers, Inc., 1985), 261; James Tent, *Mission on the Rhine* (Chicago: University of Chicago Press, 1982), 50–51; Rüdiger Liedtke, *Die verschenkte Presse. Die Geschichte der Lizenzierungen von Zeitungen nach 1945* (Berlin: Verlag für Ausbildung und Studium in der Elefanten Press, 1982), 226–28.

14. Harold Hurwitz, *Die Stunde Null der deutschen Presse. Die amerikanische Pressepolitik in Deutschland 1945–1949* (Cologne: Verlag Wissenschaft und Politik, 1972), 96–97.

15. Interview with Max Kraus, former deputy chief editor of the *Neue Zeitung*, July 6, 1991, Washington, D.C.; Hurwitz, *Stunde Null*, 101.

16. David Lerner, *Psychological Warfare Against Nazi-Germany: The Sykewar Campaign, D-Day to VE-Day* (Cambridge, Mass., London: The M.I.T. Press, 1949, c1971), 71–76.

17. "Geleitwort von General Eisenhower," *NZ*, Oct. 18, 1945, 1.

18. Hurwitz, *Stunde Null*, 105.

19. Hans Habe, a Hungarian Jew and journalist, immigrated to the United States in 1940 where he subsequently received U.S. citizenship. In 1944 he returned to Europe where he led the reconstruction of the German media system in the occupied territories. From October 1945 to March 1946 he served as editor-in-chief of the *Neue Zeitung*. Office of Strategic Services, Foreign Nationalities Branch, "Habe-Bekessy, Hans," Microfilm No. INT-15HU-522, National Archives, Washington, D.C.; Elizabeth Matz, *Die Zeitungen der US Armee für die deutsche Bevölkerung 1944–46* (Münster: Verlag C.J. Fahle GmbH, 1969), 27, 44; Habe, *Im Jahre Null*, 86; Frei, "Presse," 276.

20. One of the first measures taken by the U.S. forces in their respective occupation zone had been the destruction of the Nazi propaganda machine. Between the end of the war and the establishment of the Federal Republic in May 1949 the Allies restricted the German press market to "licensed" newspapers and magazines. Norbert Frei, "Die Presse," 278. Peter J. Humphreys, *Media and Media Policy in West Germany: The Press and Broadcasting since 1945* (New York: Berg, 1990), 27.

21. *NZ*, Dec. 24, 1945, 6; Feb. 1, 1946, 2; Feb. 22, 1946, 1; March 18, 1946, 1. The right-hand man and successor of the Führer, Adolf Hitler, Hermann Göring was the second most important leader in Nazi Germany. Prussian minister of the interior and commander-in-chief of the Prussian police and gestapo, he was coresponsible for the concentration camps for opponents and for the dramatic reduction of civil rights and press freedom. Tusa and Tusa, *Nuremberg Trial*, 497.

22. "Beweise in Nuremberg," *NZ*, Nov. 26, 1945, 1; Hans Habe, "Nürnberger Tagebuch," *NZ*, Nov. 26, 1945, 3.

23. Hans Habe, "Mißverstandene Solidarität," *NZ*, Nov. 30, 1945, 2; "Alfred statt Gustav Krupp," *NZ*, Nov. 15, 1945, 1.

24. "Göring im Kreuzverhor," *NZ*, March 22, 1946, 1.

25. *New York Herald Tribune*, reprinted in *NZ*, Feb. 2, 1946, 2.

26. "Nürnberger Verteidigung," *NZ*, July 8, 1945, 3.

27. Erich Kästner, "Nürnberg und die Historiker," *NZ*, April 4, 1946, Feuilleton.

28. Karl Jaspers, "Tagesfragen im Ausschnitt," *NZ*, April 1, 1946, 2.

29. *Baseler Nachrichten*, quoted in *NZ*, Oct. 21, 1945, 2.

30. Tusa and Tusa, *Nuremberg Trial*, 155.

31. Louis Lochner, "Über die Anklage," *NZ*, Nov. 16, 1945, 3.

32. Erich Kästner, "Schuld und Schulden," *NZ*, Dec. 3, 1945, Feuilleton.

33. "Ruckfall um zwölf Jahrhunderte: Französischer Ankläger verlangt die Todesstrafe in Nuremberg," *NZ*, Feb. 4, 1946, 1.

34. Quoted in Erich Kästner, "Splitter und Balken," *NZ*, Feb. 8, 1946, Feuilleton. Psychiatrists in the United States agreed that a "propensity to the fanatical, and even delusional, thinking in Germans is indeed striking to those who come into contact with them." Bosch, *Judgment on Nuremberg*, 223.

35. Kästner, "Splitter und Balken."

36. Field Marshall since 1940, Wilhelm Keitel was Adolf Hitler's instrument in military affairs and a member of the Secret Cabinet Council and the Council for the Defence of the Reich. Smith, *Reaching Judgment at Nuremberg*, 498. Bosch, *Judgment on Nuremberg*, 166–82.

37. "Soldatische Ehrbegriffe," *NZ*, March 8, 1946, 3.

38. "Nürnberg und die Geschichte," *NZ*, March 29, 1946, 2.

39. Martin Meier, Hofgiebing, "Die Schuld, nicht die Unschuld," *NZ*, Sept. 29, 1946, 5.

40. Paul Distelbarth, "Die Faust des Siegers," *NZ*, April 29, 1946, 5.

41. Hans Habe, "Erzwungene Solidarität?," *NZ*, Jan. 4, 1946, 2.

42. Alfons Reuß, "Kassel," *NZ*, Feb. 4, 1946, 3.

43. The concept of the crime of conspiracy, for example, that in English Common Law dates back to the late middle ages, was unknown on the Euro-

pean continent. In Nuremberg the entire evidence lay in the prosecution's hands, who were reluctant to pass it to the German defense counsels. Werner Maser, *Nürnberg: Tribunal der Sieger* (Düsseldorf: Econ-Verlag, 1977), 546, 577.

44. "Beginn in Nürnberg: 20 Angeklagte beteuern ihre Unschuld," *NZ*, Nov. 23, 1945, 45, 2.

45. Bosch, *Judgment on Nuremberg*, 50, 54, 131, 142.

46. "Der Nürnberger Prozeß," *NZ*, Nov. 12, 1945, 3, 4.

47. Letter to the editor, "Nürnberger Verteidigung," *NZ*, July 8, 1946, 3.

48. "Der verzögerte Prozeß," *NZ*, Oct. 21, 1945, 3.

49. Arnold Arndt, letter to the editor, "Mißverstandene Solidarität," *NZ*, Dec. 12, 1945, 3.

50. *Neue Presse*, quoted in *NZ*, March 15, 1946, 3.

51. "Nürnberg und kein Interesse: Eine Untersuchung der Neuen Zeitung," *NZ*, Feb. 8, 1946, 3.

52. Hans Habe, "Nürnberger Tagebuch," *NZ*, Dec. 7, 1945, 3.

53. As a later article in the *Neue Zeitung* revealed, these "German European" attorneys ran the serious risk of becoming the pariahs of the German postwar community of lawyers. The Board of Attorneys of Cologne demanded a political checkup of the Nuremberg defense counsels because they had attempted to vindicate the atrocities of the Third Reich. "Freie Verteidigung," *NZ*, Oct. 4, 1946, 5.

54. "Unterhaltungen mit Deutschen," *NZ*, Jan. 7, 1946, 2.

55. "Die Parteiführer nach Nürnberg: Aus allen vier Besatzungszonen—Das mangelnde Interesse in Deutschland," *NZ*, Dec. 21, 1945, 3.

56. Erich Kästner, "Wert und Unwert des Menschen," *NZ*, Feb. 4, 1946, Feuilleton.

57. Quoted in "Nürnberg und kein Interesse: Eine Untersuchung der Neue Zeitung," *NZ*, Feb. 8, 1946, 3.

58. Ibid.

59. Kyong-Kun Kim, "Die Neue Zeitung im Dienste der Reeducation für die deutsche Bevölkerung 1945–1946" (Ph.D. diss., Ludwig-Maximilians-University, Munich, 1974), 144–45.

60. Hurwitz, *Stunde Null*, 106.

61. Jackson's final speech was reprinted on July 27, 1946. The American prosecutor condemned the defendants' blind loyalty to the Führer as well as their attempt in court to make Hitler alone responsible for their crimes. With one exception, all of the accused pleaded not guilty. Some even claimed an intention to resist Hitler's warfare. Others tried to hide behind the organization to which they had belonged, saying that it was the notorious SS (Schutzstaffel) or the powerful Nazi party that was to blame for the abominations of the terror regime. "Die Schlußrede Jacksons: 'Die Stärke der Anklage liegt in der Einfachheit des Falles,'" *NZ*, July 29, 1946, 2ff; "Das letzte Wort vor dem Nürnberger Urteilsspruch: Jeder Angeklagte proklamiert seine Schuldlosigkeit—Sie erkennen nur eine 'historische' keine 'juristische' Schuld," *NZ*, Sept. 2, 1946, 1; "Das letzte Wort im Nürnberger Urteilsspruch," *NZ*, Nov. 2, 1946, 1; Tusa and Tusa, *Nuremberg Trial*, 501.

62. "Beim Anblick der Einundzwanzig," *NZ*, Sept. 6, 1946, 1.

63. "Weltgeschichte, Weltgericht," *NZ*, Sept. 30, 1946, 1.

64. "Das Fazit von Nürnberg," *NZ*, Oct. 21, 1946, 11.

65. "Pfeiffer leitet Verfahren ein: Spruchkammeranklage gegen Schacht und Fritzsche in Vorbereitung," *NZ*, Oct. 7, 1946, 1.

66. "Gute Zeichen," *NZ*, Oct. 7, 1946, 7.

67. For further study, see Jessica C. E. Gienow, "Cultural Transmission and the U.S. Occupation in Germany: The U.S. Newspaper *Neue Zeitung*, 1945–1955" (Ph.D. diss., University of Virginia, Charlottesville, Va., 1995).

68. The *Neue Zeitung* existed for nine more years, though its circulation declined sharply in the late 1940s. The editors continued their efforts to reconcile American and German views, and to serve as a tool for reconstruction of the German postwar society. With the advent of the cold war, however, the paper's purpose shifted from being an instrument of reeducation to representing a bulwark of democratic thought against communism. In 1955, with the departure of the last American military agents, the *Neue Zeitung* ceased to publish.

From Counterculture to Over-the-Counter Culture: An Analysis of *Rolling Stone's* Coverage of the New Left in the United States from 1967–1975

David J. Atkin

Rolling Stone magazine's early tradition of investigative reporting of controversial issues that the mainstream press ignored, downplayed or missed is an important part of postmodern American press lore. Within months of its inception in 1967, the publication emerged as a leader among the alternative, or underground, press, fusing the music and politics of America's New Left.[1] In this regard, *Rolling Stone* became the standard-bearer for a new editorial genre that historians link to "a rebellion not only against the establishment but also against its conventional mass media."[2] But within the flowering of this new underground press lay the seeds of its own demise—a heavy editorial dependency upon the antiwar rhetoric of the New Left.

As a consequence, several of these alternative publications folded or declined in circulation as U.S. involvement in the Vietnam War subsided during the early 1970s.[3] Nevertheless, *Rolling Stone's* popularity continued to grow in mainstream as well as underground circles as it "fed the imaginations of daily reporters . . . in newsrooms across the country."[4]

Against this backdrop of social and market transition, *Rolling Stone* executed a series of editorial changes that assured its survival outside of the declining alternative press market. This chapter explores the extent to which these changing market imperatives influenced the magazine's coverage of the New Left. In particular, it offers a qualitative examination of *Rolling Stone*'s coverage, in accordance with Todd Gitlin's conception of reporting frames associated with hegemonic ideology.[5]

Although the latter-day *Rolling Stone* defies classification into traditional journalistic categories, the magazine's origins are strictly underground. The term *underground* (or *alternative*) press can be defined as follows:

Underground papers were printed cheaply by offset, free swinging in style and content, uninhibited in graphic design, unrestricted in viewpoint, and in many cases unprofitable. They reflected a rebellion not only against the establishment, but also against its conventional mass media. The best of the underground papers did a capable job of criticizing both . . . the immediate stimuli were the four letter word movement, the sex revolution, the generation and credibility gaps that created the anti-Establishment ear, and above all, the bitter antiwar protest typified by the March on the Pentagon.[6]

Rolling Stone was able to incorporate all of these stylistic dimensions while generating a relatively sound financial base during its early years.

Journalism historians maintain that *Rolling Stone* was, nevertheless, different from most other underground tabloids. Most notably, it went beyond politics, extending into the realm of popular culture. In chronicling the editorial scope of the underground press, Robert Glessing divides 457 alternative press titles into two categories:

(1) **political** papers, which "emphasize radical politics and believe the underground press should be used as tools for a political revolution," and (2) **cultural** papers, which "are interested in the total complex of relations between all people in the movement and work toward a general awareness in American society."[7]

Glessing further argues that cultural papers are more profit-conscious than their political counterparts, who operate on the principle that it is impossible to be fiscally sound and editorially free at the same time. By virtue of its pop-culture orientation, *Rolling Stone* will be classified as a cultural underground newspaper at the point of her inception. In contrast, an establishment or mainstream paper would be one that serves the dominant culture's interests. Glessing's definition of the establishment includes "everybody outside the underground movement; people who run the country."[8]

Amidst the cultural upheavals of its time, then, *Rolling Stone* emerged in November 1967 to chronicle developments in rock music and politics. The magazine was founded by Jann Wenner in San Francisco with just $8,000 and a staff made up largely of part-time workers.[9] He and his staff initially operated on the assumption that "rock was not only the pied piper and national anthem but the motive force and invincible weaponry of the counter culture."[10] Over the years, though, *Rolling Stone* increased its circulation along with her editorial scope; by 1980, the publication boasted eight hundred thousand readers, deeming itself "a general-interest magazine with a particular interest in popular culture."[11]

Much was written during this time about *Rolling Stone*'s investigative tradition and reportage of specific events (e.g., the Chicago Seven murder trial).[12] Rather less attention has been paid to any changes in political voice accompanying the magazine's shift from underground to mass audience appeals. Politics played an important defining role, however, as contemporaries deemed *Rolling Stone* "a tabloid combination of rock magazine and political newspaper."[13]

By the midseventies, *Rolling Stone* and its counterculture counterpart, *Village Voice*, were both considered to "have become so successful that they can hardly be considered alternatives anymore . . . now part of the establishment press."[14] To be sure, this change was influenced by a great many staff personalities, policies and conflicts. But it is clear that they existed within a greater, increasingly commercial milieu that represents the primary explanatory factor.[15] It is important, then, to examine these content dimensions in the context of a framework that relates media content to external audience considerations.

UNDERSTANDING MAINSTREAM VERSUS UNDERGROUND REPORTING

Cultural historians describe the underground press' constituent audience as a radical movement comprised of those who were "young or wanting to be young and opposed to the social status quo as viewed by the establishment press."[16] Alan Seeger recognized that underground papers, like their mainstream counterparts, are governed by the "ways of not seeing."[17] Thus, just as a mainstream *New York Times* account would tend to overlook or underestimate oppositionary movements,[18] we see an opposing dynamic within the alternative press. In particular, Seeger found that the underground *Berkeley Barb* overemphasized the potency of the New Left, downplaying racial and class tensions within the movement itself.

By contrast, mainstream reporting fulfills hegemonic functions by legitimating existing power structures.[19] In the case of news, this might involve the journalistic commitment to "objectivity" and "balance." The resulting preoccupation with the maintenance and disruption of the social order favors dominant worldviews over those held by dissidents.[20]

Given these mass audience dynamics, we might expect that *Rolling Stone*'s market expansion would be accompanied by a mainstreaming of political voice.[21] Specifically, as its audience share grows, the magazine's treatment of issues concerning the New Left should grow less dogmatic to meet the demands of a larger, more politically varied audience.[22]

The years 1967–1975 were selected in order to trace editorial changes occurring from the magazine's charter issue on through the end of the Vietnam War, just before the publication moved its offices from San Francisco to Manhattan. The period will be divided as follows: 1967–1970 (underground period) and 1971–1975 (commercial period).

These time frames center on the year 1970—when *Rolling Stone*'s readership doubled—reaching a circulation of two hundred and fifty thousand. Since the magazine's forays into political reporting were of a relatively low and irregular frequency,[23] attention is focused on three two-week periods, falling in 1967, 1969 and 1970. Those years are of special interest because they provided a backdrop for the only theme issues concerning the New Left. We also include an examination of criterion items appearing from 1971 to 1975, which averaged less than one per year. This sudden decline in political reporting was attributed to the unpopularity of a 1970 issue devoted to politics.[24]

Articles covering the New Left during those periods serve as primary sources for this study. Potential story items are analyzed on the basis of a central focus or idea that relates to prominent figures or groups associated with the New Left. Political perspectives for each story can be evaluated according to Gitlin's concept of a media frame.

Briefly, Gitlin defines such frames as "persistent patterns of cognition, interpretation, and presentation, of selection, emphasis, and exclusion, by which symbol-handlers routinely organize discourse, whether verbal or visual."[25]

Hence an underground reporting frame would amplify the New Left's call for social "change" and "justice" in some way. And since underground publications are "advocacy publications," their reporting frames would be "bold and make no claim to impartiality" because their constituency is often a community rather than an audience.[26]

By comparison, an establishment or mainstream reporting frame would be more impartial, helping to affirm the status quo and providing little basis for a critical appraisal of society.[27] Gitlin notes that these mainstream frames treated the New Left as a social liability, accordingly deprecating it with the following set of framing devices:

- trivialization (making light of the movement language, dress, age, style, and goals);
- emphasis on internal dissension;
- marginalization (showing demonstrators to be deviant or unrepresentative);

- disparagement by numbers (undercounting);
- disparagement of the movement's effectiveness;
- emphasis on violence.[28]

Gitlin contends that such devices help maintain the relatively moderate type of worldview that the mainstream press must, perforce, represent. The application of these framing techniques toward the New Left, then, could offer evidence of an hegemonic ideology accompanying the mainstreaming of *Rolling Stone*.

CONTENTS

Underground Period

The type of political advocacy writing that characterized *Rolling Stone* during its underground period was evident from the magazine's first issue. Early stories linked rock, drugs and other elements of the New Left to notions of general social reform. Witness the following charter-issue story about a drug bust involving the rock group the Grateful Dead:

The Good Old Grateful Dead had gotten it. Eight narcotics agents, followed by a dozen newspaper reporters and television crews raided the Dead's house at 710 Ashbury Street. . . . *Rolling Stone* didn't leave. We adjourned to the porch to take a few pictures of one of the most beautiful bands in the world. . . . The cops carried no warrant and broke in the front door even after being denied entry . . . while the narcs did their work, a rooting section gathered (and) . . . filled the air with a running commentary. . . . The law (against MJ) . . . encourages the most outrageously discriminatory type of law enforcement. If the lawyers, doctors, advertising men, teachers and political officeholders who use marijuana were arrested today, the law might well be off the books before Thanksgiving.[29]

In this account, *Rolling Stone* attempts to differentiate itself from the mainstream press elements covering the event (e.g., "*Rolling Stone* didn't leave"). The story's tone is clearly sympathetic to the rock group, referring to the police as "narcs" while painting a picture of popular crowd support for the Grateful Dead. Further, the article points out a social double standard with respect to drug enforcement, claiming that the law would be changed if the extent of establishment marijuana use was disclosed. Such a partisan "us versus the establishment" perspective addresses a somewhat limited underground readership that is, indeed, more a constituency than an audience.

Shortly thereafter, the magazine fused environmental themes with an example of grassroots action. The following describes a Berkeley park that was later to become the scene of several violent demonstrations.

A muddy, debris strewn, ugly vacant lot, property of the University of California, has been transformed by Berkeley street people into a People's Park. After taking up a collection from nearby merchants, the hip community purchased 300 square yards of sod, all manner of plants and trees, rented a bulldozer and—zap—there was an instant park where previously only a lumpy parking lot had existed. Now it's clean and neat and green, with ancient church pews for park benches and winding walkways roped off. The workers got out a leaflet proclaiming the park belongs to the people. But on the bulletin board at the center of the new park there was an official looking notice indicating that the University intends to bulldoze People's Park away and put a soccer field in its place. Not disheartened, street people continued working on their park beneath brilliant sunshine the other day. "We're building a bandstand," one muscular young freak explained setting his saw aside for a moment. "Wouldn't it be great to have concerts here?"[30]

In emphasizing group cohesion, the magazine overlooks violence and drug abuse marring early park protests, exemplifying "ways of not seeing" which Seeger attributes to underground reporting. The end result is a one-sided idealism that serves as an inverse image to establishment press accounts of student protest.

Through a follow-up story, *Rolling Stone* emphasized the brutality with which police elements of the establishment "Machine" crushed the park's idealistic curators.

In Berkeley last week a long-feared nightmare suddenly achieved reality. The Machine became a weapon. Bureaucracy, bulldozers and shotguns merged in efficient unity and struck forth with insane viciousness. When the tear gas had cleared and the Machine had done its work, a sturdy chain link fence enclosed a piece of land which had once been the People's Park. In the action 47 students and street people were arrested. Over 100 were injured, at least 35 of these near death; one died. Helicopters patrolled the city, armed with tear gas. Two thousand National Guard troops marched the streets with fixed bayonets. . . . Somewhere, someone has decided that the piece of land will be a graveyard before it is a park—a graveyard for many of the ideals of this generation and possibly the bodies of those who believed that a simple dream could be made real.[31]

Just as any combatant seeks to dehumanize an enemy, this commentator characterizes the university and government "establishment" in Orwellian terms. Martial law forces, in particular, are portrayed as part of a heartless "Machine," while demonstrators are passive victims. Within that group, divisions between students and street people are downplayed, consistent with accounts in the *Berkeley Barb* and other underground papers.[32]

However, even during its underground period, *Rolling Stone* never espoused the revolutionary solutions commonly preached in radical underground papers. In this regard, it served more of a cultural than a political function. We see, instead, a consistent focus on politics as a function of music. Toward that end, Ralph Gleason wrote one of the magazine's last editorials addressing the New Left as a force for social change. "*Rolling Stone* believes today, as it did when we celebrated our first issue, in the strength of music to change the lives, the culture, and the nature of society."[33]

Consistent with other cultural underground papers, however, Gleason's definition of revolution did not favor the concept of violence. In suggesting poetry and music as nonviolent alternatives, Gleason emphatically attacks revolutionaries: "You better figure out how to make revolution without killing people, or it won't work. . . . The Beatles aren't just more powerful than Jesus, they are also more potent than S.D.S."[34]

The mainstream press took solace in *Rolling Stone*'s moderate tone, noting that the paper managed to "identify with the movement while subtly and insidiously putting down political activism."[35] This philosophy pervaded the magazine's other major political stories of that period, which included a report on Charles Manson ("Our Continuing Coverage of the Apocalypse"), a series on the misuse of concert funds at the 1967 Monterey Pop Festival and a report on the Cambodian invasion and domestic antiwar sentiment ("On America in 1970; a Pitiful Helpless Giant").

While avoiding open calls for insurgency, the *Rolling Stone* did presuppose a degree of political awareness among its readers. Editor Wenner himself shed his personal disdain for politics in writing the lead for a 1969 special issue dedicated to "American Revolution, 1969."

Our black population and our student population have finally declared themselves sick and tired of desolation row and finished with the old folks home at college. These politics are about to become a part of our daily lives and like it or not we are in it. Like it or not we have reached a point in the social, cultural, intellectual and artistic history of the United States where we are all going to be affected by politics. We can no longer ignore it. It threatens our daily lives and our daily happinesses. The new political movement we feel around us can no longer be left at the periphery of the artistic consciousness.[36]

Ironically, Wenner issues a call for readers to overcome political apathy, even though he was regarded as only a political faddist (or chic deviant).[37] Wenner was to engage in a similar struggle in the years to come, constantly reassessing the degree to which this "movement" should be left at the periphery of *Rolling Stone*.

His lead story was followed by a series of articles written by various New Left–umbrella spokespersons, including a Black Panther spokesperson, George Mason Murray. Displaying a rare political underground tenor, Murray's piece detailed the manner in which his movement hoped to "fight to the death against racism."[38] Yet, although the struggle waged by the Panthers and other groups was to continue for several years, the April 1969 issue proved to be their last editorial soapbox within *Rolling Stone*.

Commercial Period

One might expect a certain lessening in political partisanship from a magazine covering a music genre that itself grew less political over time. But *Rolling Stone*'s decision to deemphasize issues concerning the New Left seems to be more of a short-term response to market factors than a gradual evolution in political thought. The magazine's last political theme issue was a November 1970 special devoted to the Kent State murders and the Chicago Seven murder trial. Featuring editorials such as the following by Gleason, the issue proved to be an unparalleled newsstand flop:[39] "Music is the glue which has kept this generation from falling apart in the face of incredible adult blindness and ignorance and evilness. It is the new educational system for reform and the medium for revolution."[40]

Here again, we see an interest in reform politics expressed as a function of new music. There appears to be some confusion as to whether a "reform" or "revolution" framework should be followed. In the context of the earlier-reviewed articles, however, it's clear that Gleason prefers nonviolent revolution.

Thereafter, *Rolling Stone* addressed issues concerning the New Left sparingly, expanding its editorial scope to include the type of social and international coverage one might expect to find in "a sort of hip *Playboy*."[41] We see, for example, increasing use of features on such celebrities as Raquel Welch and Tony Orlando.

This isn't to say that *Rolling Stone* espoused only antiestablishment reporting frames prior to 1970. Indications of the magazine's intention to distance itself from elements of the New Left were apparent as early as 1969. Witness the following report about an Easter vacation rock festival in Palm Springs: "[the cops] exercised amazing restraint, ignoring blatant sexual activities, drinking and doping . . . until finally, the youthful vacationers asked for much of the trouble they got."[42] This account is not unlike one found in a mainstream paper and was, in fact, picked up by *Time* magazine. *Rolling Stone* stopped short of condoning marijuana use in this example, picturing the demonstrators as deviant individuals who deserved to be arrested by local police. While the account might have been more sympathetic in the case of a festival emphasizing art or politics, we see clear limits on the magazine's capacity for youth-oriented advocacy.

This apolitical tendency was, no doubt, solidified by the ill-fated Kent State issue focusing on student activism in 1970. It wasn't until years later that we see any analysis of left-wing politics. And when the movement was later revisited, the magazine highlighted unusual representatives, portraying them in a somewhat different fashion.

The following 1974 report, titled "Strange Rumbling on the Left," isolates the National Caucus of Labor Committee as a deviant leftist organization with delusions of grandeur:

The cadres of one [NCLC] are zealots with limitless ends and they plan, for a start, to take over the United States in five to six years. They say you should hope they do because you'll be enslaved and starving if they can't stop the slide into depression and fascism that is already gaining momentum.[43]

To be sure, the NCLC was marginalized even by political papers as a crackpot organization.[44] But the fact that *Rolling Stone* chose to highlight their deviance seems reminiscent of mainstream reporting styles. In particular, the article marginalizes the NCLC, referring to them as a group of strange zealots. It then trivializes the organization's stated intentions, making light of their language and goals in a somewhat sarcastic review of NCLC philosophy. The *New York Times* couldn't have done a better job of deprecating the New Left splinter group.

One could argue that, even during its underground period, *Rolling Stone* would never have condoned the type of revolution advocated by the NCLC. But, whereas seven years earlier the magazine rarely expressed apprehension about such radical groups, *Rolling Stone* was eager to defend the establishment here. As editor Wenner argued a few years earlier: "Rock and roll is now the energy core of change in American life. But capitalism is what allows us the incredible indulgence of this music."[45] As time passed, it seemed *Rolling Stone* was more concerned about pleasing readers who had money than preaching social change to those who didn't.

This isn't to suggest that *Rolling Stone* abandoned its incisive style of investigative reporting altogether. It was credited with being the first publication to detail the Patty Hearst kidnapping story in 1975. But, even here, the reporting style was more concerned with describing rather than advocating or explaining the actions of the Symbionese Liberation Army. In addition to the deprecatory techniques listed above in conjunction with the NCLC, *Rolling Stone* trivialized the SLA's effectiveness by emphasizing the group's limited size and internal dissension (as exemplified by the title of its April 1974 article—"Seven Forked Tongue in the SLA").

By 1975, it seemed as if *Rolling Stone* couldn't even condone the use of mild drugs such as marijuana, for which it had crusaded only eight years earlier. The magazine still reported about drug busts involving major recording artists. Yet such individuals were viewed as deviant offenders rather than the vanguard of a movement to change drug laws. The following story concerns the incarceration of Latin vocalist Flora Purim:

Sure, I was stupid; I used cocaine, smoked weed, took pills, all kinds of drugs. . . . That was in 1972. Since then I have not used drugs. I would like to tell people that a joint or a blow isn't worth your freedom. There are so many ways to get high without drugs. Music is one of the best, but you can do it writing poetry, painting.[46]

When comparing this to the 1967 article concerning the Grateful Dead drug bust, we see an implied acceptance of the drug laws. Rather than challenge those laws, as it had earlier, *Rolling Stone* highlights Purim's call to abstain from drug use altogether.

Such attention to rock-culture lifestyle issues, however, seemed vestigial amidst the magazine's rapidly expanding editorial menu. Part of this shift was likely due to the need to maintain readership among a new, less politically oriented generation of college-age readers.

In response to this shift in editorial focus, David Armstrong concludes the following about the *Rolling Stone* of the 1970s: "Accomplished work still appeared in the magazine . . . but it seems almost out of context in a magazine that is safely assimilated like rock and the youth culture, into the mainstream of American life."[47]

At the same time, *Rolling Stone* began to earn legitimacy within the ranks of the mainstream press. Specifically, a November 1970 account of the raucous rock festival at Altamont, California, exposed the details of a murder and subsequent cover-up attempts conducted by presiding Hell's Angels security forces.[48] The article served as a source for several mainstream critiques of the festival.[49] Again, *Rolling Stone* viewed the event as an isolated incident rather than something endemic of a greater dysfunctioning within the concert promotion establishment.

We thus see shades of *Rolling Stone*'s evolution into mainstream reporting as early as 1969 and 1970. Rather than characterizing this as an abrupt change, it is perhaps safer to observe that those years were a period of transition for the magazine. During that time, *Rolling Stone* grew away from advocacy reporting and developed a characteristic "new journalism" style that maintained personal perspectives while avoiding outright advocacy. As the decade progressed, however, the magazine's emerging *Playboy*-like agenda was accompanied by a continuing shift in perspective.

Armstrong notes the following with regard to the magazine's latter day reporting style: "In its pursuit of profit—and its promotion of the star system, competition, hedonism and, above all, a kind of sated passivity . . . *Rolling Stone* became the antithesis of what cultural and political radicals intended when they launched the underground media."[50]

The sort of hedonism to which Armstrong refers is present in a March 1972 article entitled "Sexuality Comes to the Suburbs": "Inside the room, 35 people are sprawled on the sofas and over the floor, eating dinner. Half of them are totally naked. Sipping wine and making conversation."[51] Such lifestyle features steadily replaced political stories, as no further issues were dedicated to "the revolution" after 1970. But whimsical accounts of the New Left did, nevertheless, resurface over time.

The sardonic notes of Hunter S. Thompson—no straight arrow in his own right—proved a mainstay for the magazine as its circulation grew in the early 1970s. In part of his extended series on the 1972 presidential campaign, Thompson expressed a certain "Fear and Loathing" toward elements of the Black Panthers while chiding the political left.

When you slink out of the Senate Chamber with your tail between your legs and then have to worry about getting mugged, stomped or raped by a trio of renegade Black Panthers . . . well, it tends to bring you down a bit and warn your liberal instincts . . . the people who could make McGovern President— that huge and confused coalition of students, freaks, blacks, anti-war activists and dazed drop-outs won't even bother to register, much less drag themselves to the polls on election day.[52]

Thus, where only three years earlier *Rolling Stone* had provided a forum for such groups, the magazine later chose to give center stage to those who would trivialize the effectiveness of these very same elements. Political advocacy, it seemed, was not as good a draw as Hunter S. Thompson.

CONCLUSION

When analyzing *Rolling Stone*'s metamorphosis, it seems the goal of promoting social change through incisive, partisan reporting remains incompatible with that of economic success among American media organizations. When initiated as an underground publication, the tabloid integrated music and political stories in advocating a myriad of causes advanced by the New Left (e.g., environmentalism, peace, etc.). But as *Rolling Stone* grew more popular in the early 1970s, its publishers found they could not sustain a growing audience with political stories.

Valuing its business objectives over social advocacy, *Rolling Stone* ceased trying to link events within the rock music world to those of the outside world. Stories concerning the politics and music of the New

Left gradually gave way to general items in such areas as international affairs and the economy. This, in turn, prompted a qualitative change in the tone of the remaining items on the New Left—one that indicated a heightened sense of estrangement over time. The one-time trumpet of the Left had, for all purposes, become mainstream.

Commentators maintain that the mainstream media in our society specialize in conveying national ideology; they don't challenge the main structures, ideas and established institutions to which their fortunes are attached.[53] Although the magazine did remain honest and, to an extent, critical of society, its reporting frame changed from one of advocacy to one of mere description of changes proposed by elements of the New Left. Nonetheless, as Donald Pember argues, "It no longer seems to be on the edge of a counterculture movement, but then there may not be a counterculture or movement to be on the edge of anymore."[54]

Social changes notwithstanding, it's clear that *Rolling Stone*'s market success was closely paralleled by a distinct mainstream thrust in its editorial scope and content. By leading toward conformism and providing little basis for a critical underground appraisal of society, *Rolling Stone* was effectively helping maintain the social status quo upon which its growing market share was based.

It seems, then, that the role of audience dynamics is immutable. A magazine seeking to exploit mass markets must necessarily espouse a relatively conservative, inoffensive viewpoint with respect to leftist politics. Such market forces bind much more powerfully than those related to history or advocacy. Further research should assess similar changes in coverage associated with other U.S. underground publications that survived the Vietnam War era.

NOTES

1. By the 1960s, the social base of this oppositionary "New Left" movement had shifted away from farmers and laborers to blacks, students, youth and women. See Todd Gitlin, *The Whole World is Watching* (Berkeley: University of California Press, 1980), 2.

2. Edwin Emery and Michael Emery, *The Press in America* (Englewood Cliffs, N.J.: Prentice Hall, 1978), 379.

3. Lawrence Downie, *The New Muckrakers* (Washington, D.C.: New Republic Press, 1976).

4. Michael Schudson, *Discovering the News: A Social History of American Newspapers* (New York: Basic Books, 1977), 187.

5. Gitlin, *Whole World is Watching*.

6. Emery and Emery, *The Press in America*, 379.

7. Robert Glessing, *The Underground Press in America* (Bloomington: Indiana University Press, 1970), 7.

8. Ibid., 82–23.

9. Editor and founder Jann Wenner was only twenty-one years old when he founded the biweekly rock music tabloid. Previously, Wenner had written a music column for *Ramparts* magazine and his college paper at the University of California, Berkeley. See Harold Rosengren and Karen Krieger, *The Writer's Guide to Magazine Markets: Nonfiction* (New York: Signet Publishing, 1983).

10. "Rocking the News," *Newsweek*, 28 April 1969, 70.

11. Rosengren and Krieger, *Writer's Guide*, 240.

12. Robert Draper, *Rolling Stone: The Uncensored History* (New York: Harper and Row, 1990).

13. Editors, "Rocking the News," *Newsweek*, 28 April 1969, 70.

14. Schudson, *Discovering the News*, 187.

15. Draper, *Rolling Stone*.

16. Glessing, *Underground Press in America*, 83.

17. Alan Seeger, "An Unreported Class War: Ideology and Self-Censorship on the Berkeley Barb," *Communication* (1987): 31–50.

18. Gitlin, *Whole World is Watching*.

19. Horace Newcomb, *Television: The Critical View* (Oxford: Oxford University Press, 1994).

20. Paul Lazarsfeld, "Mass Communication Content," in *Mass Communication*, ed. Wilbur Schramm (Urbana: University of Illinois Press, 1960), 60.

21. Ben Bagdikian, *The Media Monopoly* (Boston: Beacon Press, 1983).

22. The magazine's own general manager provided some insight into his publication's plan to change copy: "We had to deliver a more high-quality reader. The only way to deliver a different kind of reader is to change editorial." Elizabeth Shore and Paul Case, *Alternative Papers: Selections From the Alternative Press* (Philadelphia: Temple University Press, 1982), 1.

23. Draper, *Rolling Stone*.

24. Shore and Case, *Alternative Papers*.

25. Gitlin, *Whole World is Watching*, 6.

26. Donald Pember, *Mass Media in America* (Chicago: Science Research Associates, 1981), 261.

27. Lazarsfeld, "Mass Communication Content," 503.

28. Gitlin, *Whole World is Watching*, 27–28.

29. "Grateful Dead Drug Bust," *Rolling Stone*, 9 November 1967, 8.

30. "A New Park is Born," *Rolling Stone*, 28 April 1968, 8.

31. "The Death of a Park," *Rolling Stone*, 14 June 1969, 8.

32. Seeger, "Unreported Class War."

33. Ralph Gleason, "Music and Society," *Rolling Stone*, 11 April 1969, 10.

34. Ibid.

35. "Rolling Stone's Rock World," *Time*, 25 April 1969, 78.

36. Jann Wenner, "The Sound of Marching, Charging Feet," *Rolling Stone*, 15 April 1969, 3–4.

37. Schudson, *Discovering the News*.

38. George Mason Murray, "Fight to the Death Against Racism," *Rolling Stone*, 15 April 1969, 16.

39. Lawrence Leamer, *The Paper Revolutionaries* (New York: Simon and Schuster, 1972).

40. Ralph Gleason, "Music and Society," *Rolling Stone*, 14 November 1970, 16.

41. Leamer, *Paper Revolutionaries*.

42. "Rolling Stone's Rock World," *Time*, 25 April 1969, 78.

43. "Strange New Rumblings on the Left," *Rolling Stone*, 4 November 1974, 11.

44. Gitlin, *Whole World is Watching*.

45. "Rolling Stone's Rock World," 78.

46. "Flora Purim, Jailed Songbird," *Rolling Stone*, 24 April 1975, 13.

47. David Armstrong, *A Call to Arms* (Los Angeles: J. P. Tarcher, 1981).

48. "Let it Bleed," *Rolling Stone*, 14 November 1970, 2.

49. Armstrong, *Call to Arms*.

50. Ibid., 177.

51. "Sexuality Comes to the Suburbs," *Rolling Stone*, 6 January 1972, 6.

52. Hunter S. Thompson, "Fear and Loathing in Washington," *Rolling Stone*, 6 January 1972, 6.

53. Gaye Tuchman, *Making News: A Study in the Construction of Reality* (Glencoe, Ill.: Free Press, 1978); see also Gitlin, *Whole World is Watching*.

54. Pember, *Mass Media in America*, 106.

IV

Sources for Newspaper and Periodical History

Annual Review of Work in Newspaper History

Diana Dixon

This checklist covers material published on the history of the newspaper press and related material on an international basis up to the end of 1995. It complements and updates Annual Reviews appearing in earlier numbers of the *Journal of Newspaper and Periodical History* and *Studies in Newspaper and Periodical History*. It is hoped that coverage of books, periodical articles and dissertations published in the United Kingdom will be as complete as possible. Material that has not been included in earlier issues of the Annual Review will be incorporated to ensure continuity of coverage. Inevitably there are gaps, and wherever possible we hope to remedy these in future issues of the Annual Review.

The bibliography is arranged in four sections: bibliographies and guides to the literature, general works relating to newspaper and periodical history, studies of individual newspapers and periodicals and studies of individual journalists. Arrangement is alphabetical by author in the first two sections, and in the last two sections it is alphabetical (by subject) by the name of the newspaper or the journalist.

BIBLIOGRAPHIES AND GUIDES TO THE LITERATURE

Chapman, C. *An Introduction to Using Newspapers and Periodicals*. Birmingham: Federation of Family History Societies, 1993. 30pp.

Cloud, B. *Directory of Journalism and Mass Communications Historians.* Las Vegas: University of Nevada Press, 1994. 43pp.

Dixon, D. "Annual Review of Work in Newspaper History." *Studies in Newspaper and Periodical History 1994 Annual.* Westport, Conn.: Greenwood Press, 1996.

"The *Guardian* Index." *British Library Newspaper Library Newsletter* 19 (1995): 5.

Linton, D. "Parameters of Press Bibliography." *British Library Newspaper Library Newsletter* 19 (1995): 2–3.

Linton, D. *The Twentieth Century Newspaper Press in Britain: An Annotated Bibliography.* London: Mansell, 1994. 416pp.

Ljungquist, K. P. " 'Al Aaaraf' and the Boston Lyceum: Contributions to Primary and Secondary Bibliography." *Victorian Periodicals Review* 28 (1995): 199–216.

McCoy, R. E. *Freedom of the Press: An Annotated Bibliography.* Carbondale: Southern Illinois University Press, 1993. 441pp.

"Newsplan News." *British Library Newspaper Library Newsletter* 18 (1994–1995): 4–5.

"Newsplan News." *British Library Newspaper Library Newsletter* 19 (1995): 4.

GENERAL STUDIES OF NEWSPAPERS AND PERIODICALS

Adam, A. *The Vernacular Press and the Emergence of Modern Indonesian Consciousness* (1855–1913). Ithaca, N.Y.: Cornell University Press, 1995.

Adams, E. E. "Market Subordination and Competition: A Historical Analysis of Combinations, Consolidation and Joint Operating Agreements through an Examination of the E. W. Scripps Newspaper Chain." Ph.D. thesis, Ohio University, 1993.

Andersen, A. W. *Rough Road to Glory: The Norwegian-American Press Speaks out on Public Affairs.* London: Associated University Press, 1990. 271pp.

Andres-Galligo, J., & Pazos, A. M. "La Buena Prensa." *Hispania Sacra* 44 (1992): 139–60.

Argyris, C. *Behind the Front Page: Organization and Self-Renewal in a Metropolitan Newspaper.* Ann Arbor, Mich.: Books on Demand, 1992.

Aucoin, J. L. "IRE and the Evolution of Modern American Investigative Journalism 1960–1990." Ph.D. thesis, University of Missouri, 1993.

Ayalon, A. *The Press in the Arab Middle East: A History.* Oxford: Oxford University Press, 1995. xiv + 300pp.

Beller, S. "German Liberalism, Nationalism and the Jews: The *Neue Freie Presse* and the German-Czech Conflict in the Hapsburg Monarchy 1900–1918." *Bohemia* 34 (1993): 63–76.

Bennett, A. "A History of the French Newspapers and Nineteenth-Century English Newspapers in Guernsey." Master's thesis, Loughborough University, 1995.

Bennion, V. "Sisters under the Skin; Utah's Mormon and Non-Mormon Women and Their Publications." *Brigham Young University Studies* 33 (1993): 111–44. [*Women's Exponent* and *Anti-Polygamy Standard*]

Benton, M. "Sizzle and Smoke: Iconography of Books and Reading in Modern American Advertising." *Publishing History* 37 (1995): 77–90.

Black, J. "Continuity and Change in the British Press, 1750–1833." *Publishing History* 36 (1994): 39–85.

Boyd, K. "Exemplars and Ingrates: Imperialism and the Boys' Story Paper, 1880–1930." *Historical Research* 67 (1994): 143–55.

Brake, L. *Subjugated Knowledges: Journalism, Gender and Literature in the Nineteenth Century.* Basingstoke: Macmillan, 1994. xv + 228pp.

Brennan, P. H. *Reporting the Nation's Business: Press-Government Relations during the Liberal Years, 1935–1957.* Toronto: Toronto University Press, 1994. xiv + 250pp.

Brown, W. *John Adams and the American Press: Politics and Journalism at the Birth of the Republic.* Jefferson, N.C.: McFarland & Co., 1995. ix + 213pp.

Bryant, M., & Henage, S. *Dictionary of British Cartoonists and Caricaturists 1730–1980.* Aldershot, UK: Scolar Press, 1994. 252pp.

Capezzi, R. A. "Modernizing Democracy: Women and the Material and Discursive Practices of Culture in the United States 1800–1916." Ph.D. thesis, University of Pittsburgh, 1993.

Carlebach, M. I. *The Origins of Photo-Journalism in America.* Washington, D.C.: Smithsonian Institution Press, 1992. 194pp.

Censer, J. R. *The French Press in the Age of Enlightenment.* London: Routledge, 1994. xii + 264pp.

Clark, C. *The Public Prints: The Newspaper in Anglo-American Culture, 1665–1740.* Oxford and New York: Oxford University Press, 1994. xiv + 330pp.

Cloud, B. *The Business of Newspapers on the Western Frontier.* Reno: University of Nevada Press, 1992. 255pp.

Cloud, B. "Images of Women in the Mining Press Camps." *Nevada Historical Society Quarterly* 36 (1993): 194–207.

Coleridge, K. A. "Newspaper Advertising in a Pioneer Colony. Twenty Years in 'Port Nick' (Wellington, New Zealand)." *Publishing History* 37 (1995): 23–54.

Coleridge, N. *Paper Tigers: The Latest Greatest Newspaper Tycoons and How They Won the World.* London: Mandarin, 1994. 592pp.

Cornelbise, A. E. *Ranks and Columns: Armed Forces Newspapers in American Wars.* Westport, Conn.: Greenwood Press, 1993. 218pp.

Damon-Moore, H. *Magazines for the Millions: Gender and Commerce in the* Ladies Home Journal *and the* Saturday Evening Post, *1880–1910.* New York: State University of New York Press, 1994. 263pp.

DeBenedittis, P. *Guam's Trial of the Century: News Hegemony and Rumor in an American Colony.* Westport, Conn.: Praeger, 1993. 183pp.

Dickstein, M. "What Happened to the Little Magazine?" *Culturefront* 3 (1994): 40–42.

Dobroszycki, L. *Reptile Journalism: The Official Polish Language Press under the Nazis, 1939–1945.* New Haven, Conn.: Yale University Press, 1994. 199pp.

Doll, L. W. *A History of the Newspapers of Ann Arbor, 1829–1920.* Ann Arbor, Mich.: Books on Demand, 1994. 183pp.

Don Vann, J., & Van Arsdel, R. T. *Victorian Periodicals and Victorian Society.* Toronto: Toronto University Press, 1994.

Downie, J. A., & Corns, T. N. *Telling People What to Think: Early Eighteenth-Century Periodicals from the* Review *to the* Rambler. London: Frank Cass, 1993. 131pp.

Dubay, R. W. "The Needle of Truth." *Proceedings and Papers of Georgia Association of Historians* 11 (1990): 57–67.

Duggan, L. "The Trials of Alice Mitchell: Sensationalism, Sexology and the Lesbian Subject in Turn of the Century America." *Signs* 18 (1993): 791–814.

Emery, M. *On the Front Line: Following America's Foreign Correspondents across the Twentieth Century*. Washington, D.C.: American University Press, 1995. 356pp.

Enlund, N. E. S. "Electronic Full Page Make-Up of Newspapers in Perspective." *Gutenberg Jahrbuch* 66 (1991): 318–28.

Evans, H. J. *The Newspaper Press in Kentucky*. Ann Arbor, Mich.: Books on Demand, 1994.

Fischer, H-D. *Sports Journalism at its Best: Pulitzer Prize Winning Articles, Cartoons and Photographs*. Chicago: Nelson Hall Publishers, 1995. 146pp.

Fortin, A. *Passage de la modernité: Les intellectuals Québecois et leurs revues*. Sainte-Foy: Laval University Press, 1993. 406pp.

Gainot, B. "Bottu, *Le Republican des Colonies*." *Annales Historiques de la Révolution Française* 293–94 (1993): 431–44.

Gardiner, D. "France's African Policy under de Gaulle (1958–1960) as Seen in the American Press." *Proceedings of the Annual Meeting of the French Colonial Historical Society* 17 (1991): 115–31.

Gehman, M. *The Free People of Color of New Orleans: An Introduction*. New Orleans, La.: Margaret Media, Inc., 1994.

Gendron, B. "A Short Stay in the Sun: The Reception of Bebop (1944–1950)." *Library Chronicle of the University of Texas at Austin* 24 (1994): 137–59.

Gillmeister, H. "English Editors of German Sporting Journals at the Turn of the Century." *Sports Historian* 13 (1993): 38–68.

Hamilton, M. A. "A Pennsylvania Newspaper Publisher in Gideon's Army: J. W. Gitt, Henry Wallace and the Progressive Party of 1842." *Pennsylvania History* 61 (1994): 330.

Hardt, H., & Brennan, B. *Newsworkers: Toward a History of the Rank and File*. Minneapolis: Minnesota University Press, 1995.

Harris, B. "England's Provincial Newspapers and the Jacobite Rebellion of 1745–1746." *History* 80 (1995): 5–21.

Hoffert, S. "New York City's Penny Press and the Issue of Women's Rights 1848–1860." *Journalism Quarterly* 70 (1993): 656–65.

Hutton, F. "The Impact of the Democratic Ideals of the U.S. Constitution on the Early Black Press in America." *Journal of the Afro-Caribbean Historical and Genealogical Society* 11 (1990): 111–20.

Jackson, G. S. *Breaking Story: The South African Press*. Oxford: Westview Press, 1993. xxiii + 308pp.

Jensen, C. *Censored: The News That Didn't Make the News and Why*. Chapel Hill, N.C.: Shelburne, 1993. 248pp.

Johannigsmeier, C. "Newspaper Syndicates of the Late Nineteenth Century: Overlooked Faces in the American Literary Market Place." *Publishing History* 37 (1995): 61–82.

Johnson, D. A. *Fountain City May Have Talkie Shows: The Story of a Small Town and its Newspaper*. Basking Ridge, N.J.: Arlan Communications, 1994.

Keller, M. L. "Picturing for St. Petersburg: Spring Training and Publicity in the Sunshine City 1914–1918." *Tampa Bay History* 15 (1993): 35–53.

Kern-Foxworth, M. *Aunt Jemima, Uncle Ben and Rastus: Blacks in Advertising, Yesterday, Today and Tomorrow*. Westport, Conn.: Greenwood Press, 1994. 205pp.

Knight, O. *Following the Indian Wars: The Story of the Newspaper Correspondents among the Indian Campaigners*. Norman: Oklahoma University Press, 1993. 348pp.

Koski, S. D. "Looking for Jazz Journalism in Missouri Dailies of the 1920s." Ph.D. thesis, University of Missouri, 1993.

Kovarik, W. J. "The Ethyl Controversy: The News Media and the Public Health Debate Over Leaded Gasoline 1924–1926." Ph.D. thesis, University of Maryland, 1993.

Lambron, E. "State, Nation and Socialism in the East and West German Quality Press." Ph.D. thesis, Leeds University, 1991.

Landau, H. "First Person History: Jewish Journalism in Louisville." *Filson Club Historical Quarterly* 68 (1994): 285–92.

Lawson, L. *Truth in Publishing: Federal Regulation of the Press' Business Practices 1880–1920*. Carbondale: Southern Illinois University Press, 1993. 229pp.

Lewis, C., & Neville, J. "Images of Rosie: A Content Analysis of Women Workers in American Magazine Advertising." *Journal of Modern Culture Quarterly* 72 (1995): 216–27.

Liebovich, L. W. *Bylines in Despair: Herbert Hoover, the Great Depression and the U.S. News Media*. Westport, Conn.: Praeger, 1994. 223pp.

Lucarelli, S. "The Newspaper Industry's Campaign against Space Grabbers 1917–1921." *Journalism Quarterly* 70 (1993): 883–92.

Luciani, F. "Lous-Stanislas Freron: Liberta di stampa o liberta di Associazione." *Annali dell Scuola Normale Superiore di Pisa* 19 (1989): 1493–1503.

Lyon, W. H. *Those Old Yellow Dog Days: Frontier Journalism in Arizona*. Tucson: Arizona Historical Society, 1994. 272pp.

McEnter, J. *Fighting Words: Independent Journalists in Texas*. Austin: University of Texas Press, 1992. 222pp.

McFarland, K. T. *Hollidaysburg Records: Marriages, Deaths and Petitions from Weekly Newspapers of Hollidaysburg, Huntingdon-Blair Counties, PA 1836–1852*. Apollo, Pa.: Closson Press, 1994. 129pp.

Maidment, B. *Into the 1830s: Some Origins of Victorian Illustrated Journalism*. Manchester: Manchester Polytechnic Library, 1992. 23pp.

Martin, J. R. "Looking the Other Way: A Study of Local Press Coverage of Events Surrounding the Herrim Massacre of June 22, 1992." Ph.D. thesis, Southern Illinois University, Carbondale, 1993.

Martin, P. E. "The Press and Transformation in the Anglophone Caribbean: Constraint and Action: A Case Study." Ph.D. thesis, Leicester University, 1991.

Mayes, S., ed. *The Critical Mirror: A Study of Post-War Journalism*. London: Thames & Hudson, 1995. 240pp.

Mayne, A. *The Imagined Slum: Newspaper Representation in Three Cities 1870–1914*. Leicester: Leicester University Press, 1993. 228pp.

Meier, J. A. *Advertisements and Notices of Interest from Norristown, PA: Vol C.* Apollo, Pa.: Closson Press, 1992.

Miller, B. C. "The Press, the Boldt Discussion and Indian-White Relations." *American Indian Culture and Research Journal* 17 (1993): 75–93.

"Mirth of a Nation." *British Library Newspaper Library Newsletter* 18 (1994–1995): 3.

Mulcrone, M. P. "The World War I Censorship of the Irish-American Press." Ph.D. thesis, University of Washington, 1993.

Murray, J. *The Russian Press from Brezhnev to Yeltsin: Behind the Paper Curtain.* Aldershot: E. Elgar, 1994. viii + 280pp.

Nerone, J. *Violence Against the Press in U.S. History.* Oxford: Oxford University Press, 1994. 320pp.

Oram, H. *Paper Tigers: Stories of Irish Newspapers by the People Who Make Them.* Belfast: Appletree Press, 1993. 143pp.

Payne, P. *Zeitungen in der Bundesrepublik Deutschland: Eine Einfuhrung mit Unterrichtsmaterialen.* Rev. ed. Lancaster: Lancaster University Dept. of Modern Languages, 1993. 145 pp.

Pilgrim, T. A. "Newspapers as Natural Monopolies: Some Historical Considerations." *Journalism History* 18 (1992): 3–10.

Popkin, J. D. "Dutch Patriots, French Journalists and Declarations of Rights: The Leidse Ontweep of 1785 and its Diffusion in France." *Historical Journal* 38 (1995): 533–66.

Popular Newspapers during World War II. Marlborough: Adam Matthew, 1993. 58pp.

Quaiyurn, H. N. "The Bengali Muslim Journalism: Its Origin and Aim." *Journal of the Pakistan Historical Society* 40 (1992): 361–70.

Ranghaven, G. N. *The Press in India: A New History.* Columbia, Mo.: Gian Publishing House, 1994.

Redhead, S. *Unpopular Cultures: The Birth of Law and Popular Culture.* Manchester: Manchester University Press, 1995. 136pp.

Reynolds, D. *Editors Make War: Southern Newspapers in the Secession Crisis.* Ann Arbor, Mich.: Books on Demand, 1992.

Riffenburgh, B. *The Myth of the Explorer: The Press, Sensationalism and Geographical Discovery.* Oxford: Oxford University Press, 1994. xi + 226pp.

Riley, S. *Biographical Dictionary of American Newspaper Columnists.* Westport, Conn.: Greenwood Press, 1995. 416pp.

Roeder, George H. *Censored War: American Visual Experience during World War II.* New Haven, Conn.: Yale University Press, 1995. xi + 189pp.

Schoenberg, W. P. *The Lapwai Mission Press.* Boise, Id.: Hemingway Western Studies Center, 1994. 86pp.

Shasko, P. "The Eastern Question: An American Response to the Bulgarian Massacres of 1876." *Bulgarian Historical Review* 20 (1992): 58–74.

Shaw, M. "The Fair in Black and White." *Chicago History* 22 (1993): 54–72.

Sieb, P. *Campaigns and Conscience: The Ethics of Political Journalism.* Westport, Conn.: Praeger, 1994. 176pp.

Simon, R. J., & Alexander, S. M. *The Ambivalent Welcome: Print Media, Public Opinion and Immigration.* Westport, Conn.: Praeger, 1993. 288pp.

Sloan, W. D., & Williams, J. H. *The Early American Press 1690–1783.* Westport, Conn.: Greenwood Press, 1994. 248pp.

Sloane, D. E. E. "The Comic Workers of Philadelphia: George Hembold's *The Tickler*, Joseph C. Neal's 'City Worthies' and the Beginnings of Modern Periodical Humor in America." *Victorian Periodicals Review* 25 (1995): 186–98.

Sotiron, M. "Concentration and Collusion in the Canadian Newspaper Industry." *Journalism History* 18 (1992): 26–32.

Springhall, J. "Disseminating Impure Literature: The 'Penny Dreadful' Publishing Business since 1860." *Economic History Review* 47 (1994): 567–84.

Stein, M. L. *Under Fire: The Story of American Correspondents*. New York: Julian Messner, 1995.

Streitmatter, R. *Raising her Voice: African-American Women Journalists who Changed History*. Frankfort: Kentucky University Press, 1994.

Summers, M. W. *The Press Gang: Newspapers and Politics 1865–1878*. Chapel Hill: North Carolina University Press, 1994. 405pp.

Targett, S. "Government and Ideology during the Age of Whig Supremacy: The Political Argument of Sir Robert Walpole's Propagandists." *Historical Journal* 37 (1994): 289–318.

Tuck, J. *McCarthyism and New York's Hearst Press: A Study of Roles in the Witch Hunt*. Lanham, Md.: University Press of America, 1995. 228pp.

Voss, F. S. *Reporting the War: The Journalistic Coverage of World War II*. Washington, D.C.: Smithsonian Institution Press, 1994. 208pp.

Ward, I. *Politics of the Media*. London: Macmillan Educational, 1994. 320pp.

Watts, A. D. "The Newspaper Press in the Town of Reading 1855–90." Ph.D. thesis, Stirling University, 1993.

Wiltshire, B. C. *Mississippi Newspaper Obituaries, 1862–1875*. Big Timber, Mont.: Pioneer Publishing Co., 1994. 253pp.

Yaszek, L. " 'Them Damn Pictures': Americanization and Comic Strips in the Progressive Era." *Journal of American Studies* 28 (1994): 23–38.

INDIVIDUAL NEWSPAPERS AND PERIODICALS

The Architects' Journal *Centenary Issue, 1895–1995. Architects' Journal* 201 (March 1995): 98 pp.

Matheou, D. "Tales from Another Century." *Architects' Journal* 201 (March 1995): 14–15.

Garnett, F. M. "The Phoenix Begins to Rise; the *Atlanta Daily Intelligencer* Announces the Return of Railroads." *Atlanta History* 37 (1994): 5–8.

Sedgwick, E. *The* Atlantic Monthly *1857–1909: Yankee Humanism at High Tide and Ebb*. Amherst, Mass.: Massachusetts University Press, 1994. 338pp.

Bradley, P. "The *Boston Gazette* and Slavery as Revolutionary Propaganda." *Journal of Mass Communication Quarterly* 72 (1995): 581–96.

Richardson, R., & Thorne, R. The Builder *Illustrations Index, 1843–1883*. London: Hutton & Rostron, 1994.

Tusa, B. H. "*Le Carillon*: An English Translation of Selected Satires." *Louisiana History* 35 (1994): 67–84.

Digby-Junger, R. "A News Version of the Founding of the *Chicago Daily News*." *Illinois Historical Journal* 86 (1933): 27–40.

Ugneault, R. "*Cîté libre* et liberté." *Cultures du Canada Français* 7 (1990): 51–56.

Godbout, J. "J'ai 24 ans." *Cultures du Canada Français* 7 (1990): 13–18.

Richards, H. "Construction, Conformity and Control: The Taming of the *Daily Herald* 1921–1930." Ph.D. thesis, Open University, 1993.

DeSantis, A. D. "Selling the American Dream: The Chicago *Defender* and the Great Migration of 1915–1919." Ph.D. thesis, Indiana University, 1993.

Carter, T. J. " 'Credos and Curios': James Thurber's Practice and Spadework on the Columbus *Dispatch*." Ph.D. thesis, University of Tennessee, 1993.

Edwards, R. D. *The Pursuit of Reason: The* Economist *1843–1993*. London: Hamish Hamilton, 1993. xix + 1020pp.

Berry, N. "Encounter." *Antioch Review* 51 (1993): 194–211.

Howard, J. P. "A History of the Magazine *Encounter* 1953–1967." D.Phil. thesis, Oxford University, 1993.

Abstracts from the Engine of Liberty & Uniontown Advertiser, 1813–1815. Westminster, Md.: Historical Society of Carroll County, 1993. 84pp.

Nimmo, I. *The Bold Adventure: 125 Years of Teesside and the* Evening Gazette. Derby: Breedon, 1994. 112pp.

Harris, B. "The London *Evening Post* and Mid-Eighteenth Century British Politics." *English Historical Review* 110 (1995): 1132–56.

Smith, M. B. "South Carolina and the *Gentleman's Magazine*." *South Carolina Historical Magazine* 95 (1994): 102–29.

Wyckoff, W., & Nash, C. "Geographical Images of America's West: The View from *Harper's Monthly* 1850–1900." *Journal of the West* 33 (1994): 10– 21.

Baker, M. "Death, Disease and the Birth of a Nation: Representations of the Jewish Body in *Ha-Magid*, a Hebrew Newspaper." D.Phil. thesis, Oxford University, 1993.

Thompson, J. E. *Percy Greene and the* "Jackson Advocate"*: The Life and Times of a Radical Conservative Newspaperman 1897–1977*. Jefferson, N.C.: McFarland, 1994.

Frenkel, F. *The Press and Politics in Israel: The* Jerusalem Post *from 1832 to the Present*. Westport, Conn.: Greenwood Press, 1994. xiv + 186pp.

Cesarani, D. *The* Jewish Chronicle *and Anglo-Jewry 1841–1991*. Cambridge: Cambridge University Press, 1994. xiv + 329pp.

Dethier, K. "The Spirit of Progressive Reform. The *Ladies Home Journal* House Plans 1900–1902." *Journal of Design History* 6 (1993): 247–61.

Kattan, N. "*Liberté*, revue montréalaise." *Cultures du Canada Français* 7 (1990): 27–30.

Major. R. "*Liberté* et *Parti pris*." *Cultures du Canada Français* 7 (1990): 57– 59.

Marks, P. " 'Americanus sum': *Life* Attacks Anglomania." *Victorian Periodicals Review* 28 (1995): 186–98.

Read, D. "Truth in News: Reuters and the *Manchester Guardian*, 1858–1964." *Northern History* (1995): 281–97.

Fleischmann, T. "Black Miamians in the *Miami Metropolis* 1896–1900." *Tequesta* 52 (1992): 21–38.

Maik, T. A. *The* Masses Magazine *(1911–1917): Odyssey of an Era*. New York: Garland, 1994. 272pp.

Street, L. M. "Teaching Orientalism in American Popular Education: *National Geographic* 1888–1988." Ph.D. thesis, Syracuse University, 1993.

Keenan, J. *"Labour Opposition in Northern Ireland": Complete Reprint of Northern Ireland's First Labour Newspaper, 1925–26*. Belfast: Athol Books, 1992. 212pp.

Harcup, T. A Northern Star, *Leeds' Other Paper and the Alternative Press 1974–1994*. Upton: Campaign for Press and Broadcasting Freedom, 1994. 30pp.

Lalli, S. F. "The *Oklahoma Rural News*: Roots of an Electronic Cooperative Newspaper." *Chronicles of Oklahoma* 71 (1993–94): 438–49.

Suistola, J. *"Oulun Wiikko-Sanoma* ja Turkkie." *Faravid* 16 (1992): 183–211.

Rich, P. B. The Pickens Sentinel *Favorite Newspaper of Pickens County*. Bowie, Md.: Heritage Books, 1994. 755pp.

Ruckman, J. A. "Images of the Northern Shoshone and Bannock in the *Pocatello Tribune*." *Rendezvous* 28 (1992–93): 105–19.

Reed, D. *"Radio Times*: High or Low." *British Library Newspaper Library Newsletter* 17 (1994): 6–8.

Morris, A. *Scotland's Paper: The "Scotsman" 1817–1992*. Edinburgh: The *Scotsman* Publications, 1992. 64pp.

MacDonald, A. *The Scottish Farmer: One Hundred Years*. Glasgow: Outram Magazines, 1993. 272pp.

Griffiths, D. "Plant Here the *Standard*." *British Library Newspaper Library Newsletter* 19 (1995): 6–9.

Griffiths, D. *Plant Here the* Standard. Basingstoke: Macmillan, 1996. xiii + 417pp.

McLane, B. *Clark County: Arkansas – Obituaries and Death Notices, 1901–1913:* Southern Standard *Newspaper*. Hot Springs: Arkansas Ancestors, 1992.

Varney, A. "The Lascivious Nightingale: Mild Impropriety in the *Spectator*." *Notes and Queries* 41 (1994): 189–91.

Blondheim, M. *News over the Wires: The* Telegraph *and the Flow of Public Information in America 1844–1897*. Cambridge, Mass.: Harvard University Press, 1994. viii + 305pp.

Fulton, R. D. "The London *Times* and the Anglo American Boarding Dispute of 1858." *Nineteenth-Century Contexts* 17 (1993): 133–44.

Grigg, J., ed. *The History of the* "Times." *Vol. 6. The Thomson Years, 1966–1981*. London: Times Books, 1993. xv + 632pp.

"Collections: *Transactions of the Oregon Pioneer Association* and Related Material." *Oregon Historical Quarterly* 94 (1993): 246–353.

Altschuler, G. C., & Grossvogel, D. I. *Changing Channels: America in* TV Guide. Urbana: Illinois University Press, 1992. 214pp.

McCusker, K. M. " 'The Forgotten Years' of America's Civil Rights Movement: Wartime Protests at the University of Kansas 1939–1945." *Kansas History* 17 (1994): 26–37.

Gilbert, B. W. "Toward a Color Blind Newspaper: Race Relations and the *Washington Post*." *Washington History* 5 (1993–94): 4–27.

Yoder, E. M. "Star Wars: Adventures in Attempting to Save a Failing Newspaper." *Virginia Quarterly Review* 69 (1993): 581–606.

Cleaver, J. D. "L. Samuel and the *West Shore*: Images of a Changing Pacific Northwest." *Oregon Historical Quarterly* 94 (1993): 166–224.

INDIVIDUAL JOURNALISTS

Fraser, D. "The Life of Edward Baines: A Filial Biography of the 'Great Liar of the North.' " *Northern History* (1995): 208–22.

Sinovas, Mate, J. "La obra periodistica de Dona Emilia Pardo Bazan publicada en el diario *La Nacion* (Buenos Aires) 1879–1929." Ph.D. thesis, City University of New York, 1993.

Yow, M. "The Uncollected Stories of Virginia Frazer Boyle, Victorian magazinist." *Victorian Periodicals Review* 28 (1995): 249–68.

Organ, M. W. B. "Clarke as Scientific Journalist." *Historical Records of Australian Science* 9 (1992): 1–16.

Slater, M., ed. *Sketches by Boz and Other Early Papers 1833–39*. Columbus: Ohio State University Press, 1994. 580pp.

Lyday-Lee, K. J. "Will Allen Dromgoole: A Biographical Sketch." *Tennessee Historical Quarterly* 51 (1992): 107–12.

Mitchell, C. C. *Margaret Fuller's New York Journalism: A Biographical Essay and Key Writings*. Knoxville: Tennessee University Press, 1995. 240pp.

Lissner, W. *George and Ohio's Civic Revival: The American Democratic Philosopher Inspired a Successful Fight against Political Bossism, Ending Many Exactions of the System of Privilege*. New York: Robert Schalkenbach Foundation, 1995.

Simon, J. *Freedom's Champion: Elijah Lovejoy*. Carbondale: Southern Illinois University Press, 1994. 206pp.

Griffith, T. *Harry and Teddy: The Turbulent Friendship of Henry R. Luce and Theodore H. White: The Press Lord and his Rebellious Correspondent*. New York: Random House, 1995.

Hobson, F. *Thirty-Five Years of Newspaper Work*. Baltimore: Johns Hopkins University Press, 1994.

Frost, C. J. "The Valley of Cross Purposes: Charles Nordoff and American Journalism, 1860–1890." Ph.D. thesis, Brown University, 1993.

Pierce, R. N. *A Sacred Trust: Nelson Poyhler and the* St. Petersburg Times. Gainesville: Florida University Press, 1993. 409pp.

Baldwin, T. D. "George D. Prentice, the *Louisville Anzeiger* and the 1855 Bloody Monday Riots." *Filson Club Historical Quarterly* 67 (1993): 482–95.

Pfaff, D. W. *Joseph Pulitzer II and the* Post-Dispatch*: A Newspaper Man's Life*. University Park, Pa.: Penn State University Press, 1991. 455pp.

Cienciala, A. M. "Foundations of Polish-American Scholarship: Karol Wachte." *British American Studies* 50 (1993): 51–73.

At the Coal-Face of History: Personal Reflections on Using Newspapers as a Source

Glenn R. Wilkinson

While some modern scholarship has started to move away from the idea that newspapers are not a serious source for historians, there still seems to be a perception that newspapers are the lignite of the historical world rather than the anthracite. Lignite, an example of poor quality domestic coal, is an apt metaphor, for although newspapers are recognized as mines of information, the extractions are felt by some to be low grade and trivial. This prejudice, however, is changing, especially among social and cultural historians to whom the distinction between low-grade and high-grade measures now depends on the subject and historical orientation of the researcher.

For those of us searching for anthracite, here are some reflections that might be useful to share. What follows can be seen perhaps as not so much a call for militancy, but more as a desire to stop exploring for gold in a coal mine. It might be fruitful to begin with an examination of some of the ways that newspapers have been used in the past, to mention the multifarious nature of the source, and to discuss some general suggestions of how the press can be marshalled to aid in the historical inquiry. I shall then go on to discuss some of the problems of using newspapers as a historical source linked to some corresponding strengths. Last, some practical and perhaps more mundane helpful hints for greenhorn coal miners.

I have found that newspapers in the past have been used to gauge, among other things, the "mood" of the country. I first came across this early in my Ph.D. career when I saw a reputable historian suggesting that the Edwardian period was a more despondent and pessimistic era compared to the later Victorian period. What this historian had done to support this claim was to look at newspapers to get a sense of the way that people were thinking and feeling just prior to and after the death of Queen Victoria. Not too bad a start, but the scholar in question looked at only two leading articles in two issues of the *Times* and found, not surprisingly, that the one before was optimistic, while the one afterward was pessimistic. Therefore, the "mood" of the country had changed after the queen's death. Anyone with an gram of methodological sense will see that this is quite a flawed piece of historical inquiry. However, it illustrates many of the fallacies associated with examining the press of a historical age.

Part of the problem arises from the belief that there are only a few types of newspapers. But there are as many newspapers as there are interest groups, particularly in the Edwardian period, in which the pamphlet and the pulpit had lost their importance and new forms of communication were either just starting (like cinema) or yet to be invented (like broadcast radio). There are the national metropolitan dailies that most historians use, but even here there are Conservative, Liberal, Independent, popular, "quality," and "new journalism" papers. There are also regional leaders and the national papers for Scotland, Ireland and Wales. There are the weekly papers, which reflected all these categories and performed slightly different functions. There are trade papers, radical left-wing papers, Socialist papers, trade union papers, women's papers, juvenile papers, sports papers, society papers, illustrated papers, humor papers and the list goes on. This is also neglecting to mention that there is a rich vein of information in the periodical press, with each title representing profound differences in perceptions held by readers. How can anyone suggest that they can even guess at the "mood" of the country unless they examine at least a representative sample of a number of these titles? One expensive newspaper that targeted a small segment of society and had a dwindling circulation cannot be seen in any way as representative of the country as a whole.

There are, however, problems with the way that newspapers have been utilized in the past, and anyone who works with the press as a historical source will come across them. They can be divided into two parts: mental and physical. The mental problems center around the inability or unwillingness of historians to imagine the various ways in which newspapers can be used. The physical problems, on the other hand, are merely questions of accessibility that can be more easily overcome.

The mental problems with thinking of newspapers as a source are perhaps the most tricky to deal with. They require both a psychological shift in attitudes and an increasing openness to an imaginative process. These are not necessarily difficult, as younger scholars seem to be pointing out, but they do appear to go against the grain.

The first problem in this section can be seen as the use of a simplistic approach. Some modern research in communication theory is making it clear that the exchange between reader and author is much more complex than some historians have thought. It has often been suggested that the presence of an opinion or idea in a newspaper automatically indicates that the readers held this view. It is as if readers are empty vessels that were filled with opinions without due regard for the context in which they lived and worked. Much of this perception seems to depend on believing what the "press barons" wished to propagate about themselves. Movements such as Tariff Reform, one of Arthur Pearson's principal concerns, or the pre-1914 scaremongering of Alfred Harmsworth were seen as ways in which readers were manipulated, unsuccessful or successfully, to come around to the ideas of the proprietor.

This approach, of course, takes away from the complexity of the communication process. The consumption of a newspaper is a two-way form of communication. It is not just a question of ideas being imposed upon readers, but rather that readers play a role in ensuring what is in the content of the press by actively buying the paper on a regular basis. It seems to me that if readers found that the paper contained ideas or modes of expression with which they did not agree or semiotic signs they could not read, they would no longer buy that newspaper. This is especially important in an era of intense competition for readers in which readers had a large selection of titles from which to choose.

The second mental problem that historians need to overcome is the idea of authority. This suggestion came to me rather out of the blue as I was fielding questions after my first academic paper at the Ph.D. level. While I had prepared for questions, I was taken aback by the first question from a senior academic near retirement. She stated, in fact, that I was being too naive or simplistic to suggest that the authority of the *Daily Mail* was equal to the *Times*. Since I was examining the imagery inherent in language concerning military expeditions and linking it with the readers of each newspaper, I was somewhat amazed at the question. Newspapers create a strong bond with their readers and as such are very authoritative concerning those readers. However, this question indicates that the idea of authority still taints the way in which people read newspapers as a source whereas the quality press is seen as having some sort of authority or value lacking in the popular press. It also reveals interesting class and status issues that seem to be little changed since the Edwardian period.

A third problem that should be discussed is the tendency to use the press as merely a supplement to more traditional and reliable sources.

For some reason, historians have thought that diaries, personal papers and government records were more dependable and informative than newspapers. The subject matter will certainly play a role in this regard, but if, for example, one is looking to gauge the mood of the country or its cultural practices, then a diary, written, as its very nature suggests, by a nonrepresentative elite, will not be the best source for this form of inquiry. A newspaper, which has a daily or weekly relationship with its readers, a relationship reinforced with every purchase, will be more representative and indicative of a larger group than a single diarist who might be operating under an unknown or subtle agenda.

The fourth mental problem that has to be addressed is one of utilization. Historians have tended to concentrate on the "hard news" sections of the newspaper, such as the leading articles or editorials and the news columns. This tendency ties in with the previous problems in that it sees the relationship to the reader as somewhat simplistic, suggesting that the news section is the most authoritative part of a paper and can be used to merely supplement other real sources. There are, however, many other parts of the newspaper that can be utilized by historians depending on the research goal, some of which will be discussed later.

The second set of problems centers around the physical difficulties of dealing with the press as a source. The first and the most obvious problem is the sheer volume of the material available to examine. When one considers the amount of material found in a single title over even the shortest of life spans, one begins to realize the scope of the problem. This problem is beginning to be addressed through the use of CD-ROM indexes, but even here the amount of material is monumental and dependent on the skill of the indexer. Even with an indexed paper, such as the *Times* with its idiosyncratic use of search fields, the exploration for imagery, for example, can be difficult. The bulk of the source, one of its main strengths, can produce a feeling of inaccessibility.

Related to this feeling of inaccessibility is the more prosaic problem of actually reading the text. Most of the heavily used titles are microfilmed, and although it seems like a minor quibble, it can be difficult to read poor quality film, particularly with a machine that needs a bit of care and attention. And, as anyone who has raced for the machines at the beginning of a research day at the British Library Newspaper Archive at Colindale can attest, physically getting a machine can be a bit of a trial! There are also problems with reading film from which many people suffer, and these include eye strain and the flicker of fast-moving film, which can be unsettling.

More seriously, but again linked to the idea of accessibility, is the third physical problem, which is that of visualization. Reading a microfilmed copy of a newspaper means that we are not viewing the paper the way that it was meant to be read. For example, we see only part or half of the page at a time instead of two pages unfolded in front of us. This can be crucial if, as in my research, the association of images or the location of certain images is important. For example, my idea that war was seen as a form of sporting activity in the Edwardian period, was supported when either photographs or stories were placed next to or on the sports page. It is important to remember that the paper was consciously laid out and that reader traffic was often taken into account, particularly in the modern period. The analysis of advertisements must keep these forms of association in mind, as the place and layout of ads can often be important in determining advertiser intention and reader reaction.

Last, there is the physical problem of quantification. There seems often to be a desire to know exact numbers for circulation and readership, as if this in itself indicates something profound. While this information can be useful in determining the nature and extent of audiences, there are ways around the lack of certified numbers for circulations and readership. The need to count seems to stem also from the content analysis school of historical inquiry. Counting column inches, or in the case of microfilm, tenths of columns, is important in that it can indicate the importance of a story. Historians can follow the rule of thumb that suggests the more space and prominence of place given to an article, the more important it was to publishers and readers. However, counting lines, in addition to being extremely tedious, cannot really tell us very much in and of itself. I discovered this after writing my first rough draft chapter having counted lines and measured tenths of columns. My great revelation was that during a war military coverage goes up and during peace it goes down. I was greeted with a big "So what?" by my wise and patient supervisors. Connections had to be made to social or cultural trends in order to make the research meaningful.

These problems, however, can be addressed by examining them in relation to corresponding strengths. Again, some of these suggestions depend on the way in which historians conduct their search and the style or method of history they wish to employ. But I think that those who are able to take the time to examine the press in imaginative ways will be more than a little rewarded for the effort expended.

In dealing with the press, we must realize that the relationship between consumer and producer is a complex one. There is more to reading papers than trying to decide between the reflection/manipulation debate. Since the process of communication is two-way, historians can look at what is contained in the press as the result not simply of attempts to manipulate readers or a reflection of the sophistication of a culture, but of the way in which people express themselves or see their world.

My research examined images of military conflict and the depiction of the use of force before the First World War. By looking at images of conflict, I could examine the language and visual portrayals present in the press—whether for or against a particular war—and determine how conflict was viewed. Given the fact that readers kept buying papers and reinforcing the images they saw, this indicated to me that it was more than simply readers being told what to think or see. Certainly newspapers set the agenda, but the way in which that agenda was discussed had to be in a language understood by readers.

Since newspapers are in part constructed by their audience, it follows that one paper will not have more authority as a source than another. If we want to examine working-class culture, we do not go to the *Times* for guidance, but to the papers that working-class people actually read and consumed, be those weekly papers or trade papers. In this way, it is clear to me that to say the "quality" press has more authority than the "popular" press or any other press is facile. In fact, it is important to examine as many titles as possible in order to find representative samples of papers that carried authority by dint of them containing perceptions associated with a wide variety of groups. Then we could suggest that we can gauge the mood of the country.

In looking at this mood, we would do well to recognize that newspapers have particular advantages over other sources and can be used in their own right as more than just supplements. For example, personal diaries are often used to determine attitudes of society. But these diaries were written by people who are perhaps least representative of society as a whole, since they were written by those not only with the education to write and express themselves, but also the leisure and inclination to do so. Newspapers, however, relate directly with a large segment of society and do so on a wide scale across the socioeconomic spectrum. In addition, a newspaper edition has a life span stretching from the time it is printed to the time the next issue comes out. Newspapers do not have an eye for posterity or future reputation, which can be the case with diaries. Newspapers are also dated, meaning that, unlike diaries, there tend to be no gaps in the record, or writing after the fact, to establish an author's prescience. In addition, newspapers, unlike works of literature, cannot be "discovered" to be significant or particularly important for audiences long after their publication. The press has to strike resonances with its audience immediately.

Yet, not only can we examine a wide variety of newspaper titles to get a broad picture of society, we can also utilize the entire content of a single issue. There is so much more to a newspaper than the leading articles and hard news section. First, there are the feature articles that go into more depth on particular topics. These can be by experts, and the kind of experts employed can be revealing, or by journalists as observers. Book reviews can tell us more about the kind of literature that was popular and how certain books were received and consumed. There are cartoons, which need to be read by consumers with a minimum of effort and are loaded with cultural meaning and current significance. Advertisements are fruitful sources of information regarding the use and manipulation of acceptable imagery. Advertisers would not use an image if it offended or alienated a target audience. It is safe to assume, then, that since advertisers are dealing directly with their audience, they will be good indicators of popular tastes, particularly if the images found in ads correspond with those found in the other parts of the newspaper. Letters to the editor, if treated with care, can also be revealing in that they represent the direct voice of selected readers.

While these solutions address the need to examine the mental problems of using newspapers as a source, there still remain the physical barriers to be overcome. There are many ways in which researchers can accomplish this, perhaps the best way being to mention some of the ways in which I limited my research in order to minimize the barriers.

First, while an indexed newspaper seems to be more accessible to research techniques, this might not be the case. I was looking for imagery of military expeditions and there was no point in searching for images of war as sport, for example. And my sources, except for the *Times*, were not indexed. However, I was able to limit my search by examining the coverage of case studies.

For example, I looked to representative military conflicts during the Edwardian period and, knowing the dates of individual battles, was able to focus on those issues that would contain reports of the fighting. Soon a pattern arose in which, due to the inaccessibility of the country where the fighting was conducted and the distance to the telegraph, a delay of a day or two was to be expected. Also, more detailed and handwritten reports tended to find their way into the pages of the press usually a week or so after the initial telegraphed reports.

This pattern can be confirmed by looking at an indexed paper and comparing it to the content of other papers. The *Times* is a good example of this, since it was one of the papers from which other newspapers tended to cull information and to follow in the timing of reporting major stories. This is not to say that other papers slavishly followed its lead, but rather that a pattern of news reporting can be found and followed.

In addition, researchers can examine the articles contained in press directories. These are yearly summaries designed to inform advertisers of the trends and players in the newspaper industry throughout the country. The articles inform potential advertisers as to what was happening in the industry and can be helpful to historians looking for clues or patterns of reporting. The titles that I found most helpful were *Mitchell's Press Directory* and *Sell's Press Directory*, two of the sources with the longest run in the United Kingdom.

With respect to the problems of having to use microfilm readers, there is little anyone can do until new technology takes over. Colindale has started putting new issues of the national daily press on CD-ROM, but until past records are converted, this will not be helpful to most historians. Yet, many newspaper titles are still to be found in hard copy, bound in large and crumbling folios, which makes a welcome change from microfilm. However, it is debatable how long this will be the case unless those researchers seen licking their fingers and flicking the pages of one hundred–year-old newspapers are encouraged to think about the delicate nature of their source.

The difficulty of visualizing the source in the way that it was intended to be consumed can, of course, be alleviated when looking at the hard copy of less used papers. But it must always be kept in mind when dealing with microfilm that the placement of a story or an image on the page and within the body of the paper can tell much about the importance of a topic. For example, a story that has the upper left-hand corner column or is on or opposite to the leader page, has been given more status than other stories tucked away elsewhere in the paper. This indicates that the paper, and therefore readers, have given a value to particular topics, and this can be read by historians to gauge the views of audiences.

Association with other forms of imagery are also important to keep in mind. Items that surround a particular form of imagery help to define its meaning. For example, I discovered in an illustrated journal a photograph of Japanese soldiers firing at Russian troops juxtaposed and boxed within the same border as a photograph of King Edward shooting grouse. This grouping of imagery suggested to me connections on many levels. First, that the shooting of an enemy was related to the shooting of game—that is, a sporting event. Second, it reflected the respect that the Japanese held in Britain as allies and military models to be emulated. Further connections could be made by recognizing that in both photographs, the figures were looking toward each other and images of both the king and the Japanese soldiers were reproduced to make them the same size. There is further significance in the fact that this was a front-page piece and that the Japanese were on the left in a position of prominence. The latter suggested not so much that the Japanese were more important than the king, but that the topic, a particularly significant battle, was for the moment more newsworthy.

The final physical problem that historians face when dealing with newspapers as a source, that of quantification, can be overcome by several techniques. First, the researcher has to differentiate between circulation and readership. The former concerns how many actual issues were printed, which can be more than those sold. The latter relates to the actual number of people who read the paper or have it read to them. Before the advent of certified circulations in the mid-twentieth century, newspapers themselves supplied circulation figures to advertisers, readers and others interested in knowing the outreach of a particular paper. The possibility and temptation of stretching the truth are obvious.

However, if it is necessary to determine the distribution of newspapers and their readership, there are some ways in which this can be done. There is some scholarship that has been concerned with this problem, most notably A. P. Wadsworth's classic work "Newspaper Circulations, 1800–1954" in *Manchester Statistical Society Transactions, 1954*. This is an impressive example of scholarship that pieces together diverse collections of statistical evidence.

For our purposes, in addition to examining the work of statisticians, there is the internal evidence found within the pages of the press itself. In order to calculate circulation a researcher could examine the geographical spread of the advertisers within the paper and compare it to the population density of that region. This technique would work better for more remote and local papers, but it might very well come in handy to at least establish maximum numbers. Also, the press directories can give some indication of what a newspaper claimed as its circulation. This is, of course, assuming that circulation records are important. In many ways, the relative extent of a paper's circulation is enough, if one can determine who actually read the paper.

For my work it was readership rather than circulation that was the most important. In determining the extent of readership, the advertisements can be examined. The target audiences, whether women, middle-class families, children, commuters, or a particular political group, will be more or less revealed in the advertisements. Advertisers, for example, will not advertise items that are beyond the means of a paper's readers. In addition, the entertainments section can be utilized to find out who is reading the paper. The kind of entertainment advertised, and the cost of that entertainment, can give quite bold indications of who bought the paper. Similarly, the letters to the editor, the book reviews, the presence of a society page, and the cartoons can give more hints.

Last, there are one or two things that I found to make the process of conducting research easier and more effective. The first thing was the crucial need for tightly defined limits to the study. With all the information and bulk of the source, it is easy to get lost and to lose track of what it is you are searching for. Linked to this is the tendency, which no newspaper researcher can deny, to get sidetracked by other interesting stories, be they a particularly gruesome trial, a titillating divorce or the score in the Cup Final. While this is part of the fun of looking at the press and should not be completely denied, it is the way to an unfinished piece of research. Second, I found it also important to maintain a sense of context with what was going on in terms of cultural trends, socioeconomic changes, philosophical debates and so on. For example, while the Edwardian press rarely, if ever, directly mentioned the debate on the fear of physical degeneration, it can be seen clearly in the way in which reports were written. My research concerning military imagery was crucially informed by the fear of deterioration, which was a pan-European concern. The impact and significance of the Boer War and the Russo-Japanese War can be understood only with due regard to this context. So, while newspapers contain all the essential elements of culture, it is important to be able to recognize them when in fact they do make an appearance.

Associated with the idea of philosophical context, is the need to link newspapers to more mundane cultural changes. In my research, examining elements of the way warfare was reported gave rise to the impression that, for example, war was compared to a theatrical entertainment or a sport. These images are important in looking at attitudes and perceptions, but they must be connected to trends in society concerning the development and middle-class appropriation of both entertainment and sport. The increasing desire for realistic illusions on the stage or the demand for players to follow rules informed the way in which readers saw warfare. Therefore, the use of stage or sport imagery to report warfare was not just linguistic lightness or flowery prose. They contained real meaning that has to be connected to cultural developments in order to make sense of them.

Similarly, one has to be aware of what is not present in newspaper reports, or what is merely alluded to. War reporting, for example, minimized and hid the less desirable effects of warfare, namely death and wounding. Corpses were partially hidden by bushes, they were bodily intact and there was a minimum of blood. The absence of portrayals of death, which were not significantly different for those other than British troops, has to be examined in terms of general attitudes to death and corpses. These attitudes changed over the course of the nineteenth century. Graveyard iconography moved from skulls and crossbones to cherubic angels and broken columns, symbolizing a growing denial of death and an increasing removal of the body from the imagery.

Apart from these philosophical and cultural considerations, more mundane hints for working with papers might include taking frequent breaks, especially if using microfilm. This might seem impractical, as open hours at archives like Colindale can be quite brief, but your eyes and your research will benefit from it. Also, while many people read the paper at lunch (what else would a newspaper historian do?), take the time to chat with some of your fellow researchers and the archivists. They can give you interesting hints and can be interesting in and of themselves.

Furthermore, take a sweater, as microfilm rooms tend to be chilly, and if you are going to Colindale, take a lunch. This is not because the journey is so long (though it does take a slice of time—anywhere from forty-five minutes to an hour and a quarter—from central London!), but because there is a shortage of places to eat and drink. One would have thought that Colindale would have shared their underused staff cafeteria to exploit a captive audience of scholars, but they haven't yet. Colindale, however, is a user-friendly archive that has plenty of electrical outlets for computers as well as light and airy reading rooms for searching through hard copies. The staff is very friendly and helpful, though sometimes extremely overworked.

To conclude, newspapers can be used in new and dynamic ways to access certain kinds of historical information. While they lend themselves better to social or cultural forms of history, other historians will doubtless benefit from a more reasoned and methodological approach to the source. There are, however, things to keep in mind and imaginative applications that need to be developed. A little exploration, however, will certainly reveal some rich seams of valuable anthracite for those willing and able to get their historical hands dirty.

V

Reviews

The Atlantic Monthly, 1857–1909: Yankee Humanism at High Tide and Ebb. By Ellery Sedgwick. Amherst: University of Massachusetts Press. 1994. xi + 338 pp.

Ellery Sedgwick's history of the *Atlantic Monthly* is, in fact, a history of its editorship over five decades. It is a narrative account whose hero is the editor in seven incarnations, each allocated a chapter, headed by a telling epithet, and prefaced by a suitably emblematic photograph. From James Russell Lowell, epitome of the "Yankee Humanist" to Bliss Perry, "Liberal Humanist in the Progressive Era," Sedgwick traces the refraction of American cultural history through the pages of the Boston-based literary magazine.

The action is largely confined to the editorial office, which was, as Perry noted, "somewhat apart from the insane whirl which is miscalled 'progress.'" But Sedgwick manages to differentiate sufficiently between the characters of its occupants to suggest a dramatic pattern to historical events beyond those walls. The elevated group of New England writers who established the *Atlantic* may have launched it "on vanity and champagne," but without responsive adaptation to a rapidly changing world, the magazine would scarcely have survived these turbulent years.

It was Oliver Wendell Holmes who named it, intending to indicate intellectual commerce with European culture. But from the start, emphasis fell heavily upon American writing, and Sedgwick follows meticulously its role in granting cohesion to the various strands of literary New England, in nurturing local-color realism, and in fostering the talents of William Dean Howells and Henry James (commercial factors permitting). He takes pains to stress the magazine's enlightened attitude, throughout the period, toward writing by women; he asserts that it constituted 50 percent of published fiction. The *Atlantic* gave practical encouragement to the black novelist Charles Chestnutt, and published autobiographical writings by Zitkala-Sa, who subsequently founded the National Council of American Indians. Increasing social awareness is evidenced by the inclusion of work by these writers and others such as Booker T. Washington, W. E. B. DuBois, Abraham Cahan, Jacob Riis and Jack London.

It is doubtless part of Sedgwick's agenda to dispel any sense that the *Atlantic* catered, during this period, exclusively to the tastes of an elite. The illustrious company assembled in its early editions, with Emerson at its heart, set a particular standard and tone that was significantly modified by Howells ("Editorial Realist"), and then modernized by Walter Hines Page ("Progressive Editing"). But Page's hardheaded awareness of market values clearly sits uneasily with Sedgwick. It was his successor, Perry, who fused economic realism with intellectual integrity to make the *Atlantic* "one of the last public forums in America for discussion of major works and figures of Western humanism outside an academic context." This is a genuinely heroic achievement for Sedgwick, unsettled by today's legion of college graduates, whose knowledge might be considerable, yet is limited to "the ephemeral celebrities of commercial mass culture."

Here is the nub of this history, for Sedgwick qualifies our view of the magazine as bastion of high culture, in order to establish its continued authority as critic of "the assumptions and pieties of mass culture." He does so by systematically highlighting espousal of liberal causes—opposition to slavery, support for women's rights and exposure of the social ills accompanying industrial capitalism.

Despite the diversity of origin and of professional orientation among successive editors, Sedgwick's approach has evident limitations to its scope, and there are inevitable structural repetitions. Alternative strategies suggest themselves: more coverage of contributors, with closer attention to their work, or more explicit reference to those historical events whose reverberations were registered in the nuances and deflections of editorial policy. As it stands the book is undeniably a solid and engaged work of scholarship presenting revision of a history that merits attention.

Julian Cowley
University of Luton

Froth & Scum: Truth, Beauty, Goodness, and the Ax Murder in America's First Mass Medium. By Andie Tucher. Chapel Hill: University of North Carolina Press. 1994. ix + 257 pp.

Two notorious New York murders provide focal points for Andie Tucher's study of sensationalism and objectivity within the history of American popular journalism: the death of a prostitute in 1836, and of a tradesman, killed in 1841 by inventor Samuel Colt's brother, John. Notes and bibliography suggest a formal academic approach, yet Tucher's style aims to divert and entertain. A particularly gruesome example of her cultivated populism commences chapter 14: "When the missing printer's battered body turned up in a box aboard a cargo ship, [Horace] Greeley welcomed the story with all the fervour of a diner confronting a fingernail in his sausage." It is not always easy to reconcile such touches with the serious aspirations of the book.

A chapter on P. T. Barnum explores the essence of "humbug." Helen Jewett's murder was transformed into humbug in the hands of James Gordon Bennett. Yet, we are told, the same editor subsequently exemplified "authoritative fact-finding," in his handling of Colt's trial and conviction. Resisting the obvious temptation to assume the superiority of the latter mode, Tucher addresses "the continuing capacity of each to generate publics willing to stake their identities on its own particular truths." Her real subject, then, is the production of a readership.

Her argument does not endorse a model of the press as manipulative or exploitative; while the press generates its readership, it is readers themselves who must bear ultimate responsibility for the popular myths they endorse. Humbug and objectivity are equally methods (rather than outcomes) toward discovery, "directed by the public's need to fashion out of these discovered things a comprehensible drama that adequately explains human suffering, injustice, anger, or want." The problem here is that the nature of that need goes unquestioned; it is assumed to be a given of human society, conceived as a "community of consumers." Tucher shows no sense that suffering, injustice, anger and want might be historically determined or amenable to rational analysis. In this light, her ostensibly democratic respect for the needs of the people might be seen as unfortunate, apolitical relativism.

The claim that inventors of the penny press did not set out to invent a mass medium, but rather invented "a medium that was appealing enough to grow massive," is familiar enough, and within its own terms appears reasonable; but such appeal does not exist in a social or cultural vacuum. Popular journalism may offer "resonant, familiar, intelligible" explanations for "the curious, confusing, or troubling matters of everyday life," but an intelligent reading will ask how, in a modern democracy, do such tensions, anxieties and areas of ignorance arise? There may be validity in the claim that "a myth works for the members of a community only if it illuminates a truth important to them in a way they find congenial"; but such validity is questionable without inquiry into the terms for congeniality.

Irruption of irrational or accidental events into daily routine may be traumatic, but there are other means for coming to terms with and understanding them than the provisional and sometimes illusory coherence of a newspaper report. Tucher is right to point out that facts and truth may not always be congruent, and to identify popular myth as a form of mediation between the two. But she ignores the many factors that enter into construction of such myth and the complex ramifications of its operation within social groups.

The "froth & scum of the eternal sea" was Henry David Thoreau's evaluation of "the news." At the end of her book, Tucher asserts that it is we who must decide whether "the ascetic philosopher" was prophet or merely curmudgeon. There is rather more involved in arriving at our decision than *Froth & Scum* assumes.

Julian Cowley
University of Luton

The Builder *Illustrations Index, 1843–1883*. By Ruth Richardson and Robert Thorne. London: The Builder Group and Hutton+Rostron in Association with the Institute of Historical Research. 1994.

With the exception of certain newspapers such as *The Times*, it is unusual to find a stand-alone index to any newspaper or periodical. The illustrations index to *The Builder* is therefore a welcome addition to this field of publishing.

The Builder was one of the most important and influential architectural journals of the Victorian era. It first appeared at the end of 1842, in the same year as the *Illustrated London News* and a year after *Punch*. Its first editor was Joseph Aloysius Hansom (1803–1882) after whom the patent safety cab was named. He was also an architect of note and with his colleague Edward Welch, designed Birmingham Town Hall, still to be seen today in Chamberlain Square. Hansom published the "Precursor Issue" of *The Builder* on the last day of 1842. It was his vision to present a journal that would not only entertain and inform but would also be a mouthpiece for a national movement to sustain the rights and dignity of the building trades. Sadly, after just twenty issues, he was forced to sell the copyright to the printers J. L. Cox and Sons, although he remained editor until the end of 1843.

The second editor was Alfred Bartholomew, another architect and writer of note whose Italianate savings bank in Clerkenwell still survives. Unfortunately, ill health forced him to resign late in 1844 and he was succeeded by George Godwin (1813–1883). Godwin proved to be the most famous of *The Builder*'s editors and during his forty years of editorship the journal rose to become one of the most popular and frequently quoted of its kind in Europe.

At the time George Godwin took over as editor of *The Builder* he was a practicing architect and surveyor, like his father before him, mainly in the Kensington area of London. In 1836 he had won the silver medal of the recently established Institute of British Architects with an essay on concrete. As a consequence of this, he became a regular contributor to the *Architectural Magazine* until its demise in 1842. His interests were many and varied, and although no personal papers have survived, he can be glimpsed through the memoirs of others. Among his achievements was the founding of the Art Union of London in 1840, his election as Fellow of three major bodies—the (Royal) Institute of British Architects, the Society of Antiquaries and the Royal Society—and as a writer of numerous plays, including a farce, *The Last Days*, which was performed at the Olympic Theatre in 1840.

The Builder came out weekly and an annual index was produced, though inevitably this proved inconsistent and uneven over time. A modern, comprehensive index was needed, but to index the entire contents for even a few decades was logistically and financially impossible. Sensibly, and unusually, it was decided to concentrate on the illustrations and the time period of forty years was chosen as it corresponded neatly with Godwin's editorship.

Illustrations of any kind provide an amazing amount of information, and the beautifully engraved drawings of the Victorian period provide a clarity of image unmatched in the modern, photographic equivalent. The fine detailing of brickwork; the interior decoration of chapels; the amazing heads sculpted on Cambodian temples; the humorous corbels on cathedrals and the suggestive chairs (i.e., four chairs named after Ann Boleyn, Samuel Johnson, Lord Byron and Lady Morgan) all provide valuable insights into the architectural and furnishing history of the time.

Using the illustrations on the pages of *The Builder* and information provided in the accompanying caption and text, the index covers an enormous amount of useful, interesting and entertaining data. The contents include a Catalogue consisting of a single entry for each illustration (or group of illustrations published under the same heading) in chronological order as they appear in each volume, each entry is given a number that is then used in the six succeeding indexes to relocate the original Catalogue entry:

Places (London; Britain; World)
Illustration Titles
Names
Roles (i.e., job descriptions)
Styles
Subjects

The clearly written User's Guide explains each section, and it is recommended that this be consulted "in order to get the full benefit."

In using the index there are one or two anomalies of which one needs to be aware. For instance, it is not usual to index initials of people under the last letter even though one would suppose this to be the surname and a perfectly logical thing to do. In *The Builder Index* these initials appear at the start of each letter of the alphabet, that is, CF, TF and WGF are under the letter F. Where a person's name is known, it is usual to include this in the index even if it does not appear in the text, for instance George Frampton is listed as Frampton, Mr. And finally, there are a few odd headings for entries, for example, in the Roles Index, Head of Metropolitan Fire Brigade appears under H instead of under F for Fire Brigade (and similarly Head Teacher under H instead of T), but apart from these minor details, the index is extraordinarily comprehensive.

The whole volume is well produced with a colored frontis of a rare portrait of George Godwin himself, a foreword by HRH Prince Charles, a double introduction covering "George Godwin and *The Builder*" and "*The Builder* as Illustrated Journal" and a list of some ninety-four illustrations, all excellently reproduced and scattered throughout the text. Quotations from the text are usefully employed and are occasionally commented upon. The layout is good and easy to read; the engravings are a joy; and the information of relevance not only to architects but to geographers; archaeologists; genealogists; people interested in theatres, hospitals, railways, churches and all manner of public buildings and of course to social historians in general.

Geraldine Beare

Crime in Victorian Britain: An Annotated Bibliography from Nineteenth-Century British Magazines. Edited by E. M. Palmegiano. Westport, Conn.: Greenwood Press. 1993. ix + 165 pp.

This bibliography, drawn from forty-five periodicals published in Britain between 1824 and 1900, lists 1,614 articles and gives a brief description of the contents of each. Thus an 1898 article in the *Westminster Review* is attributed to its author; the title, "Judicial Sex Bias," is recorded; and the description—"Summarizes various laws prejudicial to women, such as one exempting marital rape from criminal prosecution"—follows. At this basic level, the volume is clearly of great benefit to researchers, directing them to sources they might otherwise overlook and sparing them wasted time by consulting articles whose promising titles might, in fact, disappoint.

The volume is concerned with crime in its broadest sense, and Professor Palmegiano thus not only lists violations of the law, whether against persons, property or the state, but also provides essays on behavior that the authors thought *ought* to be criminal. Moreover, she is not simply concerned with crime as such, but also with its detection, prosecution and punishment. Accordingly, we have a broad range of references from Edwin Chadwick's exhortation to adopt a preventive police force in the *London Review* in the 1820s to the debate on the use of "underhand" detection methods, deemed by some as essential to trap the more sophisticated criminal in the 1880s. Murder remained a fascinating topic for the Victorians, but in this context Professor Palmegiano's listing reminds us of how early the controversy over the efficacy, cruelty and dangers inherent in the application of the death penalty began. Transportation attracted its share of essayists, with speculation that the Falkland Islands would make a suitable alternative destination as the Australians became increasingly unhappy at being the recipient of Britain's criminals, and the discussion of imprisonment in the Victorian periodical press reflected arguments that are familiar today, with the ongoing debate over retribution, reform and the necessity to protect society.

The Victorians, of course, were as baffled by the causes of crime as is modern society. Their theories ranged from the environmental, to the moral, and even to the physiological. The poor were seen as sometimes culprits, occasionally as victims. Evolutionary ideas were adapted, so that the unsuppressed "criminal classes" became the agents for national degeneration. While some argued that most criminals were mentally instable, or at least the prisoners of their genes (or skull shape!), other suggested criminal behavior was a matter of choice, not infrequently inspired by drink and drugs; for modern concerns about lager, heroin or cocaine, the Victorians substituted beer and opium!

While this listing is primarily of use to the student of Victorian crime and criminology, other scholars would be unwise to neglect it. The student of Irish history, for example, will find many references to follow up, and indeed the pattern of commentary in the Victorian periodical press accurately reflects the changing perspective on the viability or otherwise of the Anglo-Irish Union. Similarly, students of women's history will find many examples both of Victorian prejudice against women and of their enlightened views, on occasion, toward them.

The volume contains a twenty-four page introduction, highlighting the changing patterns in Victorian reporting of crime and criminals, analyzing swings in fashion on a decade-by-decade basis, as well as looking at regional variations within Britain, or such areas as juvenile crime. An index is provided of authors and also of subjects covered by the articles listed. This is, in short, a valuable reference work. At this price, however, it is most unlikely to find a place on the shelves of the ordinary working scholar.

Alan Heesom
University of Durham

Paper Soldiers. By Clarence R. Wyatt. Chicago: University of Chicago Press. 1995. 272 pp.

Sadly, as it turns out for Mnemosyne or Clio, it was not her finest crop of young literateurs that America sent to Vietnam to firm up the *limes*. Those who did find themselves out on the edge of Empire choked and sputtered on the verge of articulation many long years before the first literary works, memoirs, poems or accounts of combat in Vietnam and more generally what is now known as the American "Experience" in Vietnam emerged gingerly to test the reactions of a skeptical public.

And invariably what the soldiers claimed they saw, did, felt, met was compared by that public to what *was* known about Vietnam as the *reality* of that war: reportage. The inarticulate combatants had left the field to journalists and now had to contend with a *mythos* set in place by the various media with which even recollection had to contend.

The "histories" of the Vietnam War have been so far histories of journalists' Vietnam, by journalists in Vietnam, about journalists in Vietnam, extolling journalism in Vietnam, and larded with the ill-concealed, self-righteous smugness of men or women just champing to shriek "I toooooooooold you so" as more and still more evidence emerged to suggest that the war *had* been brutal, dumb, mismanaged, futile and on and on. The veteran of that unhappy conflict, should he seek to claim his small corner of the historical stage, shall have to share even that paltry square of Destiny's *échiquier* with the journalist.

So it is *almost* gratifying to discover a history of journalism like Clarence Wyatt's *Paper Soldiers* which is *just that*, a history of the "American Press and the Vietnam War" with its formal prejudices laid out before us: "The press, for its part, remains in the popular mythology of the war an important, perhaps the decisive, influence on how the effort there eventually ended." This is an unabashed encomium of the reporters, editors, bureau-chiefs, and owners—the Sulzbergers, Bradlees, Sheehans, Halbershams, Arnetts—who sniff out the actual circumstances of the American war in Vietnam over the period from 1954 until the debacle ends with the fall of Saigon in 1975.

Wyatt's thesis is, however, that in the beginning "the press and the government/military largely cooperated," despite a "fluctuating mix of confrontation and cooperation." The gravamen of this narrative, painfully documented (fifty pages of notes), is essentially that "not politics, but the demands of journalism, motivated reporters in Vietnam and their superiors back in the United States." How the agents and purveyors of the war and its various strategies managed to alienate the press or lose the confidence of men and women who, as reporters, had often enough killed stories on their own or at the informal request of their government, is the stuff of Wyatt's tale.

Beginning with press coverage of the Bay of Pigs disaster and a first whiff of distress in the symbiotic relationship between the photogenic, eminently quotable young President Kennedy and his press corps, Wyatt follows the dissolution of government's grip—moral suasion at first, then actual contrivance and retaliation—on information and sources through the Cuban Missile Crisis and into the first halting steps of American diplomacy/intervention in Vietnam. Wyatt claims that it is in the conventional techniques of journalism—color, focus, movement—that one find the explanation of shifting Vietnam reportage, at least in the beginning: "Between the suppression of the sects in 1955 and the November 1960 coup attempt, the press covered the story as one of trends and conditions, depending on analysis, background, and contexts. . . . But with the increase in combat and American involvement in it, the Vietnam story became much more of a breaking story, composed of spot news, and demanding continuing, constantly updated coverage."

Wyatt follows the deterioration of American policy and intensifying presence of newsmen virtually year by year, though his heaviest concentration is clearly on that period from 1963 to 1968—from Ap Bac to Ap Bia (Hamburger Hill)—when things went ker-flooey. Though Wyatt's method is to cite public affairs documents and other administrative sources, he is mercifully restrained when it comes to drawers that have been ransacked already, so that Tet, for instance, and My Lai get only a light pasting, as does the tragic but decent Westmoreland. "It is incorrect," Wyatt asserts, "to blame—or credit—Tet or the press coverage of it with creating a great turn in public or press opinion" since "the coverage of Tet was the product of American journalism and government information policies that had been developing for years."

This is a book about the press. In it we find documented the critical junctures of press involvement in recording history or shaping public opinion. The book is on that score a useful compendium of the ill-chosen words of great men, the ill-cast hopes of at least two great peoples. What one need not look for is more than minimal sympathy for those engaged in the precarious imposture of making that history or leading those very peoples whose opinion seems so often to hang on which aspect of unfolding history the press shall show them.

Alan Farrell
Virginia Military Institute

Toward a Working-Class Canon: Literary Criticism in British Working-Class Periodicals 1816–1858. By Paul Thomas Murphy. Columbus: Ohio State University Press. 1994. x + 211 pp.

Let me say at the beginning that I admire the intention behind this study as well as the definitions and choices the author has made in the construction of his book. To describe what working-class periodicals (defined as "self-consciously directed toward the working class" and clearly reflecting "working-class interests" [31]) valued as literature, and why, is an important project and an overdue corrective to the "great books" notion of literary history that is so easy to take for granted in our surveys of Victorian literature. What we get here is "a record of working-class journalists, disestablishing and recanonizing established writers, or sanctioning new, unestablished writers, to fit the values of their own class" (3).

And class is the issue. The prevalent basis for literary judgment on the part of the editors and journalists that Murphy covers is whether and how the literary product supports and advances the cause of the working class, though the individual judgments about what literature does and how, differs from journalist to journalist and decade to decade. Murphy sees that there was "an important shift in awareness" from 1816 to 1858 in these working-class periodicals, a movement from "valuing overtly political literature" to "seeing the political implicit in all literature" (2–3).

Another point made in this study is that, though early working-class periodicals published much working-class poetry, it was only with the Chartist periodicals that fiction was introduced. Murphy also documents the extent of the early hostility to Scott (too aristocratic) as well as the consistent enthusiasm for Burns, Shelley and Byron. He argues that the criteria for the dramatic were established by comments on, and the transcripts of, meetings, debates, trials and elections.

The book consists of five chapters. Chapter 1 "provide[s] a sense of working-class literacy" (5). Chapter 2 quickly surveys the history of the working-class press between 1816–1858, showing an "evolution of a working-class sense of literature through three readily distinguishable subperiods: 1816–1829 (the years of the earliest working-class journalists [Cobbett, Carlile and Woolner]), 1830–1836 (the years of the "War of the Unstamped" [i.e., Hetherington and Carpenter]), and 1837–1858 (the years of the Chartist press [*Northern Star* and *People's Paper*])" (5).

Chapter 3, about views of fiction, argues that "working-class journalists before and into the thirties refused to separate fiction writers from the genre of fiction, and their reviews are almost always simultaneous attacks on one writer, usually Scott, and on fiction. From the thirties on, however, most journalists . . . recognize the fiction is not generically bad, but rather that individual works of fiction can be good, bad, or indifferent" (77). Chapter 4 is about poetry, which was more acceptable than fiction but judged in class terms—what is good poetry is what is good for the working class. The early demand was that poetry be directly political, but later it was accepted that poetry in and of itself had value for the working class. Chapter 5 touches on drama, for which there was little concern except for closet drama; Murphy says that the sense one gets is that working-class journalists found "nothing in the contemporary theater of any social relevance whatsoever" (151), even though the working-class certainly attended a wide variety of theatrical entertainments.

My reservations about Murphy's study have nothing to do with the thoroughness of his research or the soundness of his conclusions. I am convinced of the evolution of literary judgment that he lays out here. Nonetheless, the study seems thin to me, the evolution charted too uniform, the project itself perhaps undertheorized. I think of Brian Maidment's too-little-known study and anthology of nineteenth-century, working-class poets, *The Poorhouse Fugitives* (1987), in which he points out the complexity of the relationship of working-class writing to "established" (Murphy's word) writing: Many working-class poets, for example, modelled their poetry on Milton and James Thomson because that was what they thought poetry was. "Established" poetry is thus imbricated in working-class poetry. Isn't it likely that "established" aesthetics are similarly imbricated in working-class "aesthetics" even when the latter seems deliberately to oppose the former?

What's missing in Murphy's study for me is any sense of mixed motives on the part of journalists and writers or any sense that they themselves may be expressing conventional feelings and judgments (he takes them pretty much at their word). Nor is there much discussion of the issues of cooptation, cultural hegemony or a questioning of how (or if) a group can escape the cultural imperatives of which they are necessarily a part. Raymond Williams' work, especially his analysis in *Marxism and Literature* of hegemonic cultural domination that allows for both social reproduction and resistance, would be useful here; however, the only reference to Williams in Murphy's text is to the 1983 study of Cobbett.

Nonetheless, I do not want to leave the impression that Murphy's study is not a valuable survey of many of the published opinions of working-class editors, journalists and periodicals from 1816–1858. The book is a useful reference work. Its underlying politics, as implied in the last chapter's argument with E. D. Hirsch ("the persistent attempts by working-class journalists to establish a working-class canon in opposition—or at least in contrast—to that of the middle class, suggests that there is no such a thing as a 'national' canon" [167]), are important to have in the dialogue about Victorian literary values as well as an addition to our understanding of the cultural values of the Victorian working class.

Anne Humpherys
Lehman College and the Graduate School
City University of New York

Margaret Fuller's New York Journalism: A Biographical Essay and Key Writings. Edited by Catherine C. Mitchell. Knoxville: University of Tennessee Press, 1995. 240 pp.

Catherine C. Mitchell has done a valuable service to scholars of periodical history by gathering under one roof many of Margaret Fuller's newspaper columns from her two years as literary editor of Horace

Greeley's *New York Tribune*. Fuller went to work at the *Tribune* in December 1844, when it was a struggling paper for working-class readers and not yet "the great moral organ" of the second half of the nineteenth century. Despite her writing of some 250 bylined articles and editing or excerpting perhaps double that amount of copy—all the while working on her pathbreaking feminist tract *Woman in the Nineteenth Century* (1845)—history has received a poor impression of Fuller's productivity and quality as a journalist. Several belittling comments by Greeley, much later followed by disparaging criticism by some influential twentieth-century scholars, have resulted in an impression that Fuller was a weak and undependable writer and a difficult employee. Mitchell lays the groundwork for a reappraisal of that image.

Having been the editor of Emerson's transcendental magazine, *Dial*, from 1840–1842, Fuller came to the *Tribune* billed as the "most thoroughly learned woman on this continent," according to a Greeley letter. Today's publishers might have headlined her stature in other areas: her media celebrity, radical politics, equal salary with the *Tribune*'s male writers (although she did demure from working in the office to protect her "feminine" delicacy and status) and her shocking candor when criticizing even the most established and esteemed literary figures of her day.

Margaret Fuller's unorthodoxy, independence of mind and willfulness probably fueled the best of her work and the worst of her reputation. She was a leader in American women's struggle for equality. Several of the essays that Mitchell includes in the volume helped fire early women's rights agitation, most particularly Fuller's deeply felt *Dial* piece, "The Great Lawsuit," which evolved into *Woman in the Nineteenth Century*. At the same time, Fuller was conducting discussion groups in Boston, dubbed "Conversations," which, according to Elizabeth Cady Stanton, the intellectual foremother of American feminism, were "in reality a vindication of women's right to think."

Perhaps as vital to women's history, Fuller's strong-minded literary essays participated in the creation of an American national literature. Since Fuller was a celebrity in her own day, she had clout and she published influential as well as hard-hitting criticisms, even of powerful men in the 1840s. Fuller called the work of all-American poet Henry Wadsworth Longfellow, whose reputation in the English-speaking world at the time rivaled Tennyson's, "imitative," for example. This kind of revolutionary frankness drew fire from many big guns on the literary scene. She reviewed James Russell Lowell, a poet and essayist so revered in Anglo-American letters that he was awarded a commemorative plaque in Westminster Abbey, so harshly that he dropped his Brahmin proprieties and attacked her in a published poem. A ripple effect of this internecine invective, Edgar Allan Poe later called Fuller a "detestable old maid," according to Mitchell, and claimed in print that Fuller's poor reviews of

Lowell "set him off at a tangent and he has never been quite right since." Even her old boss Emerson, who apparently approved of her reformist involvement in the Europe of the 1848 revolutions, soon backed off the Fuller bandwagon. Although he dutifully acted as literary executor after Fuller's drowning in a shipwreck, he and others in elite Boston literary circles, including Nathaniel Hawthorne, tended to perceive her career as a shame verging on scandal.

Mitchell argues that Fuller's denigrated image today stems, in part, from her straight-shooting honesty, come what may; the many ad hominem attacks by her contemporaries were payback, Mitchell suggests, for her power to criticize them so potently in public—and her willingness to do it. "As an outspoken, intellectual woman ready to defend her ideas," Mitchell writes, "she no doubt disconcerted some of her male adversaries." The point is well taken, but it pays to remember that Fuller also criticized some of her female contemporaries. She decried the popular women authors of the 1840s, whose sentimental domestic novels were so dominant in the literary marketplace as to provoke the wrath of America's most canonized men. Indeed, five years before Hawthorne made his now-famous remark to his publisher that "America is now wholly given over to a d——d mob of scribbling women, and I should have no chance of success while the public taste is occupied with their trash," Fuller had similarly attacked "female scribblers." She called these other professional women writers, "the paltriest offspring of the human brain."

Fuller did not write sentimental fiction, moralistic novels or domestic advice manuals like most women writers of her day. She wrote high-minded literary essays and reviews, as well as real-world reform journalism on subjects like class economics, prison and asylum conditions, equality for women and African Americans, and other topics, all of which are represented in Mitchell's collection. Although Fuller did have a few female contemporaries in the working press, notably the abolitionist editor and writer Jane Grey Swisshelm of the *Saturday Visiter* (Swisshelm's spelling, from Johnson), Lydia Maria Child, whose professional life as a writer included a stint as editor of the *National Anti-Slavery Standard* between 1840 and 1843, and Cornelia Walter, editor of the Boston *Transcript* from 1842 to 1847, few have left the vexed and complex literary legacy that Fuller has. While Fuller certainly had her share of detractors, she also had fans. Walt Whitman is said to have read a collection of Fuller's essays to learn about literary criticism. Thomas Carlyle called Fuller's writing "the undeniable utterances . . . of a true heroic mind." Eleanor Roosevelt called *Woman in the Nineteenth Century* an "epoch-making book." Perhaps most impressive of all, Margaret Fuller merited high praise from ordinary American people who began writing laudatory accounts of her life and work almost immediately after her death in New York harbor in 1850.

The uniquely compelling qualities of Fuller's journalism—her thinking and her politics, perhaps more so than her style and grace—speak out in the essays Mitchell has collected. Leaving out Fuller's literary reviews (since they have been collected elsewhere), Mitchell provides an organized, enticing entrée into Fuller's editorial world and work. Mitchell does not offer, however, any analysis of the many fascinating issues her Introduction raises. Fuller's life, career and the chosen subjects of her journalism all confront questions of gender and gentility, for instance, but Mitchell avoids discussion of such questions in favor of a mere evocation of them. Mitchell undercuts Greeley's (and others') criticisms of Fuller's writing style on abstract and artistic grounds—their styles were so different, Mitchell explains, that they couldn't really appreciate one another's work—rather than on the more intriguing journalistic and political ones. Since so hard-edged and trendsetting a newspaperman as Greeley found Fuller's journalism so weak, one wonders about his perspective on women in the field. How did Fuller's journalism, and Greeley's criticisms of it, stack up against the work of other women journalists at the time? In what ways was Fuller's prose style consistent with or distinctive from the emergent styles of the American popular newspaper? Mitchell raises the all-important issue of audience, too, but doesn't analyze any aspects of Fuller's evolving relationship with her readers or the meaning of her growing reputation. Mitchell comments that Fuller's writing "improved because at the *Tribune* she developed a sense of audience," and that her "letters show her thinking about her newspaper readers . . . [and] the need to bend content and style for a specific audience," but ends paragraphs with these points rather than beginning them there. For a radical, strong-minded, celebrity woman of the press, in an uncommon position of professional prowess, prominence and power, finding an audience is the beginning of a story, not the end of it.

Mitchell's collection is a solid contribution to the study of newspaper and periodical history as far as it goes. Although she endeavors no commentary about the qualities of the essays themselves, Mitchell opens a book too long closed off or cast down, inviting future scholars to write or to rewrite the reputation of an eminent and enigmatic woman of the American press.

Amy Beth Aronson
New School for Social Research

Newsworkers: Towards a History of the Rank and File. Edited by
Hanno Hardt and Bonnie Brennen. Minneapolis: University of Minnesota Press. 1995. xiii + 237 pp.

What do journalists do? What do journalists think? The answers to
such questions have been a long time coming. Where they have been
attempted, sociologists not historians have done most of the prompting,
and usually about contemporary practice in broadcasting. The newspaper journalist still remains largely an enigmatic figure.

The ideology of the neutral reporter as an occupational category has
too readily transmuted into the neutralized historical figure. "Traditional press historians," Hardt and Brennen note in their introduction to this volume of essays, "have concentrated primarily on the
structure of the institution . . . as well as on the importance of protect-
ing content, instead of addressing the issue of production in terms of
labor and newsworkers."

The tone of this book is combative. The shelves groan with newspaper biographies, with antiquarianism, with the puffed-up memoirs of
celebrity writers, with treatises on the role of journalism as a component within liberal, capitalist democracies, with explications of "news
values." The burgeoning of labor history, inspired by E. P. Thompson's
Making of the English Working Class, and itself now more than thirty
years old, however, has mainly bypassed journalists.

Although the studies here address themselves exclusively to American practices and examples, the arguments have far wider application.
As historians were "expanding the past," to use Peter Stearns' phrase,
on both sides of the Atlantic, journalism increasingly became primarily
the province of a social science chiefly devoid of a historical dimension,
allowing a less complicated past to continue its existence untroubled.

One consequence has been the tendency to reify newsroom relationships. The eight essays in the volume, whose underlying debt is to cultural materialism, are a useful corrective. Collectively they illustrate
the extent to which journalists as producers constituted and reconsti-
tuted themselves in light of the development of the press as a capitalist
enterprise during the first half of the present century.

This is not the ritual "dance" of source relationships that has spawned
so much sociological literature, but the lived experience of historical individuals, whose "central concern . . . [was] the notion of work," which
theme the authors have taken for their own. It is, as Hardt and Brennen
acknowledge, "a fragmentary and incomplete project."

The avowed intention is to refocus newspaper history; one might say,
to drag it belatedly into the twentieth century. Hardt in particular is
unforgiving about the oversights and transgressions of "mainstream
media history." Generally, the volume exudes a certain anger. This may

be because at least half of the eight authors are or were practicing journalists. There is a sense here of "our" existence having been overlooked and devalued.

It is, of course, 100 years since the first publication of the *Daily Mail*, and it is thus proposed that 1996 marks the centenary of the "popular" press in Britain. This focus presupposes the preeminence of the institution of the newspaper, of considerations of popularity, of the influence of the specific individuals, such as Northcliffe and the so-called press baron, of the Fourth Estate role of the press.

The reformation of capitalist enterprise between the 1880s and 1920s exemplified by the Northcliffe press is less likely to be addressed. The impact over time of these developments on the thousands of workers in the newspaper industry will probably receive virtually no attention. Northcliffe's journalists will for the most part remain invisible.

This is the overriding reason why *Newsworkers* should be required reading on all media studies courses, in which, at least in the United Kingdom, the press as a whole is ever more marginalized within a broadly ahistorical agenda. It is, as the authors contend, impossible to understand the media without understanding the history of newspaper workers.

Michael Bromley
City University, London

The Press in the Arab Middle East. A History. By Ami Ayalon. Oxford: Oxford University Press. 1995. 300 pp.

In his study of the political activists and Islamic reformists, Afghani and 'Abduh, Elie Kedourie said that, "To appreciate literacy as a political weapon is a first necessity of the modern demagogue." In Ami Ayalon's history of *The Press in the Arab Middle East*, the development of the press was likewise entangled with political changes. The first press to come to the Middle East was contained in Napoleon's arsenal of weapons, and indeed, 'Abd al-Rahman al-Jabarti combatted this challenge with an exposition of the "literary, grammatical and lexical faults" of the French proclamations. Nonetheless, the Egyptian ruler who succeeded the French, Muhammad 'Ali, adopted the printing device and had his officials produce an official journal, *Jurnal al-Khidiwi*, in 1821 or 1822, and later the *al-Waqi'i' al-Misriyya*, edited by the first modernist Egyptian intellectual, Rifa'a Rafi' al-Tahtawi. The first part of Ayalon's informative book recounts the history of the founding of state journals, the first Ottoman program to establish an official journal appearing in 1830, and then afterward, the founding of more autonomous journals that appeared under the direction of the Christian

Lebanese subjects of the sultan. In 1855 Rizqallah Hasun set up Mirat al-Ahwal in Istanbul, beginning the long apprenticeship of Christian Arabs in the thought of Western Europe, a trend recounted in Albert Hourani's modern classic, *Arabic Thought in the Liberal Age*. It was this induction into the explosive ideas of European nationalism that Kedourie held responsible for the dislocation of a time-honored Islamic social and political system, and thus the proliferation of political unrest and instability in the contemporary Middle East.

Ayalon, however, concentrates not so much on the ideas disseminated, as on the medium of the press itself. The press played an essential part in undermining the Islamic political ethic, yet by noting the limitations within which the journalists operated in the Middle East it is clear from Ayalon's study that the press was hardly as revolutionary as the ideas themselves might suggest. First, social conditions limited the spread of the new medium and its message: The literate in the population ranged from 1 to 8 percent in the Arab provinces of the Ottoman empire before the First World War, and increased only marginally thereafter. The new political ideas were spread through social networks of the urban quarter and the village, the coffeehouses and the local shaykhs, as well through the hands of the local notables; the journalists, therefore, did not so much lead the community astray by their persuasive words as they were led themselves by the dictates of the community and circumstance. One of these circumstances was the relative poverty of the Middle East. So limited were the markets that most new journals could not survive without a patron, and therefore the communal leaders exerted considerable control over the content and reception of the message. Ayalon's reading of the press and the memoirs of journalists indicates that as late as the mid-twentieth century only 13 percent of the Arabic dailies in Egypt were able to survive without subsidies, state or private, and that, of the small number of autonomous papers, competition was such that it was necessary to put the courting of "popular opinion" (the small number of literate readers) before impartial news reportage. Egyptian journalists sat in the cafes in the fashionable squares of Cairo, negotiating with their agents and distributors, and bargaining with others who would use their services to pursue a partisan political line. The rapidly expanding press did not simply reflect a public appetite for news; rather, because of its utility as a political weapon, the press grew with political controversy and conflict. The movement against European imperialism provided a great impetus for expanding markets, as did domestic political struggles between parties, or, as in Lebanon, between contending families, clans and communal groups. Sometimes press campaigns were waged in the interest of an individual; for example, if a journalist could not find a political boss to act as his or her patron, then an independent line could be adopted by heaping abuse on a chosen political figure in order to win subventions. Ayalon includes the amusing adventures of one Egyptian journalist who, having blackmailed all prospective candidates in Egypt, toured the whole coast of Arabia to subject the petty Arab princes to similar blandishments. Or, we learn of the Syrian journalist, Muhammad Ali Khuri, who developed a liberal reformist position in Egypt, then turned to Arab nationalism against the Ottomans after his return to Syria, and finally during the war going to the side of the Ottoman military regime that executed a number of opposition press figures. After the war, Khuri was invited by King Faysal to act as his press propagandist, and after Faysal's fall, he went into government as the minister of education acting as state censor. This, according to Ayalon, was not an entirely uncommon course for an Arab journalist.

Early attempts to challenge the sacred authority of the Islamic, Ottoman state were resisted by the traditional authorities of the "ulama," that is, the notables and the ruling elites. Ayalon indicates that the ulama justly feared that the idea of freedom of speech, a newly coined phrase in Arabic, would shake the very foundations of a political and social order based not on political rights, but on a reverence for state authority. Such traditional notions of the state were common, even in the more advanced political communities of Egypt and Lebanon. Moreover, those liberation movements led by press publicists in defense of political rights and freedoms, ideas stemming from western European prescriptions for individual rights, were transformed into a movement for the "liberation of the collective." Hence the transformation of *al-Ahram* from one of the few papers with a reputation for news reportage to that of an official mouthpiece of the state, with news reporting beginning only after the virtues of the government and its leader are extolled in a manner that owes much to the traditional Islamic state-sponsored prescriptions.

Ayalon's contention that the evolution of the press had a complex political and cultural impact has, therefore, on his own authority, important qualifications. Nevertheless, Ayalon indicates that the erosion of the old Islamic social and political ethos was the result of changes brought by the press. Freedom of expression was a subversive idea, but even more dangerous for the Arab cultural legacy were the new methods and modes of discourse employed by the press. The reportage of news required a functional use of language, replacing the literary style of classical Arabic as it brought into being new literary forms, such as the political essay. Again, politics had an important impact on the evolution of a style pioneered by Afghani and Mustafa Kamil and then perfected by Muhammad Husayn Haykal, 'Abbas Mahmud al-'Aqqad, and Ibrahim al-Mazini; yet for many the press was a battleground from which to launch or join a struggle. Therefore, the political essay was more often than not nothing more than a forum for political publicists. Given Ayalon's thesis that the press transformed cultural values and his contention that language encapsulates a society's values and beliefs by harmonizing conception and expression, one would assume that the redefinition of Arabic concepts must have been the most dramatic result of the introduction of the press. In some cases the conceptual change was so fundamental that vocabulary had to be completely transformed or invented anew. According to an outstanding nineteenth-century journalist, Butrus al-Bustani, Arabic was a language that had many expressions for one notion (for example, the attributes of God) but lacked words for many other notions. Scholars such as Hourani have illustrated the importance of some key concepts such as *watan*, *umma*, *qaum*, *asabiya* and *ijtihad*, and recently Timothy Mitchell has added new insights into the transformation of this last important conception. More discussion on the redefinition of social, political and cultural categories, especially the extent to which such redefinitions were efforts to reimagine the political community, would have been welcomed by this reader.

James Whidden
School of Oriental and African Studies,
University of London

Index

About the Editors and Contributors

STUART ALLEN lectures on Media and Cultural Studies at the University of Glamorgan. He is a series editor in Cultural Studies for the Open University Press, and the deputy editor of the journal *Time & Society*, published by Sage. His publications are primarily in the areas of media sociology, cultural theory and nuclear issues, and include the book, coedited with Barbara Adam, *Theorizing Culture: An Interdisciplinary Critique after Postmodernism* (1995).

AMY BETH ARONSON received her Ph.D. from Columbia University in New York. She is currently a lecturer in Media Studies at the New School for Social Research, and has previously lectured at New York University and Rutgers University. She has also done editorial work for several American women's magazines, including *Family Circle* and *Working Woman*.

DAVID J. ATKIN, Ph.D., M.A. (Michigan State University), A.B. (University of California, Berkeley) is an Associate Professor in the Department of Communication at Cleveland State University. His research interests include the past and present diffusion of new media and the access opportunities they create for underrepresented groups.

GERALDINE BEARE is a freelance indexer. She has published a complete index of the *Strand Magazine* and is currently indexing the cartoons in *Punch*.

LAUREL BRAKE is a Senior Lecturer in Literature at Birkbeck College. She writes on nineteenth-century literature and the press, and is currently preparing a biography of Walter Pater. Recent work on journalism includes *Subjugated Knowledges: Gender, Journalism and Literature in the Nineteenth Century* (1994), "Endgames: The Politics of *The Yellow Book*" in *The Ending of Epochs* (Essays and Studies 1995), "The 'Wicked *Westminster*,' the *Fortnightly*, and Walter Pater's *Renaissance*" in *Literature in the Marketplace*, edited by John O. Jordan and Robert L. Patten (1995), *Investigating Journalism* (1990), coedited with Aled Jones and Lionel Madden, and *Defining Centres* (forthcoming 1997), coedited with Bill Bell and David Finkelstein.

PETER BRETT is a Lecturer in History and Post Graduate Certificate in Education Tutor at St. Martin's College Lancaster. He is currently writing a book on early nineteenth-century popular politics, having completed a doctoral thesis at Durham University in 1991 on reform politics in Newcastle, Bristol and York.

MICHAEL BROMLEY is Lecturer in Journalism and deputy director of the Communications Policy and Journalism Research Unit at City University, London. He is author of *An Introduction to Journalism* (1995), and coeditor of the forthcoming *Journalism Reader*.

JAMIE L. BRONSTEIN is Lecturer in Modern World History at California Polytechnic State University, San Luis Obispo. Having earned her Ph.D. from Stanford University in 1996, she is currently working on a comparative history of various aspects of the English and American working-class experience in the nineteenth century.

JULIAN COWLEY is Senior Lecturer in Literature at the University of Luton. He has written widely on aspects of twentieth-century American fiction, and most recently has published an article on the Australian novelist, Janette Turner Hospital.

DIANA DIXON is Lecturer in the Department of Information Studies at Loughborough University. She is coauthor, with Lionel Madden, of the *Nineteenth Century Periodical Press in Britain* (1976), and of various articles on newspaper bibliography.

PETER DOWLING is a postgraduate student at the National Centre for Australian Studies at Monash University, Melbourne. His Ph.D. research is on "Chronicles of Progress: The Illustrated Newspapers of Colonial Australia, 1853–1896."

ALAN FARRELL is Dean of the Faculty at the Virginia Military Institute. He served as Special Forces advisor to French-speaking montagnard tribesmen in the highlands of Vietnam from 1968 to 1970. He taught French for twenty-five years at Hampden-Sydney College in Virginia, a small liberal arts college founded by James Madison and Patrick Henry.

JESSICA C. E. GIENOW-HECHT, a graduate of the University of Virginia, is a postdoctoral fellow at the University of Bielfeld (F.R.G.). She has taught courses on German-American and Soviet History. Her particular interest is the investigation of supranational organizations and international cultural interaction. She is winner of the Goldsmith Research Award from Harvard University and the author of several articles on German-American history and culture.

CHRISTOPHER T. HAMILTON is Lecturer in the Division of Literature and Drama at Nanyang Technological University, National Institute of Education (Singapore). He received his Ph.D. in 1992 from Southern Illinois University at Carbondale, where he specializes in the eighteenth-century novel.

MICHAEL HARRIS is Senior Lecturer in History at Birkbeck College, University of London. He founded the *Journal of Newspaper and Periodical History* in 1984 and continued as executive editor until 1992 when the new format was adopted. He is now coeditor of *Studies*. As well as editing a series of books on the history of print, he is author of *London Newspapers in the Age of Walpole* (1987) and is currently working on a history of news in the period 1660 to 1750.

ALAN HEESOM is Senior Lecturer in History, University of Durham. He is a specialist in the history of North East England.

ANNE HUMPHERYS is Professor of English at Lehman College and the Graduate School, City University of New York. She is the author of *Travels into the Poor Man's Country: The Work of Henry Mayhew* and of numerous articles on the Victorian press, the novel, Dickens, and G. W. M. Reynolds. She is currently working on a book on divorce and the novel in nineteenth-century Britain.

TOM O'MALLEY is Senior Lecturer in Media Studies at the University of Glamorgan, Wales. He has coedited the 1994 and 1995 volumes of

Studies, and published on press and broadcasting history. He is currently working on media history in the United Kingdom since 1945. He is the author of *Closedown? The BBC and Government Broadcasting Policy, 1979–1992* (1994).

TODD ALEXANDER POSTOL is completing a study of the American newspaper boy for his Ph.D. in history at the University of Chicago. His writings on working children have appeared in *Labor's Heritage*, *American Educator* and the *Journal of Public Health Policy*.

ANDREW THOMPSON is Lecturer in Sociology at the University of Glamorgan, and received his Ph.D. in sociology from the University of Wales, Bangor, in 1995. His research interests are the sociology of nationalism and national identity with special attention to the politics of time and space, and the sociology of Wales.

MARK W. TURNER is Lecturer in English at Roehampton Institute, London. He is reviews editor of *Studies*, and is currently working on a study of Anthony Trollope and the periodical press. He is particularly interested in cultural theory and media history.

JAMES WHIDDEN is a postgraduate student at the School of Oriental and African Studies, University of London. He has written on Egyptian politics and has reviewed for *History*.

GLENN R. WILKINSON is Lecturer at the Acadia University, Nova Scotia. He was awarded his Ph.D. from Lancaster University in 1994 and has taught at the University of Calgary. His publications include articles on the newspaper press and war in the *Journal of Contemporary History*, the *Journal of Newspaper and Periodical History*, *Modern History Review*, and *War and Society*. His article, "Purple Prose and the Yellow Press: Tirah, 1897" will be published in *Space, Text, Identity: Negotiating India in the Periodical Press, 1840–1914* (1997), edited by D. M. Peers and D. Finkelstein.

ISBN 0-313-29052-0

90000>

EAN

9 780313 290527

HARDCOVER BAR CODE